NINTH SERIES

Also by the Author

Lamparski's Hidden Hollywood: Where the
    Stars Lived, Loved, and Died
Whatever became of . . . ? EIGHTH SERIES

Whatever became of ...?

ALL NEW NINTH SERIES
100 profiles of
the most asked about personalities from
television series, documentaries, and movies

RICHARD LAMPARSKI

CROWN PUBLISHERS, INC.

NEW YORK

Published by Crown Publishers, Inc., One Park
Avenue, New York, New York 10016
and simultaneously in Canada by General Publishing
Company Limited
Printed in the United States of America
Library of Congress Cataloging in Publication Data
Lamparski, Richard.
Whatever became of . . . ? Ninth Series
1. Television personalities—United States—
Biography.   2. Moving-picture actors and
actresses—United
States—Biography.   I. Title.
PN1992.4.A2L3   1985   791.43'028'0922
                       [B]   84-16974
ISBN 0-517-55540-9 (cloth)
0-517-55541-7 (paperback)
10 9 8 7 6 5 4 3 2 1
First Edition

For Gawain Bierne-Keyt
My young friend
who seems like
an old friend

Contents

NOTE: The superscript [8] with a name in the text indicates that this personality is profiled in *Whatever became of . . . ? EIGHTH SERIES*, by Richard Lamparski.

Acknowledgments

*The author gratefully acknowledges those who
have helped to make this book possible:*

Deborah Davis-Lipson
Wayne Martin
David Del Valle
Bob Satterfield
Phil Boroff
Chris Dietrich
Ronnie Britton
Wayne Clark
Lester Glassner
Dewitt Bodeen
Collectors Book Store
Robert F. Slatzer
Aurand Harris
Jim Brennan
Jim Janisch
Jim Jeneji
Deborah Davis
Copy King of Hollywood
Patrick Lobo
Doug Hart's Back Lot
Critt Davis
Gregory William Mank
Gary H. Grossman
Norman Lobo
Schaeffer Photo Lab
Wayne Parks
Amaryllis Bierne-Keyt
Gawain Bierne-Keyt
Paul Adrian
Allied Artists Corp.
Paramount Pictures
Steven Arnold
Michael Back
Virginia Reidy
Roy Bishop
Beverly Hills Public Library
Eddie Brandt's Saturday Matinee

Mathew Tombers
Don Schneider of the Electric Theatre
    Museum
Donna Schaeffer
Paul Schaeffer
Peter Schaeffer
Richard Schaeffer
Anne Schlosser and the staff of the Library of
    the American Film Institute
Tony Slide
Sons of the Desert
Twentieth Century-Fox Corp.
United Artists
Jon Virzi
Marc Wanamaker of the Bison Archives
United Press International Photos
World Wide Photos
Dan Patterson
Morgan Amber Neiman
Francie Neiman
Chapman's Picture Palace
Louise Brooks
Frank Buxton
Diana Serra Cary
R. T. Brier
Cinemabilia
Columbia Picture Corp.
Warner Brothers
Bob Cushman
Shelly Davis
Samson DeBrier
Walt Disney Prods.
Tim Doherty
George Eells
Richard Fletcher
Leatrice Fountain
Hal Gefsky

Aurand Harris
Michael R. Hawks
Howard W. Hays
Terry Helgesen
Charles Higham
Herman Hover
Corinne Lobo
Leatrice Joy
Michael Knowles
Don Koll
Anton LaVey
Charles Lockwood
Los Angeles Times
Dick Lynch
Bobby Downey

Luther Hathcock
Mike Marx
Metro-Goldwyn-Mayer
Iris Adrian
National Screen Service
Sloan Nibley
R. C. Perry
Dorothy Revier
Sarah Richardson
Linda Mehr and the staff of the Motion Picture
   Academy of Arts and Sciences
Bill Tangeman
Art Ronnie
Donovan Brandt

NINTH SERIES

Dayton Allen was playing a doctor and asking "Why not?" in this skit, which he did on a Steve Allen Show in 1959.

Dayton Allen

The comedian whose phrase "Why not?" swept the nation in the late fifties was born in New York City on September 24, 1919. The Allens, who were hit hard by the Great Depression, moved around Long Island before settling in Jackson Heights. Dayton says he is one of the few among the boys he grew up with who did not become a hoodlum. Another exception

is Art Carney, who was a schoolmate when Allen was voted the "wittiest boy in class."

He was not yet sixteen years old when he graduated from high school. His first full-time job was as a projectionist of 16-mm movies that were shown as recreation at hospitals, summer camps, and prisons. The other part of the program was an act by an Indian chief that included his tribal dance. Allen began introducing the man, who was named Swift Eagle, and was soon doing impersonations.

By 1935 Dayton had become a disc jockey at radio station WINS in New York City.

Then "Uncle Jim" Harkins hired him as a comedy writer for Fred Allen, whom he managed. Dayton also made frequent appearances on the star's network radio show.

He was the voice of the puppet-star of *The Adventures of Oky Doky.* The kiddie show, which was seen on the Dumont Television Network in 1948–49, was hosted by the late Wendy Barrie.

Bob Keeshan, who later became "Captain Kangaroo," was playing "Clarabell the Clown" on *Howdy Doody* when he suggested to Buffalo Bob Smith[8] that Allen do some of the voices on the show. Eventually Dayton did a dozen of the famous characters, such as "Ugly Sam," "Pierre the Chef," and "Flub-a-Dub."

The next five years were spent doing the voices of various cartoon characters on the Saturday morning TV show *Winky-Dink and You.* Mae Questel did all of the lines for "Winky-Dink."

Dayton Allen's real fame came on *The Steve Allen Show.* He first appeared in late 1958 as a last-minute substitute for the double-talking comedian Al Kelly. In a sketch in which he was being interviewed as "Congressman Dudley" Pat Harrington, Jr., asked him an unscripted question and he ad-libbed "Why not?"

"Skitch Henderson fell on the floor," recalls Allen. "And the audience howled."

He became one of the regulars and within weeks "Why not?" was heard everywhere. It was as popular as "Sock it to me!" came to be a few years hence and had almost as many spin-offs. There was the *Why Not?* book and the *Why Not?* humor album, both by Dayton Allen. British Airways tried to sell Americans on a tour of the United Kingdom with the argument "Why not?" There were hats topped by a plastic hand with the index finger pointed straight up, the gesture he always made when posing the question "Why not?"

People wrote to Allen to say that they had christened their boats or named their pets "Why not?" He is especially proud of the small towns Whynot, Mississippi, and Whynot, North Carolina.

In 1959, just as the still undeclared Democratic Presidential candidates were about to announce their intentions, Hi Rosen drew a cartoon that ran in the *Washington Post.* It showed John F. Kennedy, Lyndon B. Johnson, and Hubert H. Humphrey responding to a reporter who was asking if any of them would be a candidate in 1960. They were answering in unison, "Why not?"

There were 135 *Dayton Allen Shows* filmed in the early sixties. The five-minute programs were usually shown on local TV news shows. In them he delivered absurd monologues.

Dayton is still in touch with Steve Allen and occasionally they work together as they did at the 1973 Carnegie Hall reunion of the favorites from the TV show. At present there is interest in pairing them again on a cable television show.

In 1976 Allen was one of the first to impersonate Jimmy Carter on his *Just Plains Folks* LP.

Dayton's serious interest is money. He has done very well in real estate in White Plains, New York, and considers himself an expert on the international gold market. Mrs. Allen confirms his preoccupation with the monetary supply with the remark, "He's real cheap!"

Since 1958 he has been married to the former Elvi Daniels, who for a while was a TV personality on New York City's Channel 9.

Of the many voice-overs he has done, probably the Terry Toons characters "Heckle & Jeckle" and "Deputy Dawg" are the best known.

He is frequently recognized, which pleases him. Of the many articles that bore the phrase "Why not?", he does not own the "Why Not?" game. He hopes that eventually a fan will send him one.

Dayton Allen and his wife, the former Elvi Daniels, run a real estate business from their home in White Plains, New York.

Richard Lamparski

Fran Allison was nominated for an Emmy in 1949 as the Most Outstanding Kinescope Personality. Kukla, Fran and Ollie *received Emmy nominations seven times. In 1953 it won as the Best Children's Program.*

Fran Allison

The star of radio and television was born on November 20, in La Porte, Iowa.

Fran was graduated from Coe College in Cedar Rapids and spent the next two years teaching in a rural school.

Her brother, who was a musician, formed an orchestra that was hired to play on the local radio station, WMT. His sister joined the group that sang the vocal accompaniments. By 1934 she had left the teaching profession to appear on the radio as the station's staff singer and part-time salesperson.

An Iowa businessman brought her to the attention of radio executives in Chicago and in

1937 Fran became the staff singer at the NBC-owned and -operated station there.

It was "Aunt Fanny" that first brought her fame. She had originated the character, a gossipy spinster, on radio in Iowa. Her debut on the *Breakfast Club* came when she appeared in the studio audience one day and was interviewed by the show's host, Don McNeill. "Aunt Fanny" told of the goings-on among her relatives and neighbors, "The Smelsers." "Ott Ort" and "Bertie Beerbower" were some of the fictitious characters she made both hilarious and human to radio listeners for the next twenty-five years. She became a regular

"Clubber" and one of its most popular. "Aunt Fanny's" corny humor was perfect for the show that was a morning listening habit for much of the U.S. until it left the air at the end of 1968.

The public first saw her on October 13, 1947, when she appeared on the debut of *Kukla, Fran and Ollie*. She had first met Burr Tillstrom, the show's puppeteer, when they appeared on the same bill at shows put on at hospitals and orphanages. Although they did not work together at that time the two liked each other, and when it was suggested to Tillstrom that he use Fran as the foil to his menagerie of puppets they came to a quick agreement. Their association and friendship continue to this day.

Almost all of the *Kukla, Fran and Ollie* shows were done live. The only scripted shows were the holiday specials. Before each broadcast Tillstrom and Fran discussed the point from which they would begin and decided upon a thought or subject on which the show might conclude. The spontaneity, combined with the charm of the puppets, made for a unique experience in broadcasting. Officially designated as a children's TV show, intellectuals, childless couples, educators, and celebrities were also captivated by the pace and whimsy of the programs. Tallulah Bankhead was one of its most enthusiastic fans.

"Burr always said that we were just visiting," recalls Fran. "We went into people's homes, usually at 7:00 P.M., to chat and sing and enjoy each other. We never departed from that original concept."

Stars such as Tallulah Bankhead were astounded that Fran could stand as she did in front of the little stage where the hand-powered puppets would appear and relate to each as to another actor. The gentle quality of her voice and the concern she showed when the feelings of the characters got ruffled moved many viewers to tears. "Magical" was a word frequently

Richard Lamparski

Fran Allison is the co-host of The Prime Time, *an early morning self-help program for senior citizens seen on station KHJ-TV in Los Angeles.*

used to describe the special quality of that show.

For seven of the many years that *Kukla, Fran and Ollie* were on the air she was also the official spokesperson for Whirlpool appliances. She appeared as well on the TV specials *Pinocchio* with Mickey Rooney in 1957 and *Damn Yankees* in 1958.

After the syndicated version of *Kukla, Fran and Ollie* went off the air in 1976, Fran and her husband, a music publisher, moved to Los Angeles. At the time he died, two years later, they had been married for thirty-seven years.

Asked if she has any children, Fran responds, "Yes, all the kids in the neighborhood. They come by all day for visits and I love it!" She shares her Van Nuys home with her niece.

"I never had any career aspirations," said Ms. Allison recently. "I just fell into everything that's happened to me. I've worked hard and enjoyed every bit of it. Still do."

"Auntie Mame"

The real-life "Auntie Mame" was born Marion Tanner in Buffalo, New York, sometime around the turn of the century. Her father was an attorney. Her brother was the father of Edward Everett Tanner III, who wrote *Auntie Mame* under the nom de plume Patrick Dennis.

Marion had known Katherine Cornell from dancing class when she was very young, but did not become seriously interested in the theater until she was a student at Smith College. After receiving her master's degree in sociology in 1914 she went to New York City.

She did some work in silent films before moving to Boston for about a year, where she played ingenue roles at the Castle Square Theater. Between parts Marion supported herself in various jobs, such as hockey instructor and assistant buyer at Macy's.

In 1929, a few days after the stock market crashed, she authored a lengthy and well-written article on the disaster for a New York newspaper. During the thirties Ms. Tanner was very active in the National Labor Relations Board, mediating and conducting elections.

She was never really dedicated to a theatrical career, but managed to get small parts in *The Music Man* (1929) and *Fires of Spring* (1929), which starred Judith Anderson (single and living in Montecitio, California). In 1935 she was in a revival of *The Cat and the Canary*. In 1938 she appeared in *Knickerbocker Holiday*. Probably her largest part was as "Grandma Jeeter" in the short-lived 1960 production of *Tobacco Road*.

In 1927 Marion Tanner took possession of a red brick house at 72 Bank Street in Greenwich Village, which soon became known throughout Manhattan as a home for indigent artists and intellectuals. It was also the scene of both of her

The novel that was published in 1955 was such a success the author wrote a sequel. There followed a play, a TV special, and a movie. The Broadway musical **Mame** *was also made into a film.*

marriages. The first was to a writer and lasted approximately ten years. Then she was married for six years to an English engineer. Neither died on the Matterhorn.

Auntie Mame was a huge hit when it was published as a novel in 1955. Although the author admitted at the time that he had been partially raised by an eccentric aunt, little was known about her until Marion appeared as a contestant on *The Big Surprise,* a popular TV quiz show. Ms. Tanner came as a complete shock to Rosalind Russell, who had just begun stage rehearsals for the stage version. Both star and author felt that the publicity Marion re-

Richard Lamparski

Marion Tanner was known locally as the "Good Samaritan of Bank Street" before Auntie Mame *was published. She now resides a few blocks away in the Village Nursing Home.*

ceived after she won $20,000 on the program would detract from the play.

It was at that point that Aunt Marion and her nephew had what she later called "a falling off, not out."

"We used to be very close," Marion told journalist Sally Hammond in 1964, and admitted that Dennis had not been to see her in five years. "I think by the time Rosalind Russell appeared in the play he thought *she* was his aunt," said Ms. Tanner.

Robert E. Lee, who with his partner, Jerome Lawrence, adapted the book for the stage, said in 1983, "By opening night I think Rosalind Russell believed that *she* wrote *Auntie Mame*."

In May 1964, Ms. Tanner, who was recovering from a broken leg, was evicted from her home, which was sold at public auction. By then those staying with her were dropouts, derelicts, and people recently released from prison. The rumor at the time was that her nephew, who had been contributing to her support, objected that his money was going in-

directly to people who had been described by a neighbor as "bums and junkies."

She lived in various halfway houses until taking up residence in a community nursing home in Greenwich Village in March 1977. By then her health had deteriorated to the point where she could do little other than watch television. When First Lady Rosalynn Carter visited the facility she had lunch with its most famous resident.

During a recent interview Marion Tanner voiced no complaints about her nephew and only relative, who died in 1977, or her circumstances. She was not mentioned in his will.

As an animal lover, she wished she could be allowed to keep a dog. Childless, she worried about a teenage runaway named Sarah whom she had befriended before she was forced to enter the nursing home. The worst part of old age, she said, was "being patronized by everyone." She missed traveling throughout the world, which, like "Auntie Mame," she did several times. Her one regret in life was that she didn't write about her many adventures.

Like the famous character, Marion Tanner often wore kimonos and used long cigarette holders. One of the schools her nephew attended did hold some classes in the nude. She highly approved of nudism and was a vegetarian for many years.

Her outlook on life, too, was similar to that of the famous "Mame." "There is no need to be bored," she once told reporter Joyce Wadler. "I have always found something to be curious about. But a 'sane' life can be very boring." Her advice to people looking for a more colorful life: "Be nice to people and be open-minded about everything and everyone."

Asked directly if she thought that she was the prototype for the character that has entertained millions as a book, its sequel, a play, a movie, a TV special, a musical, and a movie musical, she replied, "No. I think I'm much nicer."

John Beal was described by Jimmie Fidler as "one of the finest actors we've ever had in Hollywood." Brooks Atkinson wrote in the New York Times *that he was "one of the best actors in our theater."*

John Beal

The "almost star" of films, theater, and television was born James Bliedung on Friday, August 13, 1909, in Joplin, Missouri, where his father owned a department store. Mrs. Bliedung had been a concert pianist. Even before he acted in school and church plays he put on shows in his parents' garage. A movie fan from an early age, he won a $50 prize from *Photoplay* magazine when he was twelve years old.

He was drawn to both acting and art as professions, but, at his father's insistence, attended the University of Pennsylvania, where he earned a B.S. degree in economics.

He took "John Beal" from the names of his two closest friends at college.

John spent a season with a repertory com-

pany before understudying and doing walk-ons in Broadway shows. He had his first lead in *Wild Waves* (1932), which soon closed, but earned him several good notices. Those reviews, seconded with the recommendation of Albert Hackett, who was then still an actor, got him an excellent part in the hit *Another Language* (1932).

When M-G-M filmed *Another Language* (1933), Beal was brought out to Hollywood to repeat his performance, this time opposite Helen Hayes. He was offered a term contract but declined and returned to Broadway for *She Loves Me Not* (1933), another hit. After it closed RKO signed him, but the roles he was assigned were not the kind that could launch a movie star's career. In two, however, he played opposite Katharine Hepburn: *The Little Minister* (1934) and *Break of Hearts* (1935). He was loaned out to make *Les Miserables* (1935) and used in low-budget productions.

He then returned to Broadway for *Russet Mantle* (1936), which ran for 117 performances.

He was next pacted by M-G-M, but they didn't make good use of him, except when he was cast as Gladys George's son in the tearjerker *Madame X* (1937). He left after *Port of Seven Seas* (1938).

Beal spent much of World War II as a staff sergeant in the motion picture unit of the Army Air Force. After V-J Day he replaced Elliott Nugent in *The Voice of the Turtle,* one of the longest-running plays of the period. When William Eythe left *Lend an Ear* in 1948, John took over for him and in 1955 he assumed the role originated by John Forsythe in *The Teahouse of the August Moon.*

As early as 1934 John Beal began appearing in prestigious radio dramatizations, such as *Lux Radio Theater, Cavalcade of America,* and *Suspense.*

On television he did some of his best work, as in the original production of *A Trip to Boun-*

tiful on the Goodyear-Philco Playhouse in 1953 and as one of the *Twelve Angry Men,* which was first presented on *Studio One* in 1954. He also appeared on the *Philip Morris Playhouse, Kraft Theater, Omnibus,* and the *U.S. Steel Hour.* He received raves as the middle-aged writer who suffers a heart attack on *The Long Way Home,* which was first seen on *Robert Montgomery Presents* and later released as a feature under the title *That Night!* (1957).

John has been in several productions of *Our Town,* including a tour with Henry Fonda. He describes the 1959 production under José Quintero's direction as "one of the highlights of my life." His other favorites from his stage career are the title role in *A Man for All Seasons* and "James Tyrone" in *A Long Day's Journey into Night.* He believes his best-known screen work is in *The Little Minister* (1934) opposite Katharine Hepburn, and the cult film *The Vampire* (1957). His part in *One Thrilling Night* (1942) which he made for Monogram in six days is his personal choice.

I Am the Law (1938), *The Cat and the Canary* (1939), *My Six Convicts* (1952), and *The Sound and the Fury* (1959) are among his other screen credits. His last were *The Bride* (1973) and *Amityville 3-D* (1983).

His other Broadway appearances include the *succès d'estime Liberty Jones* (1941), *The Long Christmas Dinner* (1966), the all-star production of *The Front Page* (1968), and *To Be Young, Gifted and Black* (1969). Also notable was his 1968 tour in *The Little Foxes* with Geraldine Page and his late friend Betty Field.

On Friday, July 13, 1934, John married Helen Craig, who created the starring role in the original production of *Johnny Belinda* on Broadway. They have two daughters. Their youngest is a dancer-choreographer with her own troupe, Tandy Beal & Company. He delights in his only grandchild, Paul Kruger, who is by Tita, his oldest.

Betty Shirley

John Beal lives in Manhattan with his wife, Helen Craig, the star of the original Broadway production of Johnny Belinda.

Long after Beal became a well-known actor he continued to study art. He has drawn and painted "people who were important in my life," including Robert Ryan, whom he liked and admired, and Pope John Paul II, who inspires him. John is a "repatriated" Roman Catholic.

He speaks without disappointment of his film career and without boast of his stage credits, which could be envied by major stars. He volunteers the fact that he "never made it into the big money." He has, however, become an actor of whom people often say, upon seeing his face, "I don't know his name and I really should because I've seen him so many times and he's always just excellent."

Tommy Bond's character "Butch" is described in Our Gang, *the definitive book on the comedies by Leonard Maltin and Richard W. Bann, as a "full-fledged, glowering meanie."*

Tommy Bond

Our Gang's heavy was born on September 16, 1927, in Dallas, Texas.

Spanky (1932) was the first of twenty-seven of the famous shorts in which Tommy Bond appeared. By the following year he was a regular, usually menacing the other "Gang" members. "Butch," the name of his character, was frequently aided in his bullying by "Woim," Leonard Kilbrick.[8]

Bond was also in several Charlie Chase comedies and is known to Laurel and Hardy fans as the brat playing football in their feature *Block-Heads* (1938). He and most of the other "Gang" members were seen in a sequence of the Eddie Cantor vehicle, *Kid Millions* (1934).

After *Bubbling Trouble* (1940), his last "Gang" two-reeler, Bond continued as an actor until 1951, when he became a television technician.

He was in *Man from Frisco* (1944) and *Tokyo Joe* (1949). In the low-budget features *The Gas House Kids Go West* (1947) and *The Gas House Kids in Hollywood* (1947) he was paired with his fellow "Gang" member and close personal friend, Carl "Alfalfa" Switzer. Tommy played cub reporter "Jimmy Olsen" in the movie serial *Superman* (1948) and its sequel, *Atom Man vs. Superman* (1950), which starred Kirk Alyn (single and living in Sun City, California) in the title role.

Since 1974 Bond and his wife, who was Miss California of 1945, have lived on a 140-acre ranch in the mountains near Dunlap, California. Tommy is a stage manager at Channel 30 in nearby Fresno. His son "Butch," although still in his teens, has worked as a producer and personality in both radio and TV.

Former "Gang" members Jackie Lyn Taylor and Tommy Bond co-host the syndicated TV program Little Rascal Theatre. *Jackie is married to a minister and lives in Reno, Nevada.*

Marjorie and Priscilla Bonner played together in the silent feature Paying the Price *(1927).*

Priscilla and Marjorie Bonner

The sisters of the silent screen were the daughters of the assistant to General Wood of the U.S. Army. Priscilla, who is the older by six years, was born in Adrian, Michigan, on July 18. Marjorie was born in Washington, D.C., on February 17.

Priscilla's father disapproved of his daughter's determination to become an actress but, after a great deal of persuasion on her part, allowed her to go to Hollywood.

"Daddy gave me one year," she said recently. "I promised to come home if I wasn't successful. It never occurred to me that I wouldn't make good. I was so spoiled as a child that I just expected all the things I wanted to come my way. To the amazement of everyone but me they did."

After debuting in *Homer Comes Home* (1920) opposite the comedy star Charles Ray, Priscilla made *Bob Hampton of Placer* (1921) with James Kirkwood (the father of author James Kirkwood), *Shadows* (1922) with Lon Chaney, *Purple Dawn* (1923) with Bessie Love (living in London, England), *Tarnish* (1923) with Ronald Colman, *Charley's Aunt* (1925) with Sydney Chaplin, *Drusilla with a Million* (1925), *Three Bad Men* (1926) with George O'Brien (living in Oklahoma), *Long Pants* (1927) with Harry Langdon, and *It* (1927) with Clara Bow.

Priscilla Bonner feels she is best remembered for *The Strong Man* (1926), in which she played the blind girl who is loved by Harry Langdon.

The one part that might have made her a star became, instead, her greatest disappointment. Warner Brothers picked her to play in *The Sea Beast* opposite John Barrymore, who was then a major star. Recently she spoke of the experience.

"It is still difficult for me to go into this. In a way its seems like yesterday instead of 1926. The studio sent me to see Mr. Barrymore. He, of course, had approval of his leading lady. When I knocked on his door I was quite in awe of him, but in person he was much less appealing than he was on the screen. He was very polite to me, but I wasn't at all drawn to him. To be perfectly frank he looked rather dirty. But he seemed to like me and told me I had the part. So, I signed a contract and it was announced in the press that I was to be teamed with the great star in what was almost certain to be a major film. Shortly after that, however, I was informed that Dolores Costello had replaced me. It seems Barrymore had seen her on the lot and that was that. He did write me a lovely letter which I still have. I received my full salary, but I felt awful about what happened. No matter what the reason, to be taken off a picture is a great professional embarrassment. At least I felt humiliated by the experience. Eventually Barrymore and Miss Costello were married. She was more beautiful than I and she was quite suitable for the role. But I lost that part the moment Barrymore realized that he would not be able to make me. It was a while before I figured that out. I was so naïve in those days."

Priscilla retired when she married a prominent physician in 1928. She never made a talkie.

"My voice was fine," she has said. "But my husband did not want me in pictures. I never stopped missing it, though. There's no substitute for that kind of attention. But I made an agreement and I kept it."

The Beverly Hills apartment which the Bonner sisters share is furnished with antiques. Both are widowed and neither has had children. They have remained friends for over sixty years with Mary Brian.[8]

Marjorie Bonner followed her sister to Hollywood and acted on and off in movies right through the thirties. For a while she was under contract to Universal Pictures but never be-

Julius Neeley

Marjorie Bonner Lowry (left) and Priscilla Bonner recently. When she saw this photograph Priscilla said, "I know that's how I look now, but I don't like it and will never let anyone take my picture again."

came the name her sister was.

"I lacked Priscilla's ambition," she once told an interviewer. "Acting was never a serious thing with me. The one chance I did get went down the drain the moment I told Harry Cohn what I thought of him. I'm not a bit sorry. I never missed pictures. In fact, I haven't even thought of myself as Marjorie Bonner in years. I'm Mrs. Malcolm Lowry and very proud to be."

When she married the writer Malcolm Lowry in 1940 he had never seen her in a movie. It was she who typed and edited the original manuscript of the novel *Under the Volcano*, considered by many to be a masterpiece. It was made into a film in 1984 by John Huston.

Dorothy De Borba's picture appeared on the tops of Good Humor ice cream cups while she was in the Our Gang comedies.

Dorothy De Borba

The little girl of the *Our Gang* comedies was born in Los Angeles on March 28, 1925. Her father was a drummer who played for a while with Paul Whiteman. Dorothy's parents got married and then divorced three times.

Although her mother was an actress, Dorothy says she was not a "stage mother." Most of the money she made was placed in a bank account for her.

Dorothy played small parts in pictures with Pola Negri, Mary Astor, Gilbert Roland, and Buster Collier, Jr. (married and living in San Francisco), before going under contract to Hal Roach. *Pups Is Pups* (1930) was the first of the twenty-eight *Our Gang* films in which she appeared.

Although she got butted by a goat while making *Hook and Ladder* (1932) and knocked out in a fall during *Spanky* (1932), Dorothy very much enjoyed being a "Gang" member. A tomboy, she played along with the boys in their games. The late "Stymie" Beard and "Wheezer" Hutchins (also deceased) and their mothers were frequent guests in the De Borba home.

After appearing in *Mush and Milk* (1933), her last in the series, Dorothy did bit parts in *Bombshell* (1933) and *Dante's Inferno* (1935), then left the profession.

She has a son by her first husband, who died three months after they were married. Her daughter is by her second marriage, which ended in divorce.

In 1976 she retired from her job of senior clerk at the School of Journalism at the University of California at Berkeley.

Dorothy and her son share their mobile home with two miniature schnauzers and a Siamese cat. Nearby on their property they keep two burros.

She is a student of Unity.

Richard Lamparski

Dorothy De Borba lives with her son on the outskirts of Livermore, which she claims is the home of "California's finest wines and biggest bombs."

Randy Boone played the ranch hand "Randy" on The Virginian *for three seasons in the mid-sixties.*

Randy Boone

The singer-actor was born on January 17, 1942, in Fayetteville, North Carolina. He is not related to either Pat or Richard Boone.

Neither of his parents nor his sister was musi-cal. Randy became interested in playing the bongo drums while he was at summer camp. Shortly after his counselor taught him the basic guitar chords Boone's foot became seriously infected. Since he had to sit for hours while it soaked in medication he utilized the time by practicing the guitar.

He enrolled in college, but soon realized that he had no real interest in anything he was studying. He dropped out and set off on a hitchhiking tour of the country with one duffel bag and his guitar. His hope was that along the way he would discover what he wanted to do with his life.

In Southern California he began appearing in the small clubs throughout the beach towns that were then showcasing folksingers. Quickly, he developed a following. One of his fans intro-duced him to the producer Peter Tewkesbury, who brought Boone to the attention of Univer-sal. He spent the next four years under contract to that studio.

On his first series, *It's a Man's World,* he played what he describes as a "laid-back guitarist" living on a houseboat with three other young men. The show lasted on NBC for only five months in 1963, but is now consid-ered to have been a bit before its time. Plots of the thirty-minute programs were frequently, but not always, humorous. At times they dealt with serious and real problems of education and personal relationships that faced college students in the sixties.

He is probably best known for his part on *The Virginian,* the first ninety-minute TV west-ern series. From 1963 to 1966 Boone played the ranch hand "Randy." Frequently he sang, sometimes with Roberta Shore.

When he returned to his hometown on a visit to his family in 1966 Randy was getting consid-erable attention from the fanzines as a coun-trified heartthrob. Childhood friends brought him together with their eighteen-year-old sister.

Three days after they met they were married. Before their divorce, eighteen months later, his only child was born.

At the height of his popularity Capitol Records wanted to produce an album of Randy Boone singing his own songs, but quickly lost interest when Universal objected. To placate him, his studio put out an album of Boone singing the songs he had performed on *The Virginian.*

"I had a black guy, who was into rhythm and blues, and a Jewish guy who loved Broadway show tunes backing me," explains Boone. "The results were God-awful!"

He feels he did his best work on *Cimarron Strip,* a series that was televised by CBS from 1967 to 1971. That its segments were ninety minutes long was one of several aspects of the show that reminded many of *The Virginian.* In support of Stuart Whitman Randy played "Francis Wilde," a young photographer of the Old West.

While he was professionally "hot" Boone guested on *Wagon Train, Laredo, Alfred Hitchcock Presents* and *Twilight Zone,* and made the features *Country Boy* (1966) and *Terminal Island* (1973) with Tom Selleck.

Randy believes that if he made a mistake it was when he fired the agent who had guided his career from the beginning. And at approximately the same time he gave away almost everything in his house and sold a luxury car for $100.

"I didn't want anything to remind me of my ex-wife, so I got rid of nearly everything and everyone who had been in my life when I was married," he said recently. "I even ripped apart entire rooms in my home and then changed them completely. That's when I learned I was good with my hands."

In a 1984 interview he described what he has been doing since the public last saw him. "Just about the time *Cimarron Strip* was taken off the air my second wife and I divorced. I spent three years trying to get established as a singer in Nashville, but nothing happened. Then I went on a very long party. It's only lately that I've seriously thought of coming back into show business. In the meantime I've started my own business."

Randy and his present companion, a legal secretary, share a house in Van Nuys with his teenage son. The boy is partnered with Boone in "Handy Randy," which is described on their business cards as "Carpentry, minor electrical and plumbing." They specialize in the repair of pleasure boats.

A few years ago Dennis Weaver, who is a fan of Randy's music, produced a single of Randy singing two of his own compositions, but it did not receive wide distribution.

Asked how he would feel if his career were to remain dormant, he replied, "Just fine. The money was always the best part of TV, anyway. The show was okay, but nothing to be really proud of. I love what I do now, being a handyman. It just doesn't pay as well."

Randy Boone still sings and composes, but he makes his living as a handyman.

Donna Schaeffer

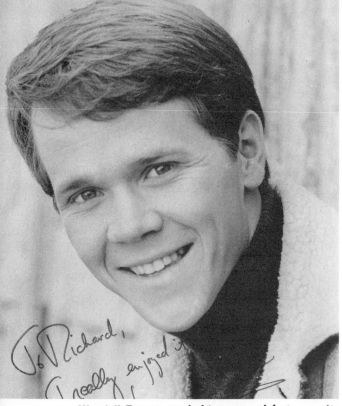

Wendell Burton made his screen debut opposite Liza Minnelli in The Sterile Cuckoo *(1969).*

Wendell Burton

The movie and television actor was born in San Antonio, Texas, on July 21, 1947. His father, a technical sergeant in the U.S. Air Force, was killed in a plane crash when Wendell was five years old. He, Mrs. Burton, and her three younger children moved from Washington State, where his father had been stationed, to Texas. His grandparents, who lived nearby, were devout Southern Baptists. Although he feels he was strongly influenced by them, he was not aware of it at that time.

Wendell went through high school with no conscious interest in going into show business. At Sonoma State College, where he majored in political science, one of his courses was public speaking. From that class he got a part in a campus production of *Oh, Dad, Poor Dad . . .*

The show's stage manager was the sister of a director who was about to cast the San Francisco production of *You're a Good Man, Charlie Brown.* At her suggestion Burton auditioned and was cast as "Charlie." He says he would have continued college with no further thoughts about an acting career had he not been "discovered" during the show's run.

Alan Pakula saw Wendell play the hung-up half-pint and asked him to audition for the role of a sensitive young man in the picture he was about to direct, *The Sterile Cuckoo.*

Much was made in the publicity of Wendell Burton as a complete newcomer who had been chosen over hundreds of experienced actors. Quite a few of those young men who were considered for the part were "names." Paramount Pictures gambled on using Wendell because while Liza Minnelli, his co-star in the movie, was well known, it was *The Sterile Cuckoo* that made her a star. She was nominated as Best Actress of 1969 by the Academy of Motion Pictures for her performance. The song from the film, "Come Saturday Morning," was also nominated for an Oscar.

Most critics thought Wendell did very well playing a young man many young men found easy to identify with. After the film was a box-office hit he was immediately up for many other movie and TV roles, including the lead in *Harold and Maude.* He chose to get more experience on the stage.

In 1970 he appeared with Eve Arden in the national company of *Butterflies Are Free.* He was aware and concerned that being seen as another "sensitive young man" might result in his being stereotyped. "I don't want to play the short-haired, shy, well-mannered college boy in everything I do," he told one interviewer at the time.

The role of "Smitty" in the screen adaptation of *Fortune and Men's Eyes* (1971) was certainly a change of pace. He played a young inmate who is raped shortly after entering prison. By the end of the film he has become a sexual aggressor, victimizing the same sort of boy he once was.

The same year he repeated his role in *You're a Good Man, Charlie Brown* on a TV special for Hallmark Cards.

He made it clear in all his public statements that he considered acting only another step along the way to his eventual goal, politics. "Burton's Ladder" is what he called his plan to become the U.S. Senator from California before he turned forty.

Wendell did feature roles on television in the early seventies, such as the TV movies *Red Badge of Courage* and *Go Ask Alice,* a particularly effective story about teenage drug abuse which is still being shown to students. He played Dick Van Dyke's son for one season, but in spite of his active career and expressed plans as to his future, Burton was beginning to have serious doubts.

In 1973 he traveled to India "looking for a guru, I guess—someone who could give me the answers to questions I couldn't quite verbalize."

He feels he found all he was seeking when he joined a small Christian congregation upon his return to the United States. By 1974, after being part of a Bible study group, Wendell Burton says that he "gave my heart to the Lord."

He was married in 1978 and is the father of a daughter and a son. The Burtons live in an apartment in the Miracle Mile section of Los Angeles.

Wendell, his wife, and a small group sing the gospel songs he has composed—at churches and on the three albums he has recorded for Lamb and Lion, his own label.

He is still available for acting roles and says his agent and fellow actors are understanding of his convictions. He admits that he is now difficult to cast, but has turned down several parts because he found the material morally objectionable. His beliefs would not permit him to-

day to be in *Fortune and Men's Eyes* even though he concedes that the statement made by the film was valid.

"I'd like to work as an actor more often," he has said. "But that, like everything else, is in God's hands. I can accept His decision, whatever it is. In the meantime I teach acting to Christians."

Wendell thinks he gave his best performance in *Sterile Cuckoo,* the TV special *East of Eden,* and as a deaf boy on a "Dr. Kildare" episode.

"But my acting is not what I take most pride in," he said recently. "It's the people I've been able to lead to Jesus that's made me happy with myself and my new life."

Richard Lamparski

Wendell Burton gives acting lessons to "Christians seeking a secular career" at Theatre/Theater on Melrose Avenue in Hollywood.

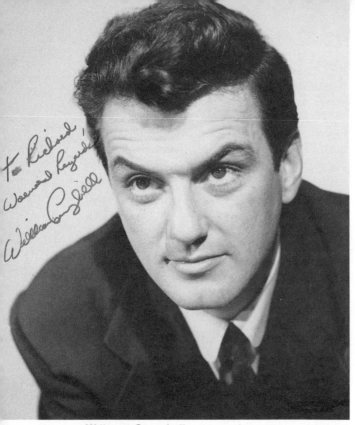

William Campbell projected a sinister kind of Cagneyish charm that made him especially effective in hoodlum roles.

William Campbell

The movie actor who starred in the TV series *Cannonball* was born on October 30, 1926, in Newark, New Jersey. His father worked for the town's water department.

Campbell says that he had not considered acting as a profession until his high school teacher suggested it. "What she told me," he recalls, "was that with my marks being what they were only an acting school would accept me. Of course, I never tell that story to other actors."

After spending most of his four-year hitch in the U.S. Navy on a minesweeper, Bill went to New York City, where he studied at the American Theater Wing. "Acting was easy for me right from the beginning," he has said. "Frankly, I doubt I would have allowed myself to starve. I just wasn't that dedicated."

He had the experience of acting in stock before being cast in the road company of *The Man Who Came to Dinner,* which starred Monty Woolley. During the run of the show at the Biltmore Theater in Los Angeles in late 1949 he was brought to the attention of Warner Brothers. After a screen test he was placed under contract. At first, as in *Breakthrough* (1950) and *Operation Pacific* (1951), he was known as Bill Campbell. The studio dropped him after only six months when he had a strong disagreement with director George Waggner.

The actor was about to return to New York when his agent heard about a part at M-G-M that sounded right for Bill. "They wanted a young guy who wasn't petrified of Spencer Tracy," he explains. "Well, I had enormous respect for him, but he didn't scare me." He got the part in *The People Against O'Hara* (1951) and before it was completed Tracy had convinced the studio of his potential. He was pacted at a starting salary of $750 a week. One of the many good notices the film received was in the *New York Times.* In it Bosley Crowther singled out Campbell for praise.

He remained at the Culver City lot until William Wellman cast him in *The High and Mighty,* a box-office smash of 1954. He got on exceptionally well with the picture's star, John Wayne. They had first met when they made *Operation Pacific.* Bill spent the next two years under contract to Wayne's production company. Their friendship lasted through the years.

The last period he spent under contract was with Universal, where he was starred in a number of B movies.

It was at Kirk Douglas's insistence that Bill was cast as the young hothead in *Man Without a Star* (1955). In the picture, which was directed by King Vidor, he more than holds his own in every scene with Douglas. Campbell considers it one of the two high points of his career. The other is his portrayal of condemned sex-offender Caryl Chessman in *Cell 2455, Death Row* (1955). For its time it was an exceptionally realistic film. Much of its mood and impact are due to Campbell's performance.

Other motion picture roles for which he is best remembered are: *Escape from Fort Bravo* (1954); *Battle Cry* (1955); *Love Me Tender* (1956), in which he played Elvis Presley's brother in the singer's screen debut; *The Naked and the Dead* (1958), and *Hush, Hush, Sweet Charlotte* (1965).

His other efforts include: *Small Town Girl* (1953); *Running Wild* (1955); *Sheriff of Fractured Jaw* (1959); *The Secret Invasion* (1964), and *Dirty Mary, Crazy Larry* (1974).

During the season of 1958–59 Campbell had his own TV show, *Cannonball*, a thirty-minute syndicated series of thirty-nine dramatizations about a long-distance truck driver. His favorite TV part, however, was opposite the late Wanda Hendrix[8] in a play they did together on *The Bigelow Theater,* a weekly presentation in 1950–51.

Bill still acts occasionally on both TV and in features. His brother, screenwriter R. Wright Campbell, frequently tailors parts for him in his scripts.

In the mid-seventies the actor received some unwelcome attention from the media. Bill has been divorced from Judith Exner since 1958, but when the press learned that she had been an intimate of two Mafia chieftains and President John F. Kennedy they descended on him.

He was gallant in all of his remarks, describing the woman he knew for six years of marriage as a "quiet, family kind of girl."

He met his present wife, Tereza, while making a film in Yugoslavia. They have been married since 1962.

Bill Campbell is the director of fund-raising and public relations for the Motion Picture and Television Country House and Hospital in Woodland Hills, California. "This is the perfect amalgam of my career," he said recently. "The people who come to this office usually recognize me. Often they're people I've worked with or whose work I remember and respect. I'm able to help a lot of members of this great industry and that is a wonderful feeling. I have two professions now and I like to think I'm good at both of them."

Zeena La Vey

William Campbell is the director of fund-raising and public relations for the Motion Picture and Television Country House and Hospital in Woodland Hills, California.

Richard Webb played "Captain Midnight," the TV hero who was described as having been "spawned in steel and weaned to the whistle of bullets." The series was played later as **Jet Jackson, Flying Commando.**

"Captain Midnight" Richard Webb

The actor best known for his portrayal of "Captain Midnight" on television was born John Richard Webb in Bloomington, Illinois, on Sep-

tember 9, 1921. After studying at Brown University and a Bible school with the intention of becoming a clergyman, he realized he did not have the calling. He then enlisted in the U.S. Army and spent two years in Panama.

After leaving the service Richard went to Hollywood, thinking he might "crash" the movies. He enrolled at the Bliss Hayden Dramatic School and was cast opposite the then unknown Veronica Lake[8] in the stage farce *She Made Her Bed.* A talent scout from Paramount Pictures brought them both to the studio as "new faces" in *I Wanted Wings* (1941). Although Webb did not make the strong impression she did in the picture, he, too, was placed under contract and was cast in *Sullivan's Travels* (1941) and *Hold Back the Dawn* (1941).

After making *The Remarkable Andrew* (1942) with William Holden, both were detailed on special duty with the First Motion Picture Unit during World War II. Their orders were handed to them by Captain Ronald Reagan. Eventually, Webb rose to the rank of major.

After leaving the service he made *Out of the Past* (1947), *The Big Clock* (1948), and *A Connecticut Yankee in King Arthur's Court* (1949).

Richard admits he never registered strongly in movies, but he was very often cast in roles as a military man or a righteous patriot. His parts in *O.S.S.* (1946), *Sands of Iwo Jima* (1949), and *I Was a Communist for the F.B.I.* (1951) made the producers of *Captain Midnight* think of him as an obvious choice for the role of "Jim Albright," the World War I air ace who joined forces with civilian patriots to expose subversion and corruption.

His agent strongly advised Webb not to accept the part of "Captain Midnight," warning him that he would be forever typecast. At first the show's sponsor, Ovaltine, was reluctant to sign Richard since he was somewhat older than the actor they had envisioned. But he very much wanted to play the hero and did for the full run of the series and at countless personal appearances during and since. He has no regrets, although the only running part he has had since was as the lead in *U.S. Border Patrol,* a series that ran during the season of 1958–59. "I'm happy and proud to be thought of as Captain Midnight," says the actor, "because I firmly believe in what I used to tell our viewers—'Be loyal to your country and obey your parents.'" He feels that young people today are looking in vain for such values from their video heroes.

The television show became so popular that it was moved from Saturday mornings, where it premiered in 1953, to Monday evenings on ABC, where it competed with *Name That Tune* and *Burns and Allen.* According to the *New York Times,* 20 million people watched it weekly. Eleven million of them were adults. The shows continued in syndication around the world for another decade under the title *Jet Jackson, Flying Commando.*

All the while Richard Webb was standing for "freedom through strength and courage" as "Captain Midnight" he was an alcoholic. "It never interfered with my career," he said recently, "although maybe if I hadn't had a glow on all the time I'd have projected more personality on the big screen. I was on the stuff in my Paramount days." He was forced to face his drinking problem after his family and neighbors witnessed him standing in the middle of his front lawn, stripped to the waist, begging the twelve policemen who had been called to his home to shoot him. One headline read: "Captain Midnight Goes Off the Ovaltine."

Richard is often recognized as either "Captain Midnight" or "Jet Jackson." "I answer to both names," he says, and adds that he enjoys encounters with old fans. He is still in touch with Sid Melton, who played his sidekick "Ichabod Mudd" on the show and occasionally hears from Olan Soulé (living in Woodland Hills, California), who was the show's science expert "Tut."

Webb is seriously interested in astrology and parapsychology. He has authored *Great Ghosts of the West* and *These Came Back,* a book on reincarnation.

He and his wife, a former publicist and scriptwriter, have been married for more than thirty years. They live in the San Fernando Valley, have two grown daughters, and are grandparents. Richard Webb has not had a drink since 1961.

Since the character is now in the public domain, Richard has written a present-day version in which he occasionally makes an appearance as "Colonel Midnight" to counsel a new, younger "Captain Midnight."

Richard Webb recently in the den of his Van Nuys home.

Carleton Carpenter was under contract to Metro-Goldwyn-Mayer from 1949 to 1953.

Carleton Carpenter

The lanky actor of movies and stage was born in Bennington, Vermont, on July 10, 1926. With no encouragement from his family he sang from the age of four. By the time he turned nine he had mastered enough magic tricks to tour with a small carnival throughout New England during the summers. He was billed in his act as "Professor Upham."

Carleton was still in high school when he went to New York for the first time by himself.

Arriving at noon on January 20, 1944, he proceeded to the theater where tryouts were being held for *Bright Boy,* David Merrick's first show. He read at 2:00 P.M. and by noon the following day was told that he had the part. The play didn't run long but he went from it directly into another, *Career Angel.*

His next show was the Ray Bolger hit *Three to Make Ready* (1944), which ran for a year and a half on Broadway. He followed it with *The Magic Touch.*

Carpenter so disliked his performance in his first picture, *Lost Boundaries* (1949), that he turned down a contract with Paramount Pictures and M-G-M's offer to play his original role in the screen version of *Three to Make Ready.* When, finally, Carleton did sign with Metro he did so, "because I was determined to make a good impression in a good picture so both the public and myself could wipe out the memory of my first botched job."

He more than accomplished his goal in his fourth film. When Carleton Carpenter sang "Abba Dabba Honeymoon" with Debbie Reynolds in *Two Weeks with Love* (1950) he all but eclipsed everything he did before or since. The song, which was a hit recording as well, is so closely associated with him that movie buffs who are oblivious of his other work know his name and face because of it.

The team of Reynolds and Carpenter was very popular and a number of vehicles were announced for them but the only other time they worked together on screen was in *Three Little Words* (1950).

During the four years he spent on the Culver City lot he made *Vengeance Valley* (1950), *Father of the Bride* (1950), *Summer Stock* (1950), and *The Whistle at Eaton Falls* (1951). In *Fearless Fagin* (1952) he had the lead. His best notices came when he played a gangling young rodeo cowboy in *Sky Full of Moon* (1952), which is his favorite screen role.

The part he very much wanted and had been told was being tailored for him went to the late Bobby Van in *The Adventures of Dobie Gillis.* Carpenter left M-G-M after *Take the High Ground* (1953), an assignment he did not enjoy.

When he asked for a release from his contract he was told that he had been scheduled to play in one of the studio's big-budget musicals, *Seven Brides for Seven Brothers.* "It was quite a thing to have dangled before you," he said recently. "But if I'd played one of the brothers I wouldn't have been in *John Murray Anderson's Almanac.* It wasn't an easy decision and I thought at the time that I might come to regret it, but I never have."

The Anderson show was very well received and Carpenter got good notices, but it was a *succès d'estime.* It firmly established him as a Broadway performer, but the momentum of his screen career was lost.

Since then Carleton Carpenter has acted in summer stock, off-broadway and on, in such shows as *Hotel Paradiso* (1957), *A Stage Affair* (1962), and *Hello, Dolly!* (1965) with Ginger Rogers. Following that engagement he was featured in the touring company of *Hello, Dolly!* which starred Mary Martin and in the Chicago engagement with Carol Channing. He was signed for the London production, too, but withdrew when he broke his pelvis.

His screen appearances, as in *Up Periscope* (1959) and *Some of My Best Friends Are* (1971), have been infrequent. He much prefers to live and work on the East Coast.

He frequently directs shows, has written several, and recently penned the music and lyrics for *Northern Blvd.,* a show currently under option. Carpenter writes mystery and Gothic novels, the seventh of which, *The Peabody Experience,* was just published.

He has done very well financially from his national television commercials.

Carleton Carpenter maintains an office in Manhattan and lives with four cats in a house on five acres in Warwick, New York.

Those with whom he has remained in close touch over the years are Jan Sterling, Van Johnson, Debbie Reynolds, and, until her recent death, the centenarian Estelle Winwood.

The 6 foot 3 inch Carleton says he has never minded being thought of in connection with "Abba Dabba Honeymoon" and does not want fans to feel shy about mentioning it. It is one of the many videotapes he shows in his home in Warwick, New York. "It's a number that's now part of movie musical history," he has said. "It's a very nice feeling to know that."

Nancy Carroll was voted the Most Popular Actress on the Screen in a New York Daily News poll of 1930. The same year she was nominated for an Academy Award as Best Actress for her performance in The Devil's Holiday.

Nancy Carroll

One of the earliest and brightest stars of the sound era in movies was born Ann Veronica La Hiff in New York City on November 19, 1906.

When barely into her teens, she was obliged to leave school and go to work. She spent several years in offices before the public saw her on stage at amateur nights. She was picked to appear in *The Passing Show of 1923*. In her next, *Tropics* (1924), Nancy was a featured dancer. Again it was her dancing that won a solo in *The Passing Show of 1924*. By then she had married journalist Jack Kirkland, who years later wrote the hit play *Tobacco Road*.

Nancy went to Hollywood with her husband and did a few stage shows. She was tested by several studios but was told each time that she was not photogenic. But when she took the lead in the West Coast production of *Chicago* she got rave reviews while Clark Gable, who appeared with her, went virtually unnoticed.

When mogul Adolph Zukor signed her for the lead in *Abie's Irish Rose* (1928), the film that made her a star, he explained that he was taking a big chance. "Girls with round faces such as you have never become stars," he said.

"Oh," replied the new contractee, "you mean like Pola Negri?"

She was told specifically that her marriage had to be downplayed in her publicity and the fact that she had a baby would not be mentioned. Yet, when she was sent to promote her hit picture she took her daughter, Patricia, along.

Singing and dancing were the rage and Nancy did both delightfully in *Manhattan Cocktail* (1928), *Paramount on Parade* (1930), and *Honey* (1930), but Paramount found her behavior troublesome. Richard Arlen, who played opposite her several times, complained repeatedly about her attitude.

Edward Sutherland, who directed her in *Dance of Life* (1929), said of Nancy many years later: "If you told her to turn her head a bit to the right she'd move to the left, or upward or downward. She'd never do what she was asked. She delighted in exasperating people."

Dorothy Revier (widowed and living in Hollywood), who was featured in *The Dance of Life*, remembers her as "sarcastic and condescending. I thought that was just the way she had when she was on a picture, but later I ran into her in a shop and she was just as snooty."

While her marriage was coming apart her career was soaring. Her red hair was photographed in color in *Follow Thru* (1930) and won her even more fans. She proved a superb dramatic actress in *Laughter* (1930), *Stolen Heaven* (1931), and *The Man I Killed* (1932). When the votes were counted for the Oscars of 1929–30 Norma Shearer was the winner, but Nancy Carroll was the closest runner-up, well ahead of Gloria Swanson and Greta Garbo.

She got a divorce and immediately married the editor of a humor magazine, disillusioning a great many Roman Catholic fans who knew she had been married in their church.

In *Scarlet Dawn* (1932) she was convincing but it was Douglas Fairbanks, Jr.'s film. Newcomers Cary Grant and Randolph Scott got all the attention in *Hot Saturday* (1932). Through no fault of hers *The Woman Accused* (1933) was not a box-office success. Most people thought her miscast in *The Kiss Before the Mirror* (1933). Her contract was terminated.

She did well with Jack Benny in *Transatlantic Merry-Go-Round* but *Springtime for Henry,* also made in 1934, was given a "Condemned" rating by the Legion of Decency.

In the early 1960s Nancy took over the lead in *Never Too Late,* which she played successfully on Broadway and on tour. She was appearing in the role opposite Bert Lahr when she was found dead in August 1965.

To many who were ardent fans throughout her career or who have discovered her appeal in recent years she seems to be the victim of either the studio system or just bad luck. Certainly her career could have been helped, saved, or revitalized by various parts. *A Farewell to Arms,* which was a great success for Helen Hayes, was meant for Nancy. She had been Samuel Goldwyn's first choice for the part that Sylvia Sydney played in *Street Scene.* Frank Capra wanted her for *Broadway Bill,* but settled for Myrna Loy when Ms. Carroll was unavailable. As late as 1944, when David O. Selznick announced that Patricia Kirkland would play the lead in *Kiss and Tell,* Nancy could have made a real comeback playing

mother to her real-life daughter. At the last minute, however, Shirley Temple accepted the star part and Nancy's daughter was dropped.

To the end of her life she continued either to totally beguile people or to alienate them completely. A journalist who interviewed her in depth during the last year of her life says of Nancy Carroll: "There was something about her in person or over the phone, in everything she said—even in her smile—that struck me as sheer contempt. Everyone and everything was beneath her."

Will Hutchins,[8] who played on Broadway with her, found her "the warmest, most helpful star I've ever worked with. She was generous in every way. I'm a better actor and person for having known her."

Nancy Carroll photographed in the spring of 1965, a few months before her death.

Edward Oleksak

Marguerite Chapman was a John Robert Powers model before going to Hollywood in 1939.

Marguerite Chapman

The leading lady of movies and television was born in Chatham, New York, on March 7. Her father was an engineer with the New York Central Railroad.

While growing up Marguerite spent more time studying the clothes, makeup, and manners of actresses than she did on schoolwork. Her allowance went to pay for acting lessons.

"One way or another," she told one interviewer, "I intended to make it." Five weeks after moving to Manhattan she signed with John Robert Powers, then one of the two top model agencies in the world. Howard Hughes was introduced to her by Sherman Fairchild, the industrialist, who was her frequent escort during that period.

On Christmas Eve, 1939, she arrived in the movie capital under contract to Howard Hughes. As she made her entrance at Jack Warner's New Year's Eve party her heel caught and she fell down a short flight of stairs. The first hand to assist her up from the floor was Errol Flynn's. "I wasn't fully up on my two feet before he had asked me to dinner," recalls Marguerite. "This was while his wife, Lili Damita [living in Fort Dodge, Iowa], was standing about three feet away. 'Well,' I thought to myself, 'I guess this is Hollywood!'"

Hughes tested her for the part that Jane Russell eventually played in *The Outlaw*. He told her that she was quite wrong for the role and "too much a lady" for him. But everyone agreed that she photographed well and her contract was sold to Twentieth Century-Fox. She made her debut in one of the "Jones Family" series, *On Their Own* (1940), and then did *Charlie Chan at the Wax Museum* (1940). Marguerite thinks she might have done well on that lot, but that she blew her chances when production chief Darryl F. Zanuck asked her to dance one evening. "I told him that I was sorry," she says, "but that I just found I couldn't dance with men shorter than I was. He didn't say anything at the time, but when my first option came up I was let go."

Her agent, Leland Hayward, sold her services to Harold Lloyd for *A Girl, a Guy and a Gob* (1941) which he produced for RKO. Marguerite was disappointed in what she felt was a lack of real progress in pictures. She returned to New York City only to be brought back immediately by Warner Brothers, who wanted to test her for *Sergeant York*. Although she didn't get that part she was placed under contract. She appeared in *Navy Blues* (1941), *You're in the Army Now* (1941), and *The Body Disappears* (1941), during the one year she spent on the Burbank lot. Then she starred in a Republic serial, *Spy Smasher* (1942).

Marguerite Chapman went under contract to Columbia Pictures in 1942. Among the nineteen features she made there are: *Submarine Raider* (1942) with John Howard,[8] who was her boy friend at the time; *Appointment in Berlin* (1943) with George Sanders; *Destroyer* (1943) with Edward G. Robinson; *Counter-Attack* (1945) with Paul Muni; *Pardon My Past* (1946) with Fred MacMurray; *Mr. District Attorney* (1947), and *Coroner Creek* (1948) with Randolph Scott.[8]

During her six years at Columbia Marguerite took acting lessons from Josephine Hutchinson (the widow of Statts Cotsworth lives in New York City). "I really wanted to become a good actress," she said recently. "I took *every* part they handed me, but eventually it dawned on me that I was just a piece of merchandise to the studio. By then I'd made so many B films I knew I was going nowhere."

Freelancing, she went to RKO for *The Green Promise* (1949), although she felt awkward in the part. The only A feature she made after that was *The Seven Year Itch* (1955), which was the next to her last movie. In the interim she worked in low-budget fare at Universal, Monogram, and Lippert.

Throughout the fifties Marguerite Chapman was seen frequently on TV programs such as *Schlitz Playhouse of Stars, Four-Star Playhouse, Lux Video Theater,* and *Climax.* After 1960 she appeared on *Marcus Welby, M.D., Hawaii Five-O, Police Story,* and lastly on *Barnaby Jones* in 1977.

She refers to her brief marriage to Bentley Ryan, a prominent attorney, as "a minor tragedy." Her second husband was the director J.

Richard Bremerkamp. She has been divorced twice, but considers herself a Roman Catholic. Marguerite donates much of her time to an organization to save stray animals, but lives in a building that does not allow pets. The walls of her apartment are decorated with her own watercolors, but she no longer paints.

Recently she spoke of her present life. "I sold real estate for years and still have a license, but I don't really need to work, so I don't. I'll always think of myself as an actress, yet I don't seem to be doing anything about reactivating my career. I used to enjoy painting, but for some reason I stopped and can't seem to begin again. I feel wonderful and I think I look pretty good. I'd like to share my life with someone, but I don't have anyone in mind. For a young woman it's tough enough, but when you're older—well, it's the pits. I guess you could say that I'm at a crossroads."

Marguerite Chapman takes aerobics classes and plays a lot of golf. She lives by herself in North Hollywood.

Dollie Tombers

Marguerite Chapman today in her North Hollywood apartment.

Mike Wallace and Buff Cobb co-hosted several local and network television shows during their five-year marriage. They were divorced in 1954.

Buff Cobb

The television personality and sometime actress was born Patrizia Cobb on October 19, 1928, in Florence, Italy, where her father was studying voice. After divorcing her mother, he married the soprano Gladys Swarthout. Buff was brought up by her mother, a novelist and scenarist. She was greatly influenced during her childhood by her grandfather, the humorist Irvin S. Cobb.

Despite strong objections from her family she married Hollywood attorney Gregson Bautzer. They were divorced within six months.

Through her family and schoolmates Buff had numerous connections in the film industry and theater. When she was offered a contract with Twentieth Century-Fox she hesitated, thinking that she should first get some experience.

"But they said they would teach me," she recalls. "The only thing I learned was how to run around Zanuck's desk faster than he could."

The only part she played was one of Rex Harrison's wives in *Anna and the King of Siam* (1946).

She married another Fox contractee, William Eythe, in June 1947 and divorced him the following January.

"I think his psychiatrist thought it would be good for him," she commented recently. "He had some real problems, poor boy."

Through Eythe she met Tallulah Bankhead, who agreed to her being cast as the young newlywed in *Private Lives*. Their national tour was playing Chicago when a young newsman named Mike Wallace interviewed her. Shortly thereafter, in 1949, she married him.

The Wallaces settled in Chicago and she continued to act on radio and in stock. They sold themselves to the local NBC-TV channel as a husband and wife team. On *The Chez Show* Mike and Buff talked with visiting celebrities and all the stars who were playing the Chez

Paree nightclub. It was a big success throughout the Midwest.

CBS brought them to New York, where they were teamed on *Saturday Night Square, Mike and Buff,* and *All Around the Town,* live programs that featured the young, attractive couple visiting places and people. At the same time they had their own morning radio program. There was a lot of bickering between them on all of their efforts, with Wallace usually getting the last word. "Smarten up, Buff!" was one of his catch phrases.

"We overdid the personal exchanges," Ms. Cobb has been quoted as saying. "It ended in our getting a divorce."

She remembers Wallace as "livid" when she alone became a regular panelist on *Masquerade Party,* a show she appeared on from 1953 to 1955.

"It became clear that he didn't want me doing anything," she recalls. "When I was offered the starring role in *The Champagne Waltz* he threw the script right out the window."

She had *The Buff Cobb Show* on her own for White Rose Tea on a New York City channel and acted on the straw-hat circuit before becoming involved exclusively with producing.

She was co-producer of *Let It Ride,* which starred Sam Levene, George Gobel, and the late Barbara Nichols in 1961. She was one of the producers of *Too True to Be Good,* a 1963 revival that got excellent notices and earned a Tony nomination. The comedy *Never Live Over a Pretzel Factory,* a 1964 Buff Cobb production, was sold to her old studio for a large sum but has never been filmed.

She was so involved in producing she had to turn down offers to host her own TV show in Chicago and to appear regularly with Charles Collingwood on the CBS *Morning News.*

Her lack of activity in recent years, she says, was due to illness and major surgery from which she is still recovering. She is a moderately heavy cigarette smoker.

During her hiatus from producing and acting Buff became fluent in French and developed into what she calls "a fantastic cook." Walter Cronkite and José Ferrer are the celebrities she sees frequently.

Her present project is to co-host a radio program with her close friend, Virginia Graham.

"We'd be heaven together," enthuses Ms. Cobb. "We agree on absolutely nothing. And Ginny always says that she has the perfect face for radio."

Buff Cobb is married to a real estate executive. She has no children.

Richard Schaeffer

The Sutton Place apartment of Buff Cobb and her fourth husband is decorated with Oriental art.

Ben Cooper and Debbie Reynolds were thought to bear a striking resemblance to each other in the fifties.

Ben Cooper

The baby-faced movie and television actor was born in Hartford, Connecticut, on September 30, 1933. He grew up on Long Island, New York.

Life with Father had been running on Broadway for more than two years when one of Ben's grammar school classmates, who was a cast member, mentioned to Mr. and Mrs. Cooper that the producers were looking for a replacement for the part of "Harlan." Cooper's father, an engineer, and his mother, a registered nurse, discussed the opportunity with their son at length. "They left it strictly up to me," he recalls. "But once I decided that I'd like to try for the part Dad coached me, using my friend's script." He auditioned along with dozens of other hopefuls, but by then he had memorized the entire play. "The fact that I had the bright red hair the part called for didn't hurt either," he added. Ben was in the show for three years, eventually growing into the role of "Whitney," one of the older sons.

While he was appearing each evening on Broadway Ben was acting on radio programs in the afternoons after school. He played on such shows as *Young Widder Brown, The F.B.I. in Peace and War,* and had the running part of "Dickie" on *Portia Faces Life.* He appeared in more than 3,200 radio broadcasts and 150 live TV shows before getting a bid from Hollywood.

Warner Brothers screen-tested him for *Retreat, Hell!* Although he didn't get the part, someone at Republic studios saw the footage and suggested him for their production of *Thunderbirds* (1952) with John Barrymore, Jr. (living in Hollywood). His next picture, *The Woman They Almost Lynched* (1953), was for the same studio. In it he played the young Jesse James. While making the film Cooper got into a conversation with the head of the studio, Herbert J. Yates. "I had no idea that he was who he was," says Ben. "He asked me if I liked my part. I told him I wanted to specialize in playing heavies. He wanted to know why and I told him that because I looked so innocent the audience would be held by the surprise of a baby-faced bad guy. The next thing I knew I was under contract to Republic Pictures."

Ben got his wish many times. In the Joan Crawford starrer *Johnny Guitar* (1954), he was "Turkey," a member of a gang of outlaws. In *Rebel in Town* (1956) he played the title role. "I was shot in Arizona, dragged through cactus, killed in Colorado, and hanged in California," he recalls. According to his count he has been killed in nineteen features and on 247 TV shows.

Republic put Ben Cooper's horsemanship to good use. It was a lot known for westerns and he had had his own horse since he was very young. He was cast in *Jubilee Trail* (1954), which starred Vera Hruba Ralston,[8] *The Last Command* (1955), *Duel at Apache Wells* (1957), and *Outlaw's Son* (1957).

He was often pictured in fanzines with starlets on dates that had been arranged by studio publicists. He was twice wrongly reported as being engaged to be married. In one instance he had never met the actress. Ben was guesting on a *Wagon Train* episode in December 1959 when Ward Bond introduced him to a young woman named Pamela who was one of the Ray Conniff Singers. That evening he told his roommate he had just met his future wife. They were married a few months later.

The Coopers bought their home in Woodland Hills after Ben had tested for "Steve" on *The Virginian*. He had been promised the part, but it went to Gary Clarke. Shortly after that experience the couple became involved in Amway, the line of consumer products sold by individual dealers. They are now distributors.

"A lot of actors I've worked with are now sitting in tiny apartments praying for the phone to ring," he said recently. "When they were at the height of their careers they never dreamed they'd need another income. I prefer to control my own future."

When he was playing a running part on *Sheriff Lobo* from 1979 to 1981 he had to be cued onto the set by a flashing light because he was unable to hear his name being called. His hearing was seriously impaired by nerve damage at about that time. After it was determined that surgery could not correct his condition he began wearing hearing aids in both ears during all of his activities, including acting. He says he has had many letters from viewers stating that seeing him wearing the devices on TV has helped them overcome embarrassment about theirs. "To me," Cooper explains, "it is like needing glasses and refusing to wear them. I don't indulge myself in such foolish vanity. People who speak to me are entitled to be heard."

Ben still acts on television. He built a large addition to his home with what he made on one series of commercials for McDonald's. In 1983 he was seen on *The Fall Guy*. "But," he emphasizes, "I'm a businessman-actor rather than the other way around."

Ben and his wife have two daughters and are grandparents.

Ben Cooper in his Woodland Hills home. The founders of Amway are in the photograph on the right.

Ron Alexander

Bob Cummings won an Emmy in 1954 for his performance in Twelve Angry Men, *a play first seen on* Studio One. *He received four other nominations during the fifties from his starring role on his own TV series.*

Bob Cummings

The star of movies and television was born on June 9, 1910, in Joplin, Missouri. His father was a physician and nutritionalist. His mother was a minister in the Church of Religious Science. Orville Wright, who was a patient and friend of Bob's father, was his godfather.

Cummings earned his first pilot's certificate when he was seventeen years old. After high school he enrolled at Carnegie Institute of Technology to study aeronautical engineering. His roommate, the scion of a wealthy family, longed to be an actor and offered Bob a trip to New York City if he would accompany him to casting offices.

A director of the American Academy of Dramatic Arts spotted Cummings in his outer office and offered him a scholarship, which he accepted only after he was assured that it would be accompanied by a small salary.

During his summer vacation he worked his way to England aboard an ocean liner. From London he mailed some eighty letters to producers and agents in New York. Since young English leading men were then very popular on Broadway Bob introduced himself as "Blady Stanhope Conway, England's youngest actor-manager-director-producer and owner of the Harrowgate Repertory Co." Three days after landing in the U.S. he was signed for the juvenile lead in Galsworthy's *The Roof* (1930).

Next he played the leading man in the *Earl Carroll Vanities.* He toned down his accent a bit and changed his name to "Brice Hutchins" before going into the *Ziegfeld Follies of 1933.*

When Bob Cummings arrived in Hollywood he passed himself off as a romantic Texan, a type in vogue at the time in movies. His screen debut was in *So Red the Rose* (1935). He followed that with *The Last Train from Madrid* (1937) and *College Swing* (1938). At the suggestion of Ernst Lubitsch he was signed for *Three Smart Girls Grow Up* (1939) and placed under contract to Universal.

Bob, who has made more than one hundred features, feels his best are *Princess O'Rourke* (1943), *The Devil and Miss Jones* (1941), and *King's Row* (1942).

Some of his other screen appearances were in *The Under-Pup* (1939), *Saboteur* (1942), *Flesh and Fantasy* (1943), *You Came Along* (1945), *The Accused* (1949), *Dial M for Murder* (1954), and *How to Be Very, Very Popular* (1955).

Where Cummings really came into his own was on television. In 1954 he won an Emmy for his performance in *Twelve Angry Men,* and was nominated for an Emmy as the "Best Actor in a Regular Series." For the next four years he was nominated in the same category for *The Bob Cummings Show,* which he often directed.

On the show, which was originally called *Love That Bob,* he played a "wolf photographer." The plots were usually built around the complications in his professional and emotional life. Sometimes he would fly his own plane back to his hometown of Joplin to visit with his grandfather, a part Bob also played.

After production ended on his series Cummings continued to make movies, such as *The Carpetbaggers* (1964) and *Stagecoach* (1966). His boyish manner and energy proved very effective in *Generation* and *Sweet Charity,* two of the stage vehicles in which he toured until recent years.

He met his wife, who is Chinese, while making *Five Golden Dragons* (1967) in Hong Kong. Their son is a high school student.

Bob Cummings considers himself retired from acting. His only close friend from the profession is Ken Murray. He has four daughters and two sons by previous marriages. Only Bob, Jr., who acts under the name Anthony Bob, followed his father's profession.

The Cummingses keep an apartment in the San Fernando Valley but live most of the year

Sarah Richardson

The license plate on Bob Cummings's Citroën sedan reads: LVMYCIT.

in their home on the shores of an island in Puget Sound. He gave up flying on his seventieth birthday rather than have the premium of his $1 million life insurance policy quadruple.

"I loved flying, but I don't miss it," he remarked recently. "That is true of acting, also. I'm keenly interested in astrology, so I'm still among the stars, you might say. I loved everything I've ever done and now I love not doing anything. I've been lucky with my career and my family. I am very thankful."

Another thing Bob is grateful for is his good health. At the height of his popularity he became one of the first celebrities to promote raw and natural foods and was often dismissed as a "health food nut."

"I'd tell all those critics how well I feel today because of my diet." He laughs. "But they're all dead."

Constance Cummings, along with Frances Dee and Joan Blondell, was named a Wampus Baby Star in 1931.

Constance Cummings

The movie actress and international stage star was born Constance Halverstadt on May 15, 1910, in Seattle, Washington. Her family moved to San Diego when she was very young. She took her brother's first name, Cummings, as her professional surname.

Constance was in her early teens and still in high school when she became a member of the Savoy Stock Company. Dancing, however, more than acting was what interested her and she went to New York City to study and work.

She was in the chorus of *Treasure Girl* (1928), which starred Gertrude Lawrence, and the first *Little Show* (1929).

"But," Constance has said, "New York was not the center of the dance world in those days. I was helping to support my mother, so when I was offered a job understudying the lead in *June Moon* I took it. And that's how I began acting."

One extremely hot day in 1930 she took over for the star at the matinee performance. A reporter she knew caught her in the part and wrote a glowing review in the New York *Sun*. When it was brought to the attention of Samuel Goldwyn he invited her to Hollywood to play opposite Ronald Colman in *The Devil to Pay* (1930). After ten days of shooting, however, it was decided that she was "unsuitable" and Loretta Young[8] replaced her. Colman, feeling that Constance needed a break, urged Myron Selznick to help her. The agent sold her services to Columbia Pictures, where she made her debut in *The Criminal Code* (1931).

She spent the next two years under contract to the Gower Street lot where she appeared mostly in programmers such as *Travelling Husbands* (1931), *Attorney for the Defense* (1932), and *The Billion Dollar Scandal* (1933). Her most notable films were *American Madness* (1932), *Night After Night* (1932), and *Movie Crazy* (1932). She got the latter only after she begged Harry Cohn to loan her out to Harold Lloyd as his leading lady. Of Mae West, who emerged as the star of the former, Ms. Cummings has said, "I did not admire her as an actress or as a person. On and off the set she struck me as someone who had no regard for anyone but herself."

By the time Constance Cummings left Hollywood in the mid-thirties she had the experience of having played with Walter Huston, Boris Karloff, and Spencer Tracy. Howard Hawks, Frank Capra, and William Wyler had directed her on the screen and on Broadway she had garnered all the notices in *Accent on Youth* (1934). She had been on the cover of several fanzines and gotten some publicity from her dates with Howard Hughes, but was still regarded by the studios as no more than a moderately pretty blond ingenue with some promise.

Constance married English playwright Benn W. Levy and settled in London.

Before the outbreak of World War II she was seen on Broadway in *Young Madame Conti* (1936), *If I Were You* (1938), and *The Jealous God* (1939), all plays Levy had written. He also authored *Return of the Tyassi,* which she did in 1950, and *Rape of the Belt,* in which she starred ten years later, also in New York City.

Constance made an occasional film and stage appearance in England, but much of her time was taken up with her two children and the running of the Levy farm fourteen miles west of Oxford. In London they lived in a large home built by Walter Gropius in Chelsea. Alfred Hitchcock was a close friend and frequent guest.

In 1964 she took over the starring role in *Who's Afraid of Virginia Woolf?* when Uta Hagen left the West End production.

Of the pictures she made away from Hollywood probably *Blithe Spirit* (1945) is the best known, although she feels the cast and Noel Coward's script never really jelled since it was made over too long a time period. Her reviews for *The Battle of the Sexes* (1960) all but

Richard Lamparski

Constance Cummings beside a sculpture of her husband, the late playwright Benn W. Levy.

eclipsed its star, Peter Sellers.

From her performances with the Old Vic and the National Theatre Company Constance Cummings has become one of the most prestigious actresses in England. Laurence Olivier chose her to play opposite him in *Long Day's Journey into Night* on stage. The immensely successful production was presented on U.S. television in 1973.

Her portrayal of a stroke victim in Arthur Kopit's *Wings* brought her the Tony as the Best Actress of the 1978–79 Broadway season.

Constance has stated that she never considered returning to live in the U.S., even after the death of her husband in 1973. "I consider myself English," she has said.

As to Hollywood and what might have happened had she stayed, she once said, "It's a wonder to me that anyone stays there who's serious about the performing arts. The atmosphere is not conducive to creative work."

NBC Photo

Dagmar has accurately described herself as "a phenomenon of the fifties."

Dagmar

The sensation of early television was born in Huntington, West Virginia, on November 29. "My age," she has said, "like my weight, fluctuates."

Her original name was Virginia Ruth Egnor. She went through school using her middle name because "it's easier to spell."

She was fascinated by show business and was in her class play every year, but immediately upon graduation married a man twelve years her senior. She moved with her husband, who was an instructor of naval cadets, to Bal Harbor, Florida, where he was stationed.

After a few years "Jenny," as she was then called, left her husband and went on the road with Olsen and Johnson. By the late forties she was divorced and appearing in the play *Burlesque* with Bert Lahr.

When she first was seen on television it was on one of Bob Hope's early shows. Her hair was then red.

In 1950 almost anyone watching late night television was tuned to *Broadway Open House,* which starred Jerry Lester (living in North Miami Beach, Florida). She was hired on a show-to-show basis and told to sit on a stool in front of Milton DeLugg's band and "look dumb." The name she was given was "Dagmar."

Having recently returned from a Florida vacation, her hair was sun-streaked. Her hairdresser used a chemical that bleached it, so that when she showed up for the first broadcast she was a 5 feet 8½ inch super-buxom blonde. From her first appearance Dagmar was a smash hit.

Bars—where most TV sets were in those days—became crowded in spite of the late hour with patrons who wanted to see the woman who was, in the vernacular of many areas of the country, a "lallapalooza."

Her deadpan readings of her poetry and "treasises" amused both genders. Two-thirds of the approximately 2,000 letters she received weekly were from women.

The July 16, 1951, issue of *Life* had an Alfred Eisenstaedt photograph of her on its cover. In the article, entitled "TV's Dagmar—from $75 a week to $3,250," she was called "an American institution" and was estimated as having a bustline of "upwards of 39 inches."

Jerry Lester gave Dagmar the exposure that catapulted her to prominence and may have named her, but her character was not one created by scripts or situations. She got most of her biggest laughs with her ad libs and the funniest thing about her was her attitude. Dagmar was her own creation.

When Dagmar and ABC-TV came to terms on a contract she was given a bonus of $10,000 upon signing. "Now wasn't that sweet of them?" she asked the press in her pronounced drawl.

With her colossal cleavage and spike heels she made the perfect partner for Frank Sinatra when he played the Paramount Theater and for Milton Berle during his stand at the Roxy. Jimmy Durante brought her on to his TV show. She co-hosted the *Mike Douglas Show,* headlined the Desert Inn in Las Vegas, and starred in road shows of *The Women* and *Gypsy.* The big disappointment of her career was when *The Amazing Adele,* the big-budget show that was expected to launch her as a Broadway star, closed out of town.

She became more and more selective about her appearances and was rarely seen on TV. Then in the early seventies her businessman husband became seriously ill. She nursed him around the clock until he died in 1977.

Although Dagmar never found the vehicle she had hoped would make her a star, she earned enough money along the way to help put her nieces and nephews through college and buy the ex-mayor's house for her parents.

Her humor was never at anyone else's expense and such diverse and prickly personalities as Gloria Swanson, Elaine Stritch, and Lili St. Cyr enjoyed working with her. The latter gave Dagmar an emerald pin after they played together.

Many ask why Dagmar, who still has the name recognition of a major star, has all but disappeared from the medium that made her a

Dagmar has homes in New York's Westchester County and Palm Springs, California. She has no children.

household word. Her explanation is: "I'd much rather have people wonder whatever happened to Dagmar than say, 'Look what's happened to Dagmar!'"

At the conclusion of a recent interview Dagmar allowed her slit skirt to fall open and said, "Honey, be sure to mention how great my legs look still. Those TV audiences never saw them. Nobody ever looked down that far."

Denise Darcel

Denise Darcel, contrary to what has been stated in some of her publicity, was never a Miss France.

The French siren of the forties and fifties was born Denise Billecard on September 8, in Paris. She and her four sisters worked in their father's bakery in the small town where they were raised.

After the end of World War II Denise moved to Paris and was working in a five-and-ten-cent store when she won the "Pygmalion Contest." The publicity that followed resulted in Denise's being called the "Most Photographed Girl in France" and the "Most Beautiful Girl in France."

She appeared in nightclubs in Paris and on the Riviera, but made no films before coming to the United States in 1947 as the bride of a captain in the U.S. Army. Out of uniform, however, Denise found him much less attractive and ended the marriage after a year.

In her first movie, *To the Victor* (1948), she sang "La Vie en Rose." The part of the cabaret singer got her quite a bit of attention but no contract offer from a major studio. To survive she played in the low-budget *Thunder in the Pines* (1949).

An agent noticed her in a little theater production and felt she was right for the film William Wellman was about to direct at M-G-M. Wellman had already cast the role by the time he met Denise but was so taken with her Gallic charms the other actress was paid off. The picture was *Battleground,* which starred Van Johnson and John Hodiak. She was the only woman in it.

Battleground (1949) was a major box-office hit and Denise was established as a busty, lusty sex symbol. It was she who devised the bit that proved to be her most memorable. William Wellman simply told her to slice some bread. She did this by placing one end of the long loaf between her breasts and cutting with the blade pointing toward them. To this day most fans she meets mention that scene.

Her other screen credits are: *Tarzan and the Slave Girl* (1950); *Westward the Women* (1951) with Robert Taylor and the late Hope Emerson; *Young Man with Ideas* (1952) with Glen Ford and Mary Wickes (single and living in Century City); *Dangerous When Wet* (1953) with Esther Williams; *Flame of Calcutta* (1953) with Patric Knowles (living in Woodland Hills, California); *Vera Cruz* (1954), and *Seven Women from Hell* (1961).

Her outstanding features were always her sense of humor about herself and her décolletage. Both worked well for her on her many appearances with Milton Berle and on her own short-lived TV show, *Gamble on Love.* They also made her a favorite with the press, bringing an extraordinary amount of publicity for someone who made fewer than a dozen features.

She thinks she lost a chance for major stardom when she rejected the advances of mogul Harry Cohn and again when she did not respond to the obvious interest of Howard Hughes. While she has no regrets about either opportunity, she now believes she made a serious error in opting to play in theaters and nightclubs rather than remain in Hollywood.

"At the time I couldn't see the sense in turning down the chance to go on the road in shows like *Can-Can*," she said recently. "I loved the live audiences and the money was very good. What I didn't realize is that if you're not in Hollywood or on Broadway you are not thought of for movie parts."

Denise co-starred in dinner theaters with Pinky Lee and Mickey Hargitay. In niteries she headlined for a while and then became the opening act for Joel Grey. In the late sixties she could command as much as $10,000 a week, but for that salary she had to strip down to pasties and bikini.

Richard Lamparski

Denise Darcel and her sons, Chris and Craig, were living together in Las Vegas in spring, 1984.

Ms. Darcel has lost none of her vivaciousness or her heavy French accent. She has been divorced three more times, raised two sons, and supported herself until recently as a dealer and shill at Caesars Palace in Las Vegas.

In June 1984 Denise and her sons were planning on moving to Los Angeles with their Doberman pinscher. Her youngest, Craig, would like to be an actor-comedian and his mother thinks she is now right for TV situation comedy.

"Right now is not the best time for my career," she said. "But as a child I almost starved to death. I know what real trouble is like, so I don't feel sorry for myself. We eat well and have good health and love each other very much. Things will be good again soon. All my life I go up, down, up, down. I am indestructible!"

Dennis Day was associated with Jack Benny from 1940, when he was first hired, until the comedian's death in 1974.

Dennis Day

The singer-comedian was born Owen Patrick McNulty on May 21, 1917, in New York City. His father was an engineer for the city. The McNulty family home was in the Bronx.

He had been in his high school glee club, but when Dennis graduated from Manhattan College his intention was to go to law school. Hoping to earn some tuition money by singing, he made a recording of "I Never Knew Heaven Could Speak." He sent copies of the record around to various radio producers. Someone played it for Mary Livingston, who insisted the tenor be considered for her husband's radio program, *The Jack Benny Show.*

By 1940 Benny was well established as the Sunday evening listening habit for much of the nation. Tenor Kenny Baker (now a Christian Science practitioner in Solvang, California) had made a name for himself as the show's vocalist, but objected to the scripts, which had him playing a likable but scatterbrained character. He gave his notice.

An audition was set and Dennis Day was one of the many singers who were called. He did not know he was being heard as a possible replacement or that the job would require comedy. When his name was called he responded with, "Yes, please!"—a phrase that was to become a familiar one to millions of radio listeners. Jack and his wife felt the moment they heard it that Dennis had the perfect attitude for the part he was to play, a good-natured schnook.

"Jack and Mary sized me up quite accurately," Day explains. "The writers did the rest. Now, I wasn't as green as they made me out to be but, frankly, I *was* naïve."

Usually in his exchanges with Benny it was Day who got the laughs. Today when he is told by former listeners of their vivid recollections of his contributions to that show Dennis is greatly flattered but says, "What people are astounded to learn is that my part on all the programs was never once more than a page and a half of script."

Dennis Day's career was managed skillfully so as to allow him to strike out on his own as a regular on other shows and to star in two of his own without leaving the Benny cast.

A Day in the Life of Dennis Day was a successful situation comedy on NBC radio for five years beginning in 1946. From 1952 to 1954 *The Dennis Day Show* was seen on TV.

His on-the-air relationship with Jack Benny was never more cleverly exploited than when the late Verna Felton would guest as Dennis's mother. Her character was that of a pushy old lady who bested Benny in every exchange.

Dennis married in 1948 and is the father of six sons and four daughters. He has eight grandchildren. His brother, an obstetrician, is the husband of Ann Blyth (living in Toluca Lake, California).

He has narrated movies for Walt Disney and worked as a single in nightclubs. Several times Dennis has toured the country as the star of *Brigadoon*. He is still active as a lecturer, which gives him an opportunity to expound on one of his favorite subjects—the defense of ethnic humor.

After taking his professional name legally in 1944 he returned to court to have the order reversed three years later. His family had strongly objected.

Dennis Day is almost as well known for being Roman Catholic as he is for being Irish. He is an outspoken opponent of anything he considers "blue." In 1962 he canceled a $5,000 booking in Seattle when he learned that he was expected to work on stage with strippers. He holds the titles of Knight of Malta and Knight of the Holy Sepulchre, both high honors in his faith.

Dennis brought up his family in a large Cape Cod house in Mandeville Canyon. For several years he was honorary mayor of that wealthy area in West Los Angeles. In 1983, when most of their children had moved away, the Days put their property on the market for $2,750,000 and planned to move to Santa Barbara. They have since decided to remain where they are, but have sold The Old House, the antique shop they owned and operated for years in Santa Monica.

When queried about Jack Benny's well-publicized stinginess Dennis answers, "To me, he was generous in every way and really happy about my success. God rest the immortal soul of my dear friend."

Dennis Day's home in the Mandeville Canyon area of West Los Angeles is furnished with fine antiques.

Donna Schaeffer

Rosie (left) and Jenny Dolly were known throughout their careers as "The Twin Hungarian Rhapsodies." Twentieth Century-Fox produced a Technicolor musical in 1945 based loosely on the lives of the sisters, who to many epitomized the Roaring Twenties.

The Dolly Sisters

The most famous and glamorous twins of the twentieth century were born in Budapest, Hungary, on October 25, 1892. Their original names were Roszika and Janszieka Deutsch. Their family migrated to the Lower East Side of Manhattan around 1900.

From an early age the sisters danced and sang for their friends and family. They ap-peared in many amateur shows before making their professional debut on a vaudeville bill in 1909. Their act was an immediate hit.

The twins were identical, as were their expressions, gestures, makeup, and costumes. In the beginning years the originality of their dances was usually emphasized in their invariably favorable reviews. If they changed little except their clothes and music during their long careers it was probably because their public did not seem to tire of what they did. Then, too, throughout most of the years they appeared on stage, merely having seen the "fabulous dancing Dollys" in person was considered a must by any serious theatergoer.

The Dollys were such a success in the *Ziegfeld Follies of 1911* that the same producer starred them in 1912 in *A Winsome Widow.* Thus launched, they headlined many times at the Palace Theater for as much as $5,000 a week. At Paris's Moulin Rouge they were paid $1,200 a day.

Their exotic beauty and huge salaries were only part of their fascination. Even in a time of great extravagance and personal liberation the Dollys seemed extreme in everything they did. "Diamond Jim" Brady gift-wrapped a Rolls-Royce in ribbons, gave it to Rosie, and then traveled around the country with both women and their husbands.

By 1918 they were known all over the world as *The Million Dollar Dollies,* the title of the movie they made for Metro Pictures. It was about that time the sisters began to share their good fortune with something their marriages, fame, and money never brought them—children. Jenny assumed the support of fifty French orphans. Rosie endowed several Hungarian orphanages.

The Dolly sisters were credited with being the first show-business personalities to be accepted socially by international society. Those who courted and escorted them were often titled men such as the Prince of Wales, Sir

Thomas Lipton, Sir Harry Lauder, Lord Beaverbrook, and King Alfonso XIII of Spain—and always rich.

They lived in Europe during most of the twenties and earned the title "First Citizens of the Riviera" from their ritzy life style and legendary nights of high-stakes gambling. Jenny claimed to have won $500,000 at baccarat in one evening. On another night she cleared $200,000 at roulette. One day at the races netted her $100,000. Four times in one year she was reported to have broken the bank at Monte Carlo.

Both Dollys loved jewels. After one particularly late night at the casino Jenny dallied over her breakfast until the doors opened at Cartier, where she spent the entire $150,000 she had won. When Rosie divorced the son of a man known as the "Canadian Rockefeller," part of her settlement was pearls valued at $750,000.

By the time they retired from performing in 1928 Rosie and Jenny had become so famous they no longer had to appear on stage to get press. Having introduced jazz to Europe and set styles with their slanted eyes and sleek black hair, they continued to be the toast of two continents until 1933, when Jenny was seriously hurt in a car crash. She had been in the midst of a stormy affair with Max Constant, a French aviator and film star. Her injuries required seventeen operations, necessitating the sale of most of her jewels, including the fifty-one-carat square-cut diamond rumored to have been a gift from the owner of London's Selfridge's department store. The extensive plastic surgery never fully restored Jenny's famous features and left deep emotional scars.

In 1932 New York's Mayor Jimmy Walker married Rosie to Irving Netcher, son of the founder of Chicago's Boston Store and a bon vivant known internationally for his lavish living. His brother Townsend and his wife, silent movie star Constance Talmadge, were witnesses.

By 1941 Jenny was separated from her second husband and living in Hollywood with her two adopted daughters. What remained of her money had been frozen in France after the outbreak of World War II. She never regained her health and described herself to a friend as "a broken shell." She left no note before making a noose from the red velvet drapes in her apartment and hanging herself.

Rosie and her husband spent the war years giving large parties in their Beverly Hills mansion. She traveled and entertained after Netcher died in 1953, but was said to miss him, her sister, and the attention they once commanded. In 1962 she made an unsuccessful attempt at suicide.

After she died of heart failure in 1970, *Variety* ran an obituary calling Rosie and Jenny "The Gabor Sisters of the Twenties."

Rosie Dolly lived out the last years of her life in a large Park Avenue apartment with her white poodle.

Jon Virzi

Ann Doran is probably best known for playing the mother on TV's National Velvet, *Phil Harris's wife in* The High and the Mighty *(1954), and James Dean's mother in* Rebel Without a Cause *(1955).*

Ann Doran

The character actress of movies and television was born on July 28, 1911, in Amarillo, Texas. Her father, an officer in the U.S. Cavalry, was gassed and wounded in World War I. The Dorans moved to Hollywood shortly afterward, hoping the climate would alleviate his condition.

Because acting, particularly in movies, was not considered respectable by many, Ann and her mother worked in films under assumed names. Mrs. Doran played leading lady to comedic stars Wally Vernon and Larry Semon. Her only child made her debut as a page in *Robin Hood* (1923), the Douglas Fairbanks, Sr., starrer. Later she worked with Fred Thompson, the star of silent westerns.

She was attending UCLA with the intention of becoming a mathematics teacher when her father died in late 1932. Needing a job immediately, she went to Fox Films because, she said, "It was the only work I knew how to do and that was the easiest studio to reach by bus from where we lived."

From a group of hopefuls Ann was chosen to play an orphan, a part with a few lines in *Zoo in Budapest* (1933).

After touring California in the chorus of *Showboat* she returned home and spent the next two years as a stand-in for Virginia Bruce.

She got a stock contract at Columbia Pictures, where she appeared in shorts with Charlie Chase and Andy Clyde. She was in a "Blondie" picture, a "Three Stooges"[8] comedy, and was leading lady to western star Charles Starrett.[8] By doing a bit part in *Mr. Deeds Goes to Town* (1936) Ann became a member of the unofficial Frank Capra stock company. She was in B pictures such as *Missing Girls* (1936) and *Women in Prison* (1938), as well as the blockbusters *You Can't Take It with You* (1938) and *Meet John Doe* (1941). At the end of three years, when the studio refused to raise her $75 a week salary, she left, intending to freelance.

She did such a good job as a nurse in *So Proudly We Hail* (1943) she was assigned a much larger role in *I Love a Soldier* (1944) and was placed under contract to Paramount.

Ms. Doran later returned to Columbia to play the mother of Ted Donaldson (single and living in Hollywood) in a series of six "Rusty" pictures.

Her screen credits include: *Penny Serenade* (1941); *The Hard Way* (1943); *Roughly Speaking* (1945); *Magic Town* (1947); *The Snake Pit* (1948); *No Sad Songs for Me* (1950); *Voice in the Mirror* (1958); *Mirage* (1965); *Once You Kiss a Stranger* (1969), and *The Hired Hand* (1971).

On television Ann had running parts on *The Legend of Jesse James, Longstreet,* and *Shirley.*

Of the more than five hundred parts Ann Doran has played in movies and on TV the one she is most frequently asked about is *Rebel Without a Cause* (1955). She was cast in the picture at the last minute, replacing Marsha Hunt, who had to withdraw because of a play commitment.

Of James Dean she says, "He was a joy to work with because he wanted so much for everything to be perfect. But such a mixed-up kid! He'd drop by at ungodly hours and I'd give him hell about racing his car and smoking that pot."

Her best work, she thinks, was as a blind woman in a short film made for the Lutheran Church and the low-budget feature *Joy Ride* (1958).

Speaking of her career recently she remarked, "I've always thought of what I did as a job—one that I loved doing. I never made big money, but I was able to look after my mother and put three young people through college. I've been up for parts that I didn't get and got others only to see them edited out of the picture, but that's the nature of my profession. I was never impressed with stars. I got to know quite a few and a great many of them had very unhappy lives only because they were so famous. I never wanted to go through life with a

Ann Doran lives with her dog and cat in a large house in Hollywood decorated with the hundreds of owls she has collected for more than forty years.

burden like that. What I call the 'leak light' was always enough for me. The light, you know, is always trained on the star. What leaks over people like me get."

Ann Doran has remained single. She is recognized frequently, but seldom for any specific role. "Often they think they remember me as a schoolteacher, someone from their childhood," she said recently. "That's very flattering because it means I must have seemed natural. But even when they know me as an actress they almost never know my name. I like that, too, because I've never aspired to be anything but a damn good, versatile actress."

Steffi Duna was chosen by Noel Coward to sing "Mad About the Boy" in the London production of his show Words and Music *(1932).*

Steffi Duna

The stage and screen personality was born in Budapest, Hungary, on February 8. Schooled in classical ballet from a very early age, Steffi joined the ballet of the Budapest Opera when she was eleven years old. She stayed with the company for a number of seasons, performing in all the major cities of Europe.

Then Steffi tired of traveling. She loved Berlin and when she had an offer to play there in *Wonder Bar* in 1929 she accepted. She began in the show as a dancer, but when the leading lady broke her leg the teenager took over her role opposite Francis Lederer,[8] who was then one of Europe's matinee idols.

When the company played London Noel Coward saw her performance and signed her for *Words and Music* (1932). It was Coward who changed her surname from Berindey. He cast her in his review as a prostitute who pines over the movie star she loves from afar with the song "Mad About the Boy."

Steffi Duna came to Broadway in the 1933 production of *The Threepenny Opera* in which she played "Polly Peachum."

Speaking of her career, she has stated, "I never made any plans. I had no goals. Things just came to me."

Her stage work had proved her talent and she had considerable film acting experience before coming to the United States. In Germany she had made movies in Hungarian and in England she had appeared in *The Indiscretions of Eve* (1932) and *The Iron Stair* (1933). Yet RKO, after putting her under contract, was unsure what to do with Steffi.

Her most memorable Hollywood work was in *La Cucaracha* (1934), a beautifully produced two-reeler which was the first live-action short made in the now abandoned three-color process. In her first feature for the studio, *A Man of Two Worlds* (1934), she played an Eskimo.

Some of her credits are: *Red Morning* (1934) with Regis Toomey (widowed and living at the Motion Picture and Television Country House); *Hi, Gaucho* (1935); *I Conquer the Sea* with Dennis Morgan,[8] who was then known as Stanley Morner; *Flirting with Fate* (1938) with Beverly Roberts (sharing a house with Wynne Gibson in Laguna Niguel, California); *Rascals* (1938) with Jane Withers; *Beasts of Berlin* (1939), and *Way Down South* (1939) with Sally Blane[8] and Bobby Breen (married and living in North Lauderdale, Florida).

Her most important American movies were *Anthony Adverse* (1936), *Waterloo Bridge* (1940) with Vivien Leigh, and *The Great McGinty* (1940).

When Steffi first went to the film capital her hopes were high. She was tested for the starring role in *The Good Earth,* but neither that nor any other important parts came her way. She returned briefly to Europe to make *A Clown Must Laugh* (1938), but a foreign film got almost no attention in Hollywood at that time, even one with as prestigious a star as the great tenor Richard Tauber.

As Ms. Duna put it, "I had great potential, but rotten luck!"

Living in California, however, was very much to her liking. Chick Chandler (living in Laguna Beach, California) and his wife, her first friends, made her feel welcome.

Her early marriage to the late John Carroll, a union she now dismisses as "ridiculous," lasted only a matter of months. It was her best friend, Virginia Field, and her boy friend Richard Greene (living in Ireland) who brought her together with Dennis O'Keefe on a blind date.

On their first evening together they discovered that they had both been signed just that morning to appear in the same motion picture, *Girl from Havana* (1940). Within months they were married and Steffi immediately retired from the screen.

Jerry Bierne

Steffi Duna, the widow of Dennis O'Keefe, lives by herself in Beverly Hills.

Dennis O'Keefe, who also wrote for the screen, died in 1968. Their son is a film editor.

Steffi is now semiretired from the real estate business and lives by herself in Beverly Hills. Virginia Field is often her houseguest. Robert Taylor's widow, Ursula Theiss, who bought her home through Steffi, is a friend, as are the Randolph Scotts and Grace Bradley, Bill "Hopalong Cassidy" Boyd's widow.

Steffi Duna-O'Keefe says her only recollection of her entire career is one night in Berlin when she failed to hear her lines and panicked. The highlight of her life was "the twenty-eight years I spent with the most amusing, thoughtful man I ever met, Dennis O'Keefe."

Johnny Eck

*Johnny Eck was billed as "The Half Boy" in
Freaks (1932), the film classic directed by Tod
Browning.*

*Standing on one hand was part of Johnny Eck's
act in side shows for three decades. It proved to
audiences that he actually ended below his rib
cage.*

Anton La Vey Collection

The man Robert L. Ripley called "The Most
Remarkable Man Alive" was born on August
27, 1911, twenty minutes after his brother. The
Eckhardt twins were identical with one exception. Older brother Robert was perfectly normal. Johnny, who weighed just over two
pounds at birth, ended abruptly at his rib cage.
Their father was a ship's carpenter and their
mother, a devout Methodist, accepted their son
as "the work of God."

Johnny soon learned to move about on his
hands and developed exceptionally broad,
strong arms and shoulders. As a young boy he
was a lead singer in the church choir and attended public school. He played baseball,
standing on one hand and batting with the
other. Until he was hired by a carnival pro-
moter Johnny had planned to earn his living as
a typist. "After all," he often asks people,
"what can you do that I can't do, except tread
water?"

When he was twelve years old the Eckhardts
permitted him to go on tour with a sideshow for
$20 a week. His twin was hired also to accom-
pany him.

"God, how we loved those big tents," he remarked recently. "We loved camping out and
all the animals. We'd stay up real late and
shoot the breeze with some of the most fasci-
nating people in the world. I got to know them
all: the Caterpillar Man, midgets and bearded
ladies and the Human Seal with little flippers
for hands and feet. Over the years I worked
with everyone from the Mule-Faced Woman to
the man with three legs. We just accepted each
other. It was a great adventure!"

Johnny Eck was, in circus lingo, a "single
O." That is, he was a show in himself. Other
freaks, such as fat ladies, giants, and tattooed
people, were exhibited together. To see "The
Half Boy," as he was billed, there was an extra
charge.

His act consisted of card tricks, juggling, and
acrobatics. Johnny swung from a trapeze,

stood on one hand, and walked a tightrope. He traveled with the Greater Sheesley Shows, Ringling Brothers and Barnum & Bailey, and many carnivals. In 1933 Ripley featured him in his *Believe It or Not Odditorium* at the Century of Progress in Chicago.

He enjoyed appearing in the movie *Freaks* (1932) and refers to its director, Tod Browning, as a "prince." The only cast member he did not get on well with was "Peter, the Skeleton Man."

"But all the freaks started wearing sunglasses and acting funny," says Johnny. "All but me, that is. In other words, they went Hollywood."

Eck was paid "about $35" for making the picture but was able to negotiate a somewhat larger salary from exhibitors after it was released. When *Freaks* was screened for him he saw himself for the first time as he appears to others. "It made me very self-conscious," he says. "Until then I never realized just how horrible I look."

He played "The Bird Man" in *Tarzan, the Ape Man* (1932), his only other screen appearance. His salary was the same.

During the fifties many states passed laws prohibiting the public exhibition of people who were then being referred to as "human oddities." The prevailing thought was that sideshows exploited those who had unfortunate afflictions. Johnny and his brother returned to Baltimore with almost no money.

"The promoters made all the money," he explains. "The only freaks I know who ever made big money were Daisy and Violet Hylton, the Siamese Twins, and they ended up down and out."

When they were very young Mrs. Eckhardt used to take her boys to an embankment near a railroad yard. Johnny in particular loved watching the trains. He wanted to be an engineer. Not long ago Robert bought his brother a miniature train from a defunct amusement park. They planned to have a park of their own

Robert Eckhardt

Johnny Eck with his Chihuahua "Major" on the steps of his Baltimore row house.

and a corral filled with miniature animals.

"All species have exceptionally small members the same as the human race," says Johnny. "Kids just love little horses and little goats because they can identify."

They ran the train for a while at church outings, but had to give it up along with their plans because teenagers jeered and stoned them.

"It would have been great," laments Johnny. "Kids are my favorite people. I love all things small."

Johnny Eck spends much of his days in good weather talking with children from the marble steps in front of his row house where he was born. He is working on his autobiography, "King of the Freaks," and paints scenic views in oil on to window screens, a long-honored art in Baltimore. His neighborhood, known locally as Highlandtown, has become a dangerous one and he and his brother, who also remained single, are often harassed.

Asked recently what he would do if he could be a full human being for one day, "The Half Man" replied, "I'd get my brother's baseball bat and beat the hell out of that son of a bitch next door who makes our lives so miserable!"

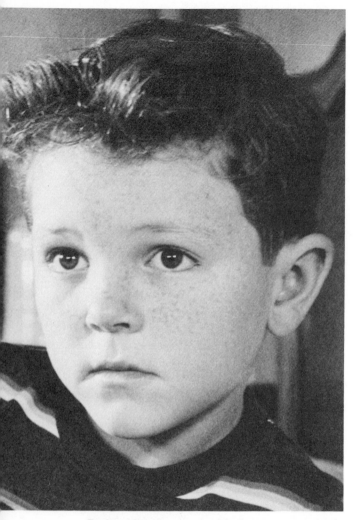

Richard Eyer was named by Parents *magazine as the "Most Talented Juvenile of 1955."*

Richard Eyer

The boy actor of the fifties was born in Los Angeles on May 6, 1945. His parents had been married over ten years when they had him, their first child. His brother Robert, who also acted for a while, was born May 6, 1948.

By the time Richard was two years old his mother had become accustomed to people remarking on how cute and well behaved he was. At the suggestion of a child talent registry Mrs. Eyer took her boy to a competition for children held in the Hollywood Bowl. Out of several thousand kids Richard was chosen as the one with the "most potential" and awarded a blue ribbon. A few months later he won a kiddie personality contest. He began getting modeling jobs and appeared with Esther Williams in advertisements for Cole of California bathing suits.

Richard's first acting was done on Roy Rogers's television show. Then he was picked by Norman Taurog, who directed him in a short made for the Community Chest, a role Richard considers to be one of his two best performances. His other favorite was in *Friendly Persuasion* (1956). In it he played a little Amish boy whose behind is constantly being nipped by a large goose named "Samantha."

It was Taurog who recommended Richard to William Wyler, who used him in *The Desperate Hours* (1955) and then *Friendly Persuasion*.

The boy supported Liberace in *Sincerely Yours* (1955) and had the title role in *The Invisible Boy* (1957). He appeared in *Slander* (1957), *Bailout at 43,000* (1957) with John Payne (who now considers himself a writer and lives in Malibu), *Fort Dobbs* (1958), and *The Seventh Voyage of Sinbad* (1958) with Kerwin Mathews,[8] and *Hell to Eternity* (1960).

On television Richard played Marie Wilson's seven-year-old nephew "Bobby Patterson" during the 1953–54 season of *My Friend Irma*. All of those shows were done live.

Richard's mother remembers him as "the best little trouper ever." "Mr. Wyler was astounded at how Richard could walk away from play and go right into a scene," she said recently. "Bogart once told me he would have given anything if his son were as well behaved as my two," she added.

Richard and his mother agree that there was never any competition between the boys who were, and have remained, very close. "I was about ten," explains Richard, "before I realized that all kids didn't act. To Robert and me playing parts was just like school or meals. Something you did."

Eyer made no friendships during his acting years. His last contact with those he worked with was in 1977 when he attended William Wyler's seventy-fifth birthday party.

The only part he did not feel comfortable with was on the *Danny Thomas Show* and he was replaced after one rehearsal. The only person he worked with that he disliked was Rusty Hamer,[8] a member of the cast of that series.

When he was sixteen years old Milton Rossner, the agent who had guided his career, died. About that time Richard had begun to weary of the restrictions placed on child actors. Recently he explained, "It took me away from sports where I was really beginning to do well in baseball and wrestling. I missed a few important games to go on what I started thinking of as 'dumb interviews.' That I didn't get to be a letterman bothered me a lot."

The last performance Richard Eyer gave was on a segment of the TV series *Combat*. He played a dying soldier. "When I saw it on the screen I didn't like my performance," he recalls. "I realized about the same time that I had become very self-conscious about being recognized. I was no longer enjoying my profession."

Richard enrolled in college and put acting out of his mind, but he now admits that his past greatly affected his future. "I was unaware of it at the time," he has said, "but I know now that two of the main reasons my wife was so determined to marry me was that I was a name to

Richard Eyer with his fraternal twin sons, Ben and Andrew, and his daughter Samantha.

Tim Doherty

some people and that I had a new Porsche which I'd bought with the money I'd earned in Hollywood. I could never make her understand that all I wanted to do was settle down in a small community and blend in. Looking back, that's really what I wanted to do even as a little kid—be just like everyone else."

Eyer and his wife, who are now divorced, share custody of their three children. He lives in Bishop, California, where he teaches third grade.

Robert Eyer lives in Los Angeles, where he owns a firm that constructs tennis courts.

Arthur Franz came to Hollywood in the late forties when he was signed to a contract by Columbia Pictures.

Arthur Franz

The star of B pictures was born in Perth Amboy, New Jersey, on February 29, 1920. He was the only child of parents who were in the real estate business.

Arthur was still in high school when he spent a summer as an apprentice with a Shakespearean stock company and won an acting scholarship. "That was it," he recalls. "I never considered another profession after that experience."

The highlight of his early years in the theater was the juvenile lead in *Ah, Wilderness,* which he did in summer stock opposite Harry Carey, Sr. Franz appeared in thirteen flop plays in a row before he landed a good part in *Hope for a Harvest,* which Fredric March starred in on Broadway in 1941. There were six more failures after that before he was cast in *Command Decision,* one of the hits of 1947. From that play he was signed to a movie contract and brought to Hollywood.

He made his screen debut in the low-budget quickie *Jungle Patrol* (1948). When he refused to join the cast of a feature that starred Rex Reason (now a real estate broker in Diamond Bar, California), his studio placed him on suspension. Reasoned Franz, "I thought that if I was going to make cheapie pictures, then at least I would insist on starring in the damn things."

Some of his many features are: *Red Stallion of the Rockies* (1949); *Abbott and Costello Meet the Invisible Man* (1951); *Invaders from Mars* (1953); *Bobby Ware Is Missing* (1955) with Neville Brand (living in Seattle, Washington), *Hellcats of the Navy* (1957) with Ronald Reagan and Nancy Davis, and *Monster on Campus* (1958).

In 1950 he toured Australia as "Stanley Kowalski" in *A Streetcar Named Desire.*

Arthur Franz is best known for playing the title role in *The Sniper* (1952). The part of a psychotic killer is his favorite among his screen roles. It was a commercially successful film and

Richard Schaeffer

Arthur Franz and his wife live in a house in Malibu overlooking the Pacific Ocean.

Franz was praised for his work in it, but no other really showy parts followed. He was, however, in some A movies: *Roseanna McCoy* (1949) with Joan Evans (now the co-owner of a private school in Van Nuys, California); *Sands of Iwo Jima* (1949); *Member of the Wedding* (1952) with the late Brandon De Wilde; *The Caine Mutiny* (1954); *The Young Lions* (1958); *The Carpetbaggers* (1964), and *Alvarez Kelly* (1966).

Franz has been married since 1947 to Doreen Lang, who was directed by Alfred Hitchcock in three of his pictures. They are the parents of three daughters and a son. Only one, Gina Franz, has gone into acting.

Arthur still sees quite a bit of Edward Dmytryk (married to Jean Porter), who directed several of his pictures. Another of his friends is Carroll O'Connor, who lives near Franz in Malibu. He was friendly with the late character actor Eduard Franz, but they were not related.

Arthur and his wife live in a home they built on a cliff overlooking the Pacific Ocean. They buy, renovate, and sell properties in the same area at considerable profit.

He speaks of his career with faint disinterest: "I became a name, so I was paid better than most actors. But I sat, like the rest of them, waiting for the phone to ring. And when I got the call it was always for the same part—the part they couldn't get a star to play. So, they'd settle for a good actor. Even the money wasn't big. Because I always needed the job. They sense that and deal with you accordingly."

Franz played a small role in *That Championship Season* (1982) as a favor to the film's director, Jason Miller. "I don't need to work anymore," is his explanation for his absence from the screen. "If I like the part and the people I'll be working with I do it. But I'm happy to tell you that I do not miss acting or the business one bit."

Jonathan Frid as the vampire "Barnabas Collins" quickly emerged as the star of Dark Shadows, *the popular daytime TV serial of the sixties and early seventies.*

Jonathan Frid

The star of television's *Dark Shadows* was born John Herbert Frid on December 2, 1924, in Hamilton, Ontario, Canada. He is the son of a prominent contractor.

Frid was drawn to acting as a profession at the age of sixteen when he became something of a hero in his prep school by turning in an exceptional performance as an irascible old man in a play. "That experience changed my whole life," he says. "The headmaster encouraged me to consider a career in the theater. I felt that I had found *something* I could do."

His training came from years spent at London's Royal Academy of Dramatic Arts, Toronto's Royal Conservatory of Music, the Carnegie Institute of Technology, and with Uta Hagen. He studied dance with Martha Graham and received a master of fine arts degree in directing at Yale.

Jonathan Frid had played many heavies such as "Cassius," the father of Elizabeth Barrett Browning, and "Macbeth" before assuming the role that would make him internationally known. He was seen in regional, repertory, and off-Broadway theater as the villainous Duke of York, an inquisitor in *The Golem,* and an evil priest in *The Burning.*

In 1966 Frid began touring in a play that starred Ray Milland. He then joined the San Diego National Shakespeare Festival, where he appeared in three plays. When he returned to his Manhattan apartment in the early spring of 1967 he had made up his mind to join the faculty of a college or university as a drama teacher. As he put his key into the lock he heard the telephone ringing. "I don't know why I rushed to answer," he said recently, "because I thought it would be for my roommate. But it was my agent who admitted that he didn't expect me to be back in town yet. He wouldn't have called again and I wouldn't have phoned him because I had decided to retire from acting."

The part offered him intrigued Jonathan sufficiently that he agreed to read for it, but when he did the script seemed to be poorly written and his character was not clearly defined. "I wasn't really interested in doing it and I think that's what got me the role," he has admitted.

When Jonathan Frid joined the cast of *Dark Shadows* the TV series had been on ABC for several seasons. Its ratings had dropped and it was well known that the network was seriously considering canceling the daytime serial. The introduction of the character "Barnabas Collins" brought the show an immediate flurry of publicity, an overnight jump in ratings, and a deluge of fan mail addressed to Jonathan. Most of it was from housewives who found his character romantic and college students who thought he was campy.

The soap opera that had seemed about to go off the air continued for another four seasons and is still playing in reruns. There were *Dark Shadows* comic books featuring the vampire "Barnabas," posters of Frid in character, and even replicas of the famous fangs he wore. M-G-M produced the feature *House of Dark Shadows* (1971) in which Jonathan co-starred with Joan Bennett (married and living in Scarsdale, New York), who was also in the series.

He was neither surprised nor disappointed when *Dark Shadows* left the air in 1971. "We had done all the basic plots of the great horror stories," he says. "The scripts seemed to get worse and worse. I felt relieved."

He has turned down all of the many offers he has received to play vampires on stage and screen since then. He does not, however, rule out doing "Barnabas Collins" again, providing he likes the script.

Jonathan has spent a great deal of time with his family in Toronto and lived for a year in Mexico.

"Richard III," not "Barnabas Collins," is his favorite role. He does not pursue an acting ca-

Richard Lamparski

Jonathan Frid in 1984 in the living room of his Manhattan apartment.

reer but would like to do a one-man show at some point. At present the bachelor is studying Spanish in preparation for his eventual move to Spain.

Frid attributes the huge popularity of his character to "people wanting to be frightened of something." He said recently, "The God who was once thought of as fearful is now, we are told, a loving God. I think I scared people because I was scared myself. I never felt I really got a firm grasp on 'Barnabas' and I was always afraid I wouldn't remember my lines."

He was never a fan of horror films, has no belief in the occult, and still becomes uncomfortable at any reference to his fangs or the scenes in which he was supposed to bite another player. He does, however, appear as the guest of honor at the annual gathering of the *Dark Shadows* fans who hold their convention in Los Angeles.

John Gary had a network variety program before the syndicated John Gary Show *in the sixties.*

John Gary

The singer–talk-show host was born John Gary Strader in Watertown, New York. His birth date was November 29, 1932.

John's mother began entering him and his sister in amateur contests when he was very young. He was nine years old when he won a three-year scholarship to the choir of the Cathedral of St. John the Divine in New York City.

A USO tour took him to Hollywood when he was fourteen years old. His stepfather, who was managing his career, brought the boy soprano to the attention of Hedda Hopper and the columnist got him a small part in the James Cagney starrer *The Time of Your Life* (1948). In *Our Very Own* (1950) he sang "Happy Birthday" to the film's star, Ann Blyth.

He joined the cast of Ken Murray's *Blackouts,* where he remained until his voice changed—right in the middle of "When Irish Eyes Are Smiling," which he was singing on stage to Marie Wilson.

Both of Gary's brothers were career Marines and John spent three years in the Marine Corps before going to New York City in search of work as a singer.

He became friendly with a group of songwriters who often used him to test their lyrics and make demonstration records of their work. He takes great pride in the fact that he was the first person ever to sing "My Secret Love," which won the Oscar as the Best Song of 1953.

For one season he was the vocalist on *Don McNeill's Breakfast Club* and then hosted his own show on a television station in New Orleans. It was during this period that he operated a marine salvage business. He still holds two world records for underwater endurance: 78 hours 45 minutes in fresh water; 41 hours 1 minute in salt water.

In 1962 his career began to take off. His first album for RCA, *Catch a Rising Star,* sold very well after Jack Paar presented him on *The To-night Show.* He headlined at many of the top nightclubs in the country, including the Fairmont Hotels in San Francisco, New Orleans, and Dallas, and the Persian Room at New York's Plaza.

In 1965 he was booked into the Crescendo on the Sunset Strip as Phyllis Diller's opening act. His claim to fame up until then was his hit record of "More," the theme from the film *Mondo Cane.* Then he was taken up by Walter Winchell, who predicted major stardom and got him an engagement at the Coconut Grove as the headliner. CBS-TV signed him as the summer replacement for Danny Kaye. After that he starred in his own syndicated program which emanated from Florida for thirteen ninety-minute shows, followed by another thirteen from Hollywood.

Gary had clean-cut good looks and a three-octave vocal range. His repertoire was middle-of-the-road material which he delivered without gimmicks. By the end of the sixties he had a fan club of 2,000—mostly women over forty. The demographics that became so important in TV programming during the seventies dictated his professional eclipse.

John had a son by his first marriage, which ended in divorce in 1965. The same year he married an ardent fan, a widow with children. He and his second wife settled in her hometown, Dallas, where they manage her family's extensive real estate holdings.

John Gary still plays nightclubs occasionally, such as Maldonado's in Pasadena. His first na-

Diane La Vey

John Gary and his wife live in Dallas, Texas.

tional exposure in some time came in the fall of 1982, when he appeared with Marvin Hamlisch on *The Magic of Mercer,* a TV salute to the songwriter Johnny Mercer.

"I got that only because Andy Williams turned it down," he admits. "These are not the best of times for balladeers, especially when you're trying to reactivate your career from Texas."

Gale Gordon has no favorite role. One of his best known was "Mr. Wilson," the next-door neighbor to the mischievous "Dennis the Menace" on television.

Gale Gordon

The blustery, overbearing comedic actor was born in New York City on February 20, 1906. His father was Charles T. Aldrich, a vaudevillian. His mother, Gloria Gordon, played in light opera and musical comedy. During the fifties she became quite well known as one of the old ladies who had a crush on Jack Benny and as "Mrs. O'Reilly," the landlady on *My Friend Irma.* Gale, who was born with a cleft palate,

was taken to England for corrective surgery when he was a baby. After his parents were divorced, when he was still a boy, he stayed with his mother and took her surname.

Gordon never considered a career other than acting and, while there have been periods of unemployment, he has always been able to support himself with his craft.

He and his mother were returning to the United States aboard an ocean liner in 1923 when he struck up an acquaintance with Baron Rothschild. The financier gave the teenager a letter of introduction to the Shuberts. Gale made his Broadway debut under their auspices in *The Dancers* (1923) in support of Richard Bennett.

By 1929 Gale and Mrs. Gordon had settled in Los Angeles. He played "Judas Iscariot" in *The Pilgrimage Play* that year.

Gale Gordon's career changed and prospered with the development of radio. He returned to Broadway to play in *The Daughters of Atreus* (1936) with Maria Ouspenskaya, but from then on he was essentially a radio performer.

For nine years he was leading man to Irene Rich (living in Pinyon, California) on the series she did for Welch's Grape Juice. He was "Paradine, the Master Spy" on *Stories of the Black Chamber,* and played the title role on *Flash Gordon.* For five seasons he was on *Junior Miss* as the father of Barbara Whiting (married and living in Birmingham, Michigan). The district attorney on *Big Town* was another part he had for years. Gale played the cantankerous sponsor on *The Phil Harris—Alice Faye Show.* Probably his best-known roles in the medium were as "Mayor La Trivia" on *Fibber McGee and Molly* and "Rumson Bullard," the obnoxious neighbor of *The Great Gildersleeve.* The job he remembers most fondly, however, was as leading man to Mary Pickford on her own show.

It was on radio that Gordon honed the characterizations and formed the relationships that made him world famous on television. His portrayal of "Osgood Conklin," the combustible principal on *Our Miss Brooks* began in 1948 on radio and continued throughout its years on TV. He was a regular on *My Favorite Husband,* Lucille Ball's first radio program. Later Gale supported her on TV for twelve years and considers the star "a very dear friend."

He played a few heavies on television, such as a general on *Playhouse 90,* but it is for comedy that he is remembered. He is considered the medium's premier slow-burn artist and the highlight of his appearances was when he blew his stack after prolonged smoldering. Although never really unpleasant, the characters he played were even in the best of moments stuffy and pompous.

Gale Gordon and Virginia Curley have been married since 1937, shortly after they first acted together on *Death Valley Days.* For a while she played "Mrs. Conklin" on *Our Miss Brooks.* She always accompanies him to Canada on his annual stints at a theater in Edmonton, Alberta, now and then appearing in a play with him. *On Golden Pond* was their last together.

He has had long runs in recent years in *Second Time Around* and *Norman, Is That You?* He used to prefer acting on TV to radio, but of late has turned down a number of TV roles, including a guest appearance on *Love Boat.*

"Most of it's just garbage," he has said, referring to television. "I don't miss working on it and I seldom watch it."

The childless couple have a home in the Hollywood Hills, but live most of the time on their "Tub Canyon Farm" in Borrego Springs, California. He served as the small town's mayor for a decade and headed the Chamber of Commerce for six years. His neighbors almost never mention his career and regard him as "just another old man in dirty overalls." Gale does all of the maintenance on his property. The Gordons' pets are a menagerie of stray dogs and their shared pastime is reading biographies.

During a recent interview he said, "Lucy and Eve Arden were both absolute joys to work with, but we seldom see each other anymore. When I'm not working I'm not around show business people. I have no regrets about my career, because I have been very, very lucky. But I also have no illusions about my capabilities. A 'Hamlet' I never was. From time to time someone needs a character actor who can yell. That's my specialty, yelling—at stars, mostly."

Gale Gordon outside his home in the Hollywood Hills.

She often played dutiful daughters, "Nancy Drew," or someone's girl friend, but no one was ever better than Bonita when she was bad.

Bonita Granville

The child actress of movies and television was born in New York City on February, 2, 1923. Her father had been featured in several editions of the *Ziegfeld Follies*. Her mother was a dancer. For a time Bonita was part of their vaudeville act.

The Granvilles went to Hollywood when her father was signed to play opposite the late Winnie Lightner in a series of two-reelers at Warner Brothers. Bonita, too, had made an appearance in a short for that studio before she was "discovered" in the lobby of the Alta Nido Apartments where her family was living. RKO's casting director noticed a striking resemblance between the child and the late Ann Harding,

who was the top star at the time on that lot. She was cast as the daughter of Ms. Harding and her husband, who was played by Laurence Olivier in *Westward Passage* (1932). After a small part in *Silver Dollar* (1932) she became one of the few cast members of the Oscar-winning *Cavalcade* (1933) who was not English. Then she did *Cradle Song* (1933) before Ann Harding brought her back to RKO for *The Life of Vergie Winters* (1934). *A Wicked Woman* (1935) and *Ah, Wilderness* (1935) followed.

She was one of the last of many children to be considered for the part that established her as a serious young actress. William Wyler cast her as the lying adolescent in *These Three* (1936), the first screen adaptation of Lillian Hellman's *The Children's Hour*. Her performance brought her an Oscar nomination as the Best Supporting Actress and proved Bonita to be a player capable of projecting a meanness seldom seen in one so young. It was followed by other characterizations almost as hateful and equally convincing. In *Maid of Salem* (1937) she falsely accuses someone of witchcraft. She taunted a pathetic Bette Davis in *Now, Voyager* (1942). When she was beaten by Nazis in *The Mortal Storm* (1940) members of some audiences broke into applause. *Beloved Brat* was the title of a picture she made in 1938 and it was the way much of the public thought of her. Other unofficial titles were "the girl you love to hate" and "the face you'd love to slap."

Yet, in some of her screen appearances she was quite likable. A few examples are: *White Banners* (1938); *Merrily We Live* (1938); *Forty Little Mothers* (1940), and *Song of the Open Road* (1944). In spite of weak scripts she was a believable "Nancy Drew" in four features that starred her as the teenage sleuth.

Much was made by studio publicists of her steady dating with Jackie Cooper. False reports of their elopement hyped the box office of *Gallant Sons* (1940), which they made together.

Hitler's Children (1943) was a surprise hit of the war year 1943. RKO wanted Martha Scott to play the lead, but, unlike Bonita, she had no contract with the studio and was thought to be too high-salaried for the low-budget film. It is the favorite of Ms. Granville's fifty-four features.

Of her screen acting she has said, "I had the best teachers in the world. It's impossible to work with the stars and directors I did and not learn a great deal." The one director she feels hindered rather than helped her performance was Irving Rapper.

In 1947 when Bonita married Texas multimillionaire Jack Wrather, Ann Rutherford[8] was her maid of honor. They are still close friends. The Wrathers are the parents of two sons and two daughters.

She has appeared in only three features since her marriage, the last being *The Lone Ranger* (1956). She continued, however, to act on television regularly for more than ten years. She was especially effective in *Guest in the House,* a 1953 television production which she did live. Bonita played the part of the neurotic invalid, which had been taken by Anne Baxter in the movie version.

"I just let my acting career slip away," she explained recently. "I can't say I miss it, but I must admit that it would be nice to be thought of for a good part now and again." In spite of her prominence within the entertainment industry she has not been offered a single movie or TV role in twenty years.

The Wrathers number among their many holdings extensive oil properties, rights to *The Lone Ranger, The Green Hornet,* and *Lassie.* They own the Spruce Goose and hold the lease on the *Queen Mary.* They have a home in Palm Springs and apartments in London, New York City, San Francisco, and at the Disneyland Hotel, which they also own.

Mrs. Wrather is very much a part of her husband's business ventures and drives her cream-

Allan J. Studley

Bonita Granville-Wrather is a member of the board of directors of her husband's conglomerate, Loyola University, and St. John's Hospital. She has two grandchildren.

color Rolls-Royce from their Holmby Hills mansion to the office building they own in Beverly Hills. On the wall behind her desk are photos signed to her by Richard M. Nixon, Gerald R. Ford, and Ronald and Nancy Reagan. Bonita and Jack Wrather spend much of their free time aboard their yacht.

From 1958 to 1972 Bonita was associate producer of TV's *Lassie* series, which she occasionally directed.

Two parts she would have liked were "Vita" in *Mildred Pierce* (which went to Ann Blyth) and "Sophie" in *The Razor's Edge.* The latter was a severe disappointment because when the role was promised to her it was predicted that whoever played the tragic, young Jewish woman would be bound to get the Oscar. But Twentieth Century-Fox had neglected to pick up Anne Baxter's option and she refused to resign with the studio unless she was allowed to play "Sophie." It brought her the 1946 Academy Award as Best Supporting Actress.

"For a brief time it seemed like the worst thing that could possibly ever happen to me," Bonita recalled in 1983. "But, as it turned out it was the luckiest. Because had I done that picture I would have not been where I was when I met my husband. Now that would have *really* been the very worst!"

Jack Wrather died in November 1984.

Alexander Gray and Bernice Claire in a scene from their early screen musical Song of the Flame *(1930).*

Alexander Gray and Bernice Claire

Hollywood's first singing team was co-starred in three musicals. They were all big-budget productions and two of them were in Technicolor. Not one was successful at the box office.

Alexander Gray was born in Wrightsville, Pennsylvania, on January 8, 1902. Until he joined the glee club at the University of Pennsylvania he was unaware of what a rich baritone voice he had.

After earning a B.A. degree in engineering he taught school and for a while worked as a laborer to pay for vocal lessons and dramatic training. The great prima donna Louise Homer encouraged him to persevere and eventually he came to the attention of Flo Ziegfeld. The producer first put him in his *Midnight Whirl,* which he presented on the roof of the New Amsterdam Theater in 1921. He was in the *Ziegfeld Follies of 1922* in which he sang the hit "'Neath the South Sea Moon" and then went on the road in *Ziegfeld's Frolic.* When Marilyn Miller went on tour in her Broadway hit *Sally* he was her leading man.

Gray had a featured role in the Gershwin show *Tell Me More* (1925) and was offered another in *Good News,* but turned it down. On July 27, 1927, Alexander took over the role of the "Red Shadow" in Sigmund Romberg's *The Desert Song* opposite Vivienne Segal.[8]

When Marilyn Miller requested him as her leading man in the movie version of *Sally,* Warner Brothers asked Gray to take a screen test. He chose a scene from *The Desert Song* and the young soprano Bernice Claire, who had become his leading lady in the show, played in the test with him. When Jack Warner saw the test he felt she would be right for *No, No, Nanette,* which his studio was about to film.

Bernice Claire was born on January 27, in Oakland, California. Her father was a stage electrician. "I never knew anything but show business" is how she describes her background.

Claire was well trained and had been signed by a top agent before she made her professional debut. She was in vaudeville for less than a month when she appeared on the bill of the Palace Theater in New York City. From that engagement she went into *The Desert Song* opposite Gray.

He made *Show of Shows* (1929) and *Sally* (1929) before being paired on screen with Bernice Claire in *No, No, Nanette* (1930), *Spring Is Here* (1930), and *Song of the Flame* (1930).

The Gray-Claire pictures were well produced and received good notices. But by 1930, as John Springer explained in his book *All Talking, All Singing, All Dancing:* "When all musicals had become anathema, those stagey ones with lush songs and ultraromantic plots were the first to go. Bernice Claire and Alexander Gray and the rest found themselves unwanted by Hollywood."

Alexander and Bernice did one more picture together, *Moonlight and Pretzels* (1933), although they were not its stars. It, too, flopped.

Bernice made three other films without Gray, who remained active on stage in dashing hero roles well into the forties.

They continued to perform both together and separately for some time on radio and in vaudeville and revivals of Broadway musicals.

In 1929 Gray's wife was killed in an auto crash that seriously injured Bernice's brother. For a time they went together. Their last duets were sung in *The Firefly* in Louisville, Kentucky, in 1940. In later years they kept in touch only at Christmastime.

In 1945 Bernice Claire and her husband, a singer, were returning from the Orient on a ship when he died suddenly. She has never sung since. Her second husband was a physician. Now widowed, she lives by herself in Mill Valley, California.

Alexander Gray was living by himself when he died in 1976.

Jon Virzi

Alexander Gray died on October 4, 1976, in Northshore, California, at the age of seventy-four.

Howard W. Hays

Bernice Claire lives by herself in a condominium in Mill Valley, California.

Most film historians believe the pair to have been victims of the times and agree with John Springer, who wrote: "If the moment had been right it might have been Alexander Gray and Bernice Claire as the King and Queen of movie operettas instead of Eddy and MacDonald."

Bronco *was televised over ABC from 1958 to 1962 with Ty Hardin playing "Bronco Layne," a former captain in the Confederate Army turned Western adventurer.*

Ty Hardin

The actor made famous by the TV series *Bronco* was born Orison Whipple Hungerford, Jr., on New Year's Day, 1930, in New York City. His father, an acoustical engineer, moved his family to Austin, Texas, six months after his son's birth. Four years later he left them.

"I grew up with nothing" is how Hardin once described his childhood.

When he moved to Los Angeles in 1957 to take a job in the engineering department of an aircraft manufacturing firm Ty was married to his high school sweetheart. She declined, however, to accompany him.

He was at Western Costume in Hollywood renting a gun to wear to a Halloween party when a Paramount Pictures executive spotted him. The studio signed him to a stock contract and he made brief appearances in pictures such as *The Space Children* (1958) and *I Married a Monster from Outer Space* (1958).

When Clint Walker (married and living in Grass Valley, California) quit his starring role on *Cheyenne,* Warner Brothers bought up Hardin's contract and put him in the series for a while. When Walker returned Ty was given his own show, *Bronco.*

He also made features for Warners but, in the sixth year of his contract, when the studio had no part for him, he went to Europe, where he lived for ten years.

"Looking back, that was a big mistake," he says now. "I hadn't really established myself in movies with a big box-office hit and many of the films I made over there weren't being seen in this country, so my name was not kept alive. But in Europe I was making between $35,000 and $40,000 a picture and I worked constantly. My big chance, although it sure didn't look promising at the time, was an offer of $10,000 to star in an Italian version of a samurai movie. When I turned it down I recommended they use an actor named Clint Eastwood. The picture was called *A Fistful of Dollars.*"

Ty thinks another reason he did not "reach my full potential" was his reputation as a ladies' man.

"Some producers figure they should have first pick of all the gorgeous young actresses," he said recently. "I guess they were jealous of me."

One of Hardin's six wives was actress Andra Martin, who is the mother of his twin sons. Another was Marlene Schmidt, who had been Miss Universe in 1961. There was also a starlet who attempted suicide when their romance ended.

His Hollywood movies were *Merrill's Marauders* (1962), *The Chapman Report* (1962), *PT-109* (1963), *Palm Springs Weekend* (1963), and *Wall of Noise* (1963).

In Europe he made *Battle of the Bulge* (1965), *Savage Pampas* (1967), *Custer of the West* (1968), *One Step to Hell* (1969), and *The Last Rebel* (1971).

Hardin has said of Joan Crawford, his co-star in *Berserk!* (1968): "She was a very dominating sort of woman. She'd invite me over and over again to her place for dinner. Well, I like to do the choosing when it comes to women. So we didn't hit it off too well."

The following year he played opposite Veronica Lake[8] in an English production of *A Streetcar Named Desire.* Her name for him during the run of the play was "Try Harder."

Ty lived mostly in Spain, running a chain of Laundromats and, for a while, a restaurant and bar with a Wild West decor on the Costa Brava. He returned to the U.S. shortly after being fined $9,200 on a charge of dealing in hashish.

It was in 1976 that he admitted to himself that there was "something missing in my life." He attended church for the first time in many years and "became a Christian." Not long after that he was ordained a minister and began appearing regularly on television as a preacher. The show was seen for several years throughout the Western part of the U.S.

"I went into the ministry with a clean heart," he said in a 1984 interview. "But I got out rather than compromise my principles. I'm against what I call 'preachers for profit.'"

He met his present wife, a divorcee with three children, during his time as a clergyman.

Richard Lamparski

Ty Hardin in his Prescott, Arizona, home holding a photo taken at the time of his sixth marriage.

They own a house, six cows, and two bulls in Prescott, Arizona, but are planning to move to Northern California.

Ty is uncertain how many grandchildren he has because, of the children by his earlier marriages, his youngest daughter is the only one he hears from.

He maintains he would never again live in Hollywood, but admits he would like to act and thinks he would be a "natural" for a series such as *Dallas.*

Hardin is deeply involved in a citizens movement that publishes *The Arizona Patriot,* a magazine currently under investigation by several federal agencies. His religious and political beliefs are proclaimed in stickers on the back of his car: JESUS CHRIST IS LORD and ABOLISH THE I.R.S.

In spring 1984 Ty Hardin announced his candidacy for the U.S. Presidency on the Populist Party ticket.

Phil Harris and Alice Faye were one of America's most popular married couples when they had their network radio program for eight years.

Phil Harris

The musician-comedian was born on June 24, 1904, in Linton, Indiana. He says his real first name is "Wonga," meaning "swift messenger" in Cherokee.

Harris's mother was a clothes buyer. His father played clarinet, professionally. Phil was raised mostly by his grandparents, who allowed him to take a job when he was eleven years old playing drums and creating sound effects as an accompaniment to silent movies. When he was sixteen he joined his father, who was working with a band in Nashville.

Phil's first job of note was with Henry Halstead's band, which had a youthful Lew Ayres [8] playing banjo.

By the late twenties Harris had acquired a widespread reputation among professionals as a drummer and was beginning to develop a following as a jazz singer.

In 1928, shortly after he became co-leader of the Lofner-Harris band, the group was the first to play the Rendezvous Ballroom in Balboa. The following year they were such a hit at the St. Francis in San Francisco that the hotel held them over for three years.

Their next engagement was at the Coconut Grove. By this time it was called the Phil Harris Orchestra. They caught on immediately with the movie crowd who frequented the Los Angeles nitery. Harris's asides to his musicians had a lot to do with their success. They were audible to the dancers and, on some nights, to those listening to their radios. It was on those programs that the Phil Harris radio personality, which later became such an important ingredient of *The Jack Benny Show,* emerged and developed.

His greeting "Hiya, Jackson!" soon became known throughout the country. Thanks to Benny's writers he became the personification of the jazz-talking, hard-drinking musician with little education and a huge ego. He often referred to his own "wavy hair and baby blue eyes."

When Harris growled, "Oh, you dawwwwg!," listeners knew that he was gazing at himself in the mirror. Probably the biggest laugh Jack Benny ever got on the air was when

Phil's name was mentioned during a meal, prompting Benny to exclaim, "*Please,* not while we're eating!"

Phil Harris and Alice Faye first met in New York City in 1933. At the time she was the vocalist with Rudy Vallee's orchestra. Both barely remembered that encounter when they were brought together again years later by Jack Oakie.

When Alice and Phil married in 1941 after a brief courtship, even some of their close friends were stunned and negative predictions were rampant. She was the reigning queen of Twentieth Century-Fox, where her public image had been carefully shaped. Her studio and many of her fans were very disappointed that she had become the wife of a man who was thought of as a carousing lush.

The pair who at first seemed so poorly matched have proved their critics to be mistaken. Not only has the marriage lasted, but Phil and Alice starred as themselves for eight years on their own radio program. Her warmth and down-to-earth attitude complimented his brashness perfectly. Their attraction to each other was obvious and understandable even to those who had heretofore found Harris only flashy and coarse.

Phil Harris has been in more than two dozen movies, beginning with *So This Is Harris,* a three-reeler that won the Oscar as the Best Short Subject-Comedy of 1932–33. He made many guest appearances on television over the years, but now prefers to live quietly in Palm Springs.

The Harris-Faye home is on the green at the Thunderbird Country Club. His office is a few miles away at the Ironwood Country Club and also faces the golf course. Phil, though still interested in the game, now limits his playing to Scrabble.

His close friend as well as hunting-fishing-business partner and drinking companion was

Richard Lamparski

In March 1984, three months away from his eightieth birthday, Phil Harris said, "I've never endorsed any brand of booze. Wouldn't want to slight the others. They're all just great!"

Bing Crosby. The Crosby sons, with the exception of Gary, stay with him whenever they are in the desert. Of Gary Crosby's controversial book about his upbringing, *Going My Own Way,* Phil says, "I couldn't finish it. Maybe it's all true. Bing *was* very hard on those boys, but he meant well and he took care of all of them financially."

Harris never became the jazz singer many thought he could have been, although his records of "That's What I Like About the South" and "The Thing" were both big hits.

He says he has no regrets about his career, although, before Robert Preston accepted the role in *The Music Man,* Phil turned it down as being "too corny to work." It was Phil Harris who suggested Forrest Tucker when he rejected the national company, as well.

***"Geoffrey Horne To Be A Star"* was the heading of the Louella O. Parsons column of February 2, 1958.**

Geoffrey Horne

The promising actor of the fifties was born in Buenos Aires, Argentina, on August 22, 1933. His father was an executive with Standard Oil. Much of his youth was spent in Cuba, being, according to Geoffrey, "incredibly spoiled" by his mother. Considered by teachers to be a difficult and undisciplined boy, he was educated in a succession of private schools. It was while studying at the University of California at Berkeley that he decided to become an actor. He went to New York in the fall of 1954 and was accepted at the Actors Studio.

Horne acted on live television shows before he made his movie debut in *The Strange One* (1957), the screen adaptation of the Broadway play *End as a Man.* Geoffrey's youth and intensity were well suited to the script, which was about emotionally disturbed military cadets.

When Sam Spiegel, who had produced Horne's first picture, decided he wanted a "new face" for the role of "Lt. Joyce" in *Bridge on the River Kwai,* his wife suggested Geoffrey. It was one of the biggest money-making films of all time and the winner of the Best Picture Oscar for 1957.

Otto Preminger immediately hired him at $1,000 a week, twice his previous salary, to play opposite Jean Seberg in *Bonjour, Tristesse* (1958). But Geoffrey "detested" making the film because of the manner in which Preminger treated most of the cast. A mild flirtation with his co-star was ended abruptly when Ms. Seberg learned that Nancy Berg, a top fashion model and Horne's lover, was about to join the company, which was shooting in the south of France. The two enjoyed a European holiday with his earnings, but when he saw the movie he thought it and his performance were both "awful."

M-G-M tested him for the title role in *Ben-Hur* and offered the lead in *The Reluctant Debutante.* He turned that down as he did several other movie roles as well as some offers from Broadway. Another part he refused brought Robert Vaughn an Oscar nomination for *The Young Philadelphians.*

Twenty-five years later he explained these decisions by saying, "I was doing my best to mask my immaturity and insecurity."

Another opportunity for stardom came when he played Silvana Mangano's lover in *The Tempest* (1959). Although the costume epic flopped in the U.S. it was a major hit abroad.

"The sensible thing would have been to stay in Europe," mused Horne recently. "I think I did my best work in *Esterina,* which I made in Italy. Everyone advised me to remain there and take advantage of my popularity at the time, but I was falling in love or out of love then—I don't remember which—and wouldn't listen to anyone."

Joseph and His Brethren (1962) might still have put him over. It was originally planned as a big-budget film with Rita Hayworth as his co-star, but Columbia Pictures sold the property and Horne's commitment to a European company. What was finally produced was a disappointment on every level.

By then he and Nancy Berg were married and their combined incomes were enough for what he now describes as a "lot of partying." After their daughter was born they were divorced.

Geoffrey and actress Colin Wilcox adopted three children and took a foster son during the years they spent together. He appeared from time to time on TV shows such as *Alfred Hitchcock Presents* and in a few plays, but was unable to reactivate his career.

He worked as a dialogue director on *Catch 22, The Babymaker,* and on other movies as an assistant to the director. Then he spent six months at a stand on the Pacific Coast Highway selling fruit.

Returning to New York City he got a running part on *As the World Turns* that lasted for eighteen months. His next marriage was to a nonprofessional. It produced one child and ended in divorce.

Geoffrey teaches acting at the Lee Strasberg Institute and occasionally does an off-Broad-

Geoffrey Horne, his wife, and their two children share an apartment in Greenwich Village.

way play, TV soap opera, or commercial. He played a role and understudied one of the leads in the 1983 Broadway production of *The Caine Mutiny Court-Martial.*

When he was interviewed by Louella O. Parsons in 1958 he seemed on the brink of stardom, yet he told the nationally syndicated columnist, "I'm not sure that I have what it takes to be a star."

When he played opposite Jane Fonda on Broadway in *Strange Interlude* in 1963, their billing and salaries were identical. "But," he recalls, "Jane always thought of herself as a star. I never did."

Geoffrey Horne concluded an interview in late 1983 by saying, "I've lived my life expecting things to take care of themselves. I told myself that all I had to do was to be a good actor. Believe me, that's not the way it works."

"Lana's greatest thrill yet!" was what columnist Walter Winchell called him when Bob Hutton carried on a well-publicized romance with Lana Turner.

Robert Hutton

The movie actor was born in Kingston, New York, on June 11, 1920. His original name was Robert Bruce Winne. His father was a movie fan and encouraged his son's early interest in acting. He graduated from the tony Blair Academy and then spent two years at the Fagin School, which specialized in training actors for motion pictures.

After spending a season at the Woodstock Playhouse he left for Hollywood with his father's blessing and financial assistance. Hutton's social skills were of considerable help to him in his first abortive attempt to "crash the movies." He had known Gloria Morgan, the mother of Gloria Vanderbilt, and her twin sister, Thelma, from their summer house in Woodstock. Through them he was invited to a party at Pickfair in honor of Lord and Lady Mountbatten. Everyone seemed to like the handsome teenager and he had an enjoyable time. But when he realized he was making no progress professionally Robert returned home.

He put in another season at the Woodstock Playhouse, but received no offers of paying jobs. Somehow he managed to get Louis Shur, who was then a very influential agent, to represent him. Shur got him a Paramount screen test but the studio would not meet the agent's salary demands. Warner Brothers bettered Paramount's offer and Hutton left for the film capital on the same train with another hopeful, Charles Drake (living in East Lyme, Connecticut).

Hutton attended the sneak preview of his first important role with great trepidation. In *Destination Tokyo* (1944), he played a young sailor who, because he was the most slender crew member on a submarine, is the one who must crawl into a narrow chute to defuse a torpedo.

"I entered that theater a nobody," he says today. "And I left a celebrity."

The *Life* review cited him as carrying off his role "with immense conviction." He was described in the same piece as "a soft-spoken actor who looks amazingly like Jimmy Stewart."

Bob thinks he also did good work in *Hollywood Canteen* (1944) with his occasional date, Joan Leslie.[8] Their studio cast them together in

Too Young to Know (1945) and *Janie Gets Married* (1946).

Warner Brothers attempted to make a young screen team of Hutton and Joyce Reynolds (widowed and living in Holualoa, Hawaii) when he was given the part of her boy friend in *Janie* (1944). Although they never got along well, they were paired again in *Always Together* (1947) and *Wallflower* (1948).

He was unaffected in all of his appearances and was especially believable in scenes requiring tenderness toward women.

Bob Hutton left Warner Brothers after eight years to freelance in television. He was immediately signed to play with Charles Laughton and Patricia Roc (married and living in the Hampstead area of London) in *The Man on the Eiffel Tower* (1950). Between making such movies as *The Steel Helmet* (1951), *Casanova's Big Night* (1954) with Bob Hope, and *Cinderfella* (1960) with Jerry Lewis, he made guest appearances on the TV shows *General Electric Theater, Schlitz Playhouse of the Stars, The Millionaire,* and *Ford Theater.*

Among his screen credits are: *Roughly Speaking* (1945); *Time Out of Mind* (1947); *The Younger Brothers* (1949); *Beauty on Parade* (1950); *The Racket* (1951) with Lizabeth Scott (single and living in Los Angeles); *The Colossus of New York* (1958); *The Jailbreakers* (1960); *You Only Live Twice* (1967); *Cry of the Banshee* (1970), and *Trog* (1970).

Bob Hutton moved to London in the early sixties and dabbled in producing, directing, and writing. He starred in *The Slime People* (1963) with Susan Hart (married and living in Beverly Hills), helped rewrite the script and directed it. He co-produced *The Secret Door* (1964) which had him in the lead.

Robert and his fourth wife, Rosemary Wooten, received screen credit as the writers of *Persecution* (1974), a vehicle for his old flame Lana Turner.

The Huttons returned to Bob's hometown in the mid-seventies and have since divorced. In 1980 he broke his back in a fall. Although for several years he was an invalid, he now sees the incident as "the best thing that ever happened to me." Hutton is using the period of recuperation as a time to reacquaint himself with his son, daughter, and four grandchildren and, as Bob puts it, "to take a personal inventory of my life."

He corresponds with Bette Davis, Ken Murray, and Lana Turner and admits he would like to work again in Hollywood as an actor or writer.

"I'd do whatever I was asked to do," he said recently. "And I'd consider myself very fortunate, whatever it was."

Robert Hutton now lives in Kingston, New York, the town where he was born. The photograph on the upper right was autographed and sent to him recently by another former Warner Brothers contractee, Ronald Reagan.

Peter Schaeffer

Leila Hyams in the early thirties.

Leila Hyams

The leading lady of silents and early talkies was born in New York City on May 1, 1905. She was the only child of the vaudeville team Hyams and McIntyre. Leila began appearing on stage at an early age. At first she worked with her parents, a popular comedy act of the day. For a while she toured with William Collier, Sr., in a one-act play.

When her parents were cast in the touring company of *No, No, Nanette* Leila remained in New York City, studying dramatic acting while she supported herself by modeling. Oliver Clive, a noted artist of the time, called her "The Golden Girl" because of the delicate coloring of her skin and hair. According to the *New York Times* she was the first model to appear in advertisements for Listerine mouthwash.

As early as 1924 Leila was acting in silents. She made *Sandra* that year with Barbara La-Marr, but felt her film career really was set in motion when director Alan Dwan cast her with Madge Bellamy in *Summer Bachelors* (1926). She always considered it her best work. The same year she supported Clara Bow in *Dancing Mothers* and signed a contract with Metro-Goldwyn-Mayer, where she remained for almost a decade.

Although Leila Hyams was never more than a leading lady, she played opposite some of the most prominent male stars of the period: Conrad Nagel in *The Idle Rich* (1929); Buster Keaton in *Spite Marriage* (1929); John Gilbert in *Way for a Sailor* (1930) and *A Gentleman's Fate* (1931). Bing Crosby wooed her in *The Big Broadcast* (1932). While her looks and personality always pleased on the screen, they never distracted from the men she supported.

She was the female lead in *Alias Jimmy Valentine* (1928), her studio's first venture into sound, and *The Big House* (1930), a prison picture that was a box-office smash. Her good friend Jean Harlow stole Leila's husband in *Red Headed Woman* (1932).

Three of her films are considered screen classics: *Freaks* (1932); *Island of Lost Souls* (1933), and *Ruggles of Red Gap* (1935). Of *Freaks* she once said, "This was certainly not the kind of picture M-G-M was known for. But they had no control over the director, Tod Browning, and until he showed them the final print I don't think they knew just how strange the film was. The studio was very embarrassed by it and I must admit I'm surprised that it is still popular. I never got to know the real freaks well but the midgets were delightful. They were great fun on the set and I had them to dinner in my home several times.''

The only two roles Leila turned down were ''Jane'' in *Tarzan* and the part that Edwina Booth (married to a bishop of the Mormon Church and living in Long Beach) played in *Trader Horn*. Neither script appealed to her and she didn't want to be separated from her husband, the agent Phil Berg, whom she married in 1927.

Leila Hyams retired from acting in 1937. After World War II her husband sold his interest in the Berg-Allenberg Agency for several million dollars. He had represented such stars as Clark Gable, Kay Francis, and Loretta Young and established the practice of deducting his 10 percent commission before the clients received their salaries, a practice now standard throughout the industry. He always referred to his marriage to Leila as ''the best deal I ever made.''

The Bergs had no children and lived in an ultramodern hilltop estate in Bel-Air. Their collection of modern art and archeological artifacts was so extensive that much of it was on permanent loan to museums. The couple were avid sports fans. Leila devoted much of her time to the American Red Cross.

A few years before Leila Hyams died in December 1977, she explained her early exit from pictures: ''I was never stagestruck. Acting was to me simply the profession I was born into. I never developed the driving ambition which you really need if your goal is stardom. I did enjoy making movies at first but after talkies came in no one seemed to know what he was

Jon Virzi

Leila Hyams shortly before she died in December 1977.

doing. It became more and more like hard work. There I was with a huge beautiful home and a wonderful husband. But I wasn't able to enjoy much of either. For a while I missed the attention. We'd go to parties or premieres and the microphones and cameras were always turned to one of Phil's clients—not me anymore. But I knew I could have worked if I'd really wanted to and whenever I found myself unhappy I'd just remember all those long, long days of shootings and the separations from Phil. Believe me, it's worked out fine.''

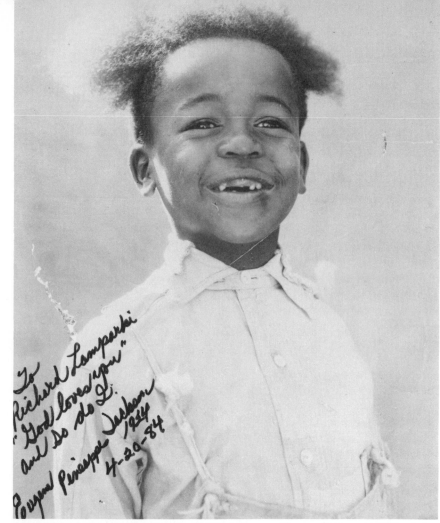

Eugene Jackson appeared in the all-black feature Hearts of Dixie (1929) *while he was making* Our Gang *shorts.*

Eugene "Pineapple" Jackson

The boy who replaced "Sunshine Sammy" in *Our Gang* was born in Buffalo, New York, on Christmas Day 1916.

Eugene went to Los Angeles with his widowed mother and brother in 1923. Since he was already an accomplished dancer, the Jack-sons often lived all week on the groceries he would win as first prize in amateur contests doing the "shimmy."

"Pineapple" played the late Allen "Farina" Hoskins's older brother in the two-reelers. They both left the series in the early thirties.

Michael Knowles

Eugene "Pineapple" Jackson acts still and runs the New Stage Workshop, which he owns in Compton, California.

Jackson has not worked in anything but show business, has fond memories of his career, and feels especially grateful for the $75 a week he made as a "Gang" member.

He supported Mary Pickford in *Little Annie Rooney* (1925) and had an important role with Irene Dunne[8] and Richard Dix in *Cimarron* (1931). He was in several Gene Autry[8] westerns and played "Uncle Lou" on the TV show *Julia*.

In the late thirties he was one of the "Harlem Tuff Kids," stars of a series of pictures with all-black casts. After World War II he was the leader of the Jackson Trio, a popular musical group.

Eugene and his wife of thirty-nine years live in Compton in a house they own which is near their commercial property and his New Stage Workshop, a dancing school. They also have real estate in Watts, California. Their son is a motion picture camera operator.

Younger blacks have attempted to admonish "Pineapple" for having played roles that they felt degraded their race. His response to them is: "I'm here to tell you that we were all damn glad to take those roles and get paid so well. Yes, we portrayed bootblacks and chauffeurs and janitors and if we hadn't been lucky enough to get those parts we'd have considered ourselves very fortunate to be able to get those kind of jobs. Those days were *tough*, baby!"

Mary Ann Jackson appeared in more than thirty Our Gang *comedies, both silent and sound. Here she is shown with fellow "Little Rascals." From left: Harry Spear, Joe Cobb, unidentified actor, Wheezer Hutchins, Jean Darling, Mary Ann Jackson, Allen "Farina" Hoskins, and Pete the Pup.*

Mary Ann Jackson

The tomboy of *Our Gang* (now seen under the title of *Little Rascals* on television) was born in Los Angeles on January 14, 1923.

Dorothy, her brother, sister, and widowed mother were all in movies as bit actors and extras before she made her first appearance as a featured "Gang" member in *Crazy House* (1928). Unlike the rest of her family, she left the profession shortly after outgrowing her part in the early thirties. Her last prominent part in the series of shorts was *Fly My Kite* (1931) with the late Matthew "Stymie" Beard.[8]

Later she worked as stand-in for her friend Edith Fellows[8] for about five years. That was her only connection with Hollywood. She does not like to be interviewed about her childhood experiences because her recollections are, for the most part, unhappy ones.

Mary Ann had a son and a daughter by her first marriage. After a divorce she married her present husband. They live in Newbury Park, California.

Edith Fellows, who has remained in touch with her through the years, recently explained Mary Ann's attitude: "It was never her idea to be in pictures. Like many of us, it was a matter of her family's survival. Eventually, she rebelled. By then her sister 'Peaches' was a Goldwyn Girl, so her mother relented and Mary Ann worked instead at the May Company. She preferred that to acting. That should tell you what she felt about the profession."

Jon Virzi

Mary Ann Jackson disliked the bangs she had in Our Gang *and has not worn her hair in that style for fifty years.*

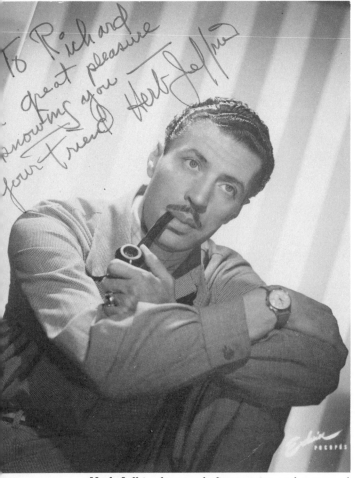

To Richard a great pleasure knowing you your friend Herb Jeffries

Herb Jeffries has made five movies and appeared on such TV shows as Hawaii Five-O *and* The Virginian.

Herb Jeffries

The singer-actor was born Herbert Jeffrey on September 24, 1914, in Detroit, Michigan. His mother was an Irish widow. His father, who died when Herb was eleven years old, was of mixed ancestry. Herb once told *Life* magazine that he was three-eighths Negro.

By the time he was sixteen he knew he wanted to be a singer. He often appeared with the Howard Buntz Orchestra at small ballrooms around Detroit. In 1933 Erskine Tate took him on as a vocalist with his group at the Savoy Dance Hall in Chicago. Earl Hines heard him and hired him for the Grand Terrace where Hines's dance music was broadcast throughout the Midwest. He made some recordings with Hines but left him to go on tour with Blanche Calloway's band. During their engagement at Sebastian's Cotton Club Herb decided to remain in Los Angeles and found work as a vocalist-emcee at the Club Alabam.

Being handsome, 6 feet 1½ inches tall, and light-complexioned, Herb was ideal to play in what was usually referred to then as "sepia movies." His smoky blue eyes were never photographed in color in his pictures, which played only in ghetto theaters and were advertised as having an "All Colored Cast." His debut, *Harlem Rides the Prairie* (1938), was the first black western since talkies started. Following the trend of the times, Jeffries was a singing cowboy. Next he made *Bronze Buckaroo* (1939) and *Harlem Rides the Range* (1939). He also starred in the crime melodrama *Two-Gun Man from Harlem* (1939).

It has been said of Herb Jeffries and "Flamingo" that the song "made" the singer and the singer "made" the song. He recorded it on December 28, 1940. It was one of the biggest hits of the era.

"In My Solitude," "I Got It Bad and That Ain't Good," and "When I Write My Song" are other hits he recorded, but "Flamingo" has remained the one most closely associated with him.

Jeffries recorded a piece of Khachaturian that got little notice. A few years later it became a hit with different lyrics as "Stranger in Paradise." He passed up a chance to be the first to record "Love Letters," because he was unimpressed. He could have recorded "Nature Boy" at approximately the same time that Nat King Cole cut what became the definitive version and a phenomenal hit. Herb shrugs today when asked why he waited six months to record his rendition.

He spent part of the fifties in Europe, where his voice, which has been described as "black velvet baritone," and vaguely Latin looks won him many admirers. He was considered the rage throughout France for a while and had his own nightclub in Paris.

Herb sang with Duke Ellington before and after his "Flamingo" success and was featured in the Duke's hit revue *Jump for Joy.* He considers the band leader to have been a very important influence in his life personally as well as professionally. It was Ellington who suggested that Herb, who was at the time besieged with troubles, "try God."

Jeffries is a yogi and a student of Eastern philosophies. The concert he does, "The Guru," is a blend of classical and jazz music with a soft rock beat. In it he sings only his own compositions with the exception of "Nature Boy," which was written by Eden Abhez (widowed and living in Sunland, California).

In his nightclub act Jeffries sings standards and recent hits, as well as jazz, which is now his specialty. He sings only a few bars of "Flamingo" during a medley. Many of his younger fans are unaware that he was ever anything but a jazz singer.

Herb has a son by his first marriage and two daughters by his second. He and exotic dancer Tempest Storm, his third wife, have one daughter. His son Michael Patrick was born in 1981. His present wife is a nonprofessional. They live in Van Nuys, California.

Peter Cury

Herb Jeffries recently with his daughter and granddaughter. He has another daughter by the exotic dancer Tempest Storm.

During years when many of non-Caucasian ancestry were "passing" for white in the U.S., Jeffries, who could easily have done so, refused to. Western star Buck Jones, who also produced, offered to stake him to a year in South America where he could learn Spanish and acquire a new name and identity. Jones then intended to star Herb in a series as a white cowboy.

In a lengthy article on him in *Life* magazine entitled "He would not cross the color line," Herb said to the reporter, "I decided sometime ago that the Negro people need all the good, intelligent, unbelligerent representatives they can get and I try to be one."

Tyrone Power (right) proposed to Evie when they were very young and remained a close friend until his death. Van Johnson (left) married her the same day she divorced his intimate friend Keenan Wynn. This photo was snapped by Gary Cooper.

Evie Johnson

Hollywood's social leader was born Eve Abbott in Buffalo, New York, on May 8. Her father operated theaters, as did his friend, the father of Katherine Cornell. Through him Evie spent six years as an apprentice with Katherine Cornell's stock company and then made her Broadway debut in support of Fredric March and Florence Eldridge in *The American Way* (1939). The same season she originated the role in the stage version of *Key Largo* that later brought Claire Trevor an Oscar. But by then Jim Backus had introduced her to Keenan Wynn. When they got married she retired from acting.

"You did that then," she said with a shrug in 1984. "It was either-or."

The Wynns arrived in Hollywood in 1942 and almost immediately became very much a part of the social scene, thanks mainly to Evie's parties. They were considered an ideal young couple.

Of all the luminaries who were friendly with the Wynns, Van Johnson, who by 1946 had surpassed even Clark Gable in popularity, seemed the closest. "Just like a family member" is how one fanzine described the handsome young bachelor's relationship with fellow M-G-M contractee Keenan Wynn and his wife. The announcement, then, that Evie was divorcing her husband because she and Van had fallen in love was front-page news in 1947.

Van Johnson's marriage to Evie had the blessing of Louis B. Mayer, head of Metro-Goldwyn-Mayer. The studio chief assured them that the millions of fans who thought of Van as "the boy next door" would understand, as he did, that the star needed a wife.

The newlyweds settled into the Art Deco dream house that art director Cedric Gibbons had built for Dolores Del Rio.[8] Johnson's career flourished, their daughter was born, and they continued to entertain, but with a bigger budget.

Her parties were dressy without being stuffy and always star-studded. The biggest names in Hollywood could "be themselves," make invaluable professional contacts, and be envied by most of filmdom all at the same time.

In her heyday Evie and Gary Cooper, whose birthdays were close together, took turns giving each other parties. Roz Russell was so fond of her she insisted Evie play a part in her picture *Never Wave at a Wac* (1952). Ronald Colman and his wife, Benita Hume, the William Powells, Lana Turner, Ronald Reagan and Jane Wyman were regulars at her soirees. Betty Grable was her closest friend.

Then, in 1963, without warning or, she insists, any suspicions that anything was wrong, Evie was notified that Van would no longer be living with her. The only time she has seen him since was five years later when they appeared in court for a divorce. Their daughter saw him once years later when she presented herself at his hotel suite. According to Evie, he was "less than friendly" to the girl, his only child.

Although she no longer gives them, Evie still enjoys parties. But even when she is invited there is the matter of an escort, no easy challenge for a matron in youth-oriented Hollywood. Old friend Caesar "Butch" Romero is a frequent date, but Evie says many hostesses make it a rule never to invite widows or divorcees.

"They're all so afraid you're going to steal someone's husband," laments Mrs. Johnson. "Having been on both sides of that game it's something I could never, ever do."

Rocky Cooper, the widow of Gary Cooper, has remained a good friend, as have Jim Backus and Keenan Wynn.

Of the many others who were frequent guests in her home she says, "I thought they were really my friends. But when I run into

Bryan Joseph Donahue

Evie and Schuyler, her daughter by Van Johnson, share an apartment in Beverly Hills.

them now about the best I get is a vague invitation to lunch. Lunch! I gave black tie dinners, dinner-dances, and big parties. It's a 'What have you done for me lately' town, believe me."

Evie has sold the house, jewelry, and art she got in the divorce settlement. She worked for a while in an art gallery and does an occasional part in a movie. Her last was in *California Dreaming* (1979), which was written by her son Ned Wynn. The writing of her other son, Tracy Keenan Wynn, has brought him two Emmy awards.

Evie says it was her family who paid for her daughter's college education. Van Johnson's rejection of them both is due, she believes, to the hatred he had for his mother. It was for quite another reason, however, that the star left his family so abruptly more than twenty years ago. She intends to tell why and to describe life at the top in Hollywood in her autobiography, which will be called "All About Evie."

He was still being billed as "Dickie Jones" when this photograph was taken in the late thirties. The hat he is holding was given to him by western star Buck Jones, whom the boy supported in eleven westerns.

Dick Jones

The child actor of westerns was born in Snyder, Texas, on February 27, 1927. His father was the editor of the local newspaper.

Dick had his own pony at a very early age and was encouraged to imitate the adult males around him. Horsemanship was held in high esteem in his area.

The boy became so expert in the saddle that he was billed as the "World's Youngest Trick Rider and Trick Roper" at the Dallas Centennial Rodeo. The western star Hoot Gibson, who was making a personal appearance at the event, was struck by Dick's skills. He offered to help get the boy into the movies.

Mrs. Jones and her son went to Hollywood with Gibson and stayed with him until they got settled. Although the star did help Dick get established, they never made a picture together.

Mr. and Mrs. Jones never lived together again and eventually were divorced. Dick stayed with his mother who guided his career. He has described her as a "typical Hollywood mother."

He made A features as well as B westerns, but his parts in the former were usually small. Some of them are: *Little Men* (1935); *Daniel Boone* (1936); *Stella Dallas* (1937); *Destry Rides Again* (1939); *Brigham Young—Frontiersman* (1940); *The Howards of Virginia* (1940), and *Heaven Can Wait* (1943). In *The Adventures of Mark Twain* (1944) he played Fredric March as a boy.

In his most successful picture, *Pinocchio* (1940), he was heard but never seen. All of the famous puppet's dialogue was spoken by Dick.

In 1942 when Ezra Stone (now a prominent television director) went into the service Jones took over the title role of "Henry Aldrich" on radio.

Jones wanted better roles in more important films, but says he was never considered for the sort of part that might have changed his career. "There were some good roles in big-budget features that were right for me," he once explained. "But they all went to Dickie Moore."[8]

When he returned after serving in the Army, work in movies was so scarce he made his living for a while as a carpenter. But Gene Autry,[8] whom Dick had supported in several features, used him in two TV series he produced.

Although he was the sidekick to Jock Mahoney on *Range Rider,* Dick prefers that show to *Buffalo Bill, Jr.,* in which he starred in the title role. He takes pride in the fact that he did all his own stunt work on both programs.

He did very little after his five years under contract to Autry. "When I got that contract it seemed like a great break," recalls Jones. "But it was actually the kiss of death professionally. By the time it was over I had been typecast as an actor for low-budget cowboy things. And no one was making B westerns anymore."

He runs into Jock Mahoney from time to time and receives a card from Gene Autry every Christmas. That is the extent of his links with the entertainment industry. After *Requiem for a Gunfighter* (1965) he went into real estate full-time.

Dick Jones is a senior loan officer with Home Savings and Loan. He lives with his wife, his childhood sweetheart, in Northridge, California, and has a weekend home in Balboa.

He would not permit any of his four children to act while they were in school and feels his attitude did much to discourage any interest they might have had in such a career.

When asked if he had many close friendships

Juan-Carlos Roberts

Dick Jones has some mementos of his career on display in his Northridge, California, home.

with any of his fellow child actors Dick said that he had left the professional children's school after one week, dismissing his classmates as "a bunch of damn phonies." He never dated an actress.

His hobbies are fishing and water skiing. He cannot recall when he was last on a horse, an animal he describes as "stupid and untrustworthy."

James Kriegsmann

"Swing and sway with Sammy Kaye" has been his slogan for almost half a century, yet he never played swing music.

Sammy Kaye

The orchestra leader of the Big Band era was born Sam Zarnocay on March 13, 1910, in Lakewood, Ohio. His father, a laborer, and mother were Czech immigrants. Neither encouraged their son's early interest in music.

In high school he played the saxophone and banjo in his band, Sammy's Hot Peppers, and earned extra money in semiprofessional baseball. By the time he enrolled at Ohio University with an athletic scholarship he had changed his name to Kaye and that of his group to "Kaye's Ohioans."

While earning a degree in civil engineering Sammy and his Ohioans began playing at The Varsity, a dance hall popular with college students. With $500 borrowed from his sister, Kaye took over the lease and, charging a nickel a dance per couple, made a tidy profit. His manager, Harry Friedland, who later led his own band under the name Blue Baron, started booking Sam and his men into other college spots as well as nightclubs in Cleveland.

During a lengthy engagement at a club in Pittsburgh Kaye made an agreement with the Mutual Broadcasting System whereby his aggregation were on standby to do remotes. Although they worked on short notice for little money, these broadcasts made Sammy Kaye and his music well known up and down the East Coast.

He was playing Cleveland's Cabin Club in the mid-thirties when he coined the slogan that became one of the most famous in show business. "Swing and sway with Sammy Kaye" clicked with the press and public immediately.

His radio show *Sunday Serenade* was a network feature for over twelve years. It was his broadcast on December 7, 1941, that NBC announcer Ben Grauer interrupted to inform millions of Americans that Japanese planes had just bombed Pearl Harbor. Within a week Sammy had co-authored the music for what immediately became one of the most popular songs of World War II, "Remember Pearl Harbor."

The audience-participation gimmick that has worked well for him from its inception, "So you want to lead a band," is still part of his evening's entertainment. It was the title of one of his TV shows and an important feature on all seven of them as well as his specials. The person who receives the most applause from the audience for his conducting receives a baton engraved with the name Sammy Kaye in gold letters. He claims to have given out over 500,000 over the years. Sammy loves to tell of the night Horace Heidt[8] tried his luck at leading the Kaye men and lost to an amateur.

In the two movies Sammy and his boys made they played music but he had no dialogue. But when *Iceland* (1942) opened on Broadway the theater's marquee had him top-billed over the picture's star, Sonja Henie. Their other screen appearance was in *Song of the Open Road* (1944).

The late Guy Lombardo was quoted as saying that Sammy Kaye "bastardized" his music and he is still usually dismissed by critics as being "Mickey Mouse." Kaye shrugs off such criticism with his motto, "The tone is greater than the technique." His men were always thoroughly rehearsed and their music precise.

Shortly after Kaye debuted in New York City in 1938 musicologist George Simon described his sweet, soothing sound as "effective dance music. It's soft, unobtrusive, and capable of producing a fairly mellow mood upon the majority of its listeners." He still plays in much the same manner. Don Cornell (married and living in Miami) is often his featured vocalist at the fifty-some bookings a year he accepts. His trumpet player, Butch Oblake, has been with him since 1933.

Although he has no gold records, Sammy had big hits with his recordings of "It Isn't Fair" and "Harbor Lights." As well as playing music, he publishes it through one of the several firms he owns.

Early in his career Perry Como offered his services to Kaye for $31 a week. Sammy offered $28 and the singer went elsewhere. Years later Kaye turned down an opportunity to break the song "A—You're Adorable." "I just

Sammy Kaye in his Manhattan office in front of a photo of himself when he led "Kaye's Ohioans."

didn't like it," he says today. It became one of Perry Como's biggest-selling records. They still play golf together in Florida.

The late Jimmy Dorsey was Sammy's closest friend in the music business. They shared a keen interest in golf. Jackie Gleason is another friend and partner on the links.

Sammy's wife divorced him many years ago, citing grounds that he fully understands. "In my heyday I played as many as 365 dates a year," he admits. "I was literally never at home. No woman could put up with that."

Sammy, who is a cigarette smoker, says he feels "great all the time" and has no intention of ever retiring.

His home is a Park Avenue apartment. His Manhattan office is looked after by a woman who has been his employee for more than thirty years. It contains more golf trophies than music awards and has on its walls photographs signed to Sammy by the late Terence Cardinal Cooke and Richard M. Nixon.

Arthur Kennedy won the Tony as the Best Supporting Actor in the play Death of a Salesman *in 1949. For his performance in the movie* Trial *(1955) he received the Golden Globe Award and an Oscar nomination, one of the five times he has been up for an Academy Award.*

Arthur Kennedy

The distinguished screen and stage star was born John Arthur Kennedy on February 14, 1914, in Worcester, Massachusetts. His father was a dentist.

He studied drama at Carnegie Tech and,

after graduation in 1936, became part of the Globe Theatre, a small group that performed Shakespeare throughout the Midwest. As a result of that training he was cast in *Richard II* (1940), making his Broadway debut in support of Maurice Evans. His performance in a play presented by the WPA brought Kennedy a Warner Brothers contract.

He was in Sidney Howard's last play, *Madame, Will You Walk?* Although it never reached Broadway, its star, George M. Cohan, praised Kennedy's acting to many, including James Cagney. Arthur made his screen debut in support of the star in *City for Conquest* (1940), at Cagney's request.

His abilities were recognized and he was frequently cast in well-written parts. Directors such as David Lean, who guided him in *Lawrence of Arabia* (1962), felt fortunate to have such a natural actor in their pictures. His own personality was never projected, whether he played a lovable man or a loathsome one. And even his villains had a certain integrity.

His other movies include: *High Sierra* (1941); *They Died with Their Boots On* (1941); *Air Force* (1943); *Boomerang* (1947); *The Window* (1949); *The Glass Menagerie* (1950); *Rancho Notorious* (1952); *The Lusty Men* (1952); *A Summer Place* (1959); *Fantastic Voyage* (1966); *The Sentinel* (1977); and *Covert Action* (1978).

If Arthur Kennedy never became a major star, as some had predicted, he was one of the most versatile. He did not change his voice dramatically or use heavy makeup and yet each character he portrayed varied a great deal from the others. Not one of his performances is at all dated when viewed today.

He seemed completely lacking in glamour and, although rather nice-looking, had no strong sex appeal. Yet audiences and critics alike found him extremely effective on screen and stage.

Arthur Miller insisted on Kennedy in his plays *All My Sons* (1947), *Death of a Salesman* (1949), *The Crucible* (1953), and *The Price* (1968). He won raves for all four roles and again when he replaced Anthony Quinn in *Becket* opposite Laurence Olivier in 1961.

He did almost no socializing in Hollywood and received very little personal publicity, which may be why he has never received an Academy Award. Arthur was nominated as the Best Supporting Actor in 1949 for *Champion,* in 1955 for *Trial,* and in 1957 for *Peyton Place,* and in 1958 for *Some Came Running.* He also received an Oscar nomination as Best Actor in 1951 for *Bright Victory.* It was his performance in that picture that brought him the New York Film Critics Award as Best Actor.

He acted on television on many dramatic programs and in 1974 was a regular on the western series *Nakia.*

Kennedy drifted away from his profession during the early seventies. At the time he was running his farm in Nova Scotia. That and his winter home in Palm Beach have since been sold. He and his wife of forty-five years have a house on Jekyll Island, Georgia, and a condominium on the west coast of Florida where they live during cold weather. Their son has been institutionalized due to a mental disorder. Their daughter, Lori Kennedy, is an actress who lives in New York City.

While he is getting accustomed to his recent cornea transplants he has substituted treading water for his favorite exercise, swimming.

Asked if he is retired he replied, "I ask myself that frequently. It seems the theater has been on the downcline since the mid-fifties. The pace of television shows is very unappealing to me. I will not live in Hollywood or New York anymore and if they don't see you around they just don't think of you for roles. I guess I'm retired, but then if Tony Quinn told me that there

Arthur Kennedy is known to his friends and family as "John" or "Johnny."

was a hell of a part for me in a picture or a play I'd probably do it. Because I'd believe him and I miss his company. I like to work with old friends and there are fewer and fewer of them left."

Kennedy has long been considered within his profession as the "actor's actor." But perhaps one of his directors paid him an even greater compliment when he said, "Arthur is too real for Hollywood. He is not the stereotyped idealization of a man . . . he's a human being and he's not an 'actor.'"

Peggy King was the Queen of the Mardi Gras in 1954 and chosen Best New Singer of 1955–56 by both Downbeat *and* Billboard *magazines.*

Peggy King

"Pretty, perky Peggy King," as George Gobel used to call her, was born in Greensburg, Pennsylvania, on February 16, 1930.

Her father encouraged her interest in singing but could not afford to pay for lessons. Instead, she listened constantly to singers on the radio.

Peggy was still in her teens when she won an amateur contest judged by Lex Barker. The prize was a week under salary singing over radio station WGAR in Cleveland. She ended up staying a year, doubling in the evenings as the band singer at the Hotel Cleveland.

Just before her nineteenth birthday she joined Charlie Spivak's band as the vocalist and immediately left on a tour of sixty-one one-nighters in as many days.

The Spivak aggregation was playing the Capitol Theater in New York City when Twentieth Century-Fox offered her a screen test. She left the band, hoping for the best. When she was not offered a contract she went with Ralph Flanagan, singing with his band for the next year.

She got six months' work and some very good experience singing on Mel Tormé's television show before producer Arthur Freed saw her during an engagement at the prestigious Blue Angel nightclub.

Freed brought her to M-G-M and set in motion a campaign to launch her as the "new Judy Garland." Instead it proved a real career obstacle when it became obvious that most Garland fans resented the title. Then Vincent Minnelli directed her in *The Bad and the Beautiful* (1952) so that she seemed to be imitating Judy. When she opened at the Mocombo on the Sunset Strip critics and public compared the two singers. Ironically, Judy Garland caught her act and liked her.

"I took singing, acting, dancing lessons at the studio," she explained recently. "I went on personal appearance tours around the country with Metro stars. I spent an entire month entertaining GIs in Korea. I even worked as a stand-in for stars just to get experience and appear cooperative. But in the end they dropped me."

She was then the wife of musician Knobby Lee. When her former coach at the studio suggested Peggy as a last-minute replacement for an ailing Ethel Merman on a radio commercial she and her husband were very hesitant. Finally she accepted $110 for the three hours it took to record an advertisement for Hunt's Tomato Sauce. She remembers that as she left home that day she said to Lee, "Well, this is it.

I've no TV offers and I failed in the movies. I'm going to be one of those singers with a really good voice who makes a living at commercials."

Instead, the jingle was a national sensation and became so popular that at one point disc jockeys were playing it as they would a top ten song.

Signed for Columbia Records, Ms. King had a great success with her first single, "Hotentot," and with *Boy Meets Girl,* an album with Jerry Vale.

When she was divorced in 1956 Peggy had been separated for some time.

During the mid-fifties Peggy King's was one of the most familiar faces and voices in America as the singer on the popular *George Gobel Show.* Hal Kantor, who won an Emmy for his work on the show, said that she did the impossible in making Gobel sexy. During the three seasons they were teamed and for years afterward she made guest appearances on virtually every top TV show, both as a singer and an actress. She starred in two TV specials and sang one of the nominated songs on the three-network simulcast of the Academy Awards show in 1955. She was nominated for an Emmy as the Best Female Singer of 1955 and in 1958 co-hosted the Emmy Awards show.

She was signed for *How to Succeed in Business Without Really Trying* but left the cast before it reached Broadway.

"I thought my heart would break at the time," she admitted twenty years later. "But I went immediately into a booking at Mr. Kelly's in Chicago. If I hadn't played that date I'd never have met the man I married and, I can assure you, I've found more security and happiness in this marriage than I ever knew in show business."

In 1961 Peggy became the wife of the president of After Six, the men's clothing manufacturer. Their son is a musician and their

Jack Mitchell

Peggy King and her husband have a home in Philadelphia and a co-op in Manhattan. She is a convert to Judaism.

daughter is a university student.

She is still in touch with George Gobel and speaks of him with fondness. Vic Damone, Debbie Reynolds, Pat Carroll, and Kaye Ballard are others she has remained friendly with during her retirement.

In late 1983 Peggy King played a well-received engagement at Michael's Pub in Manhattan.

"I'm together now," she said in a recent interview. "My husband has retired and loves the idea of my working again. We don't need the money, so I won't take anything I'm not absolutely comfortable with. And I can afford to try new things—like Broadway, where a lot of people think I've always belonged."

Harry Lauter played "Ranger Clay Morgan" on Tales of the Texas Rangers, a TV series produced in 1958–59. Dubbed into Portuguese, German, Spanish, and Japanese, the fifty-two half-hour shows still play around the world.

Harry Lauter

The character actor of movies and television was born in New York City on June 19, 1914. His mother, who died when Harry was four years old, wrote for the *Literary Digest*. His father was a graphic artist. Most of his childhood was spent in rural Colorado.

Harry spent several years studying at the Balboa Academy of Fine Arts in San Diego before he decided to be an actor.

For a while he followed the rodeo circuits through the Western states. Those years served him well later when he was cast in westerns because he was capable of doing all his own horseback riding and much of the stunt work required for his parts.

Prior to going into the service in World War II he was part of Elitch's Stock Company in Denver. Then he spent a season in summer stock on Martha's Vineyard. After V-J Day he went to New York City and was cast in *The Story of Mary Surratt* (1947), a play that starred Dorothy Gish.

Twentieth Century-Fox placed him under contract and brought him to Hollywood, where he spent a year under salary, but with no film assignment. Finally, he demanded his release.

By his own count Harry has appeared in more than nine hundred western films, including TV shows. He was a member of Gene Autry's [8] stock company and had another contract with the late Russell Hayden for the series of oaters he produced. Lauter was usually killed or arrested in the last reel, but not before he had started fights, broken laws, and killed some good guys. He claims that in one role his character was responsible for seventeen violent deaths.

"I loved to play villains, especially in horse operas," he said recently. "That's what I'm best in and what I like most. I can ride anything that moves on four legs and it never bothered me one teeny bit that I didn't get to wear the white hat or win the girl at the end. When I was a kid I always remembered the varmint better than the hero anyway."

In his first TV series, *Waterfront,* Lauter supported Preston Foster, playing the son of a tugboat captain and a member of the crew. Douglas Dick[8] and Lois Moran (widowed and living in Sidona, Arizona) were also in the cast of the seventy-eight half-hour shows that were first seen in 1954.

On *Tales of the Texas Rangers* Harry was co-starred with Willard Parker (married to Virginia Field and living in Palm Desert, California). The program was originally telecast just before *Fury* and had a huge audience among children. Lauter and Parker played members of the famous law-enforcement agency during various periods of its long history.

Harry Lauter has been semiretired from acting for over a decade. He and his wife, seascape artist Doris Gilbert, live in a mobile home park in California's Ojai Valley. His hobby is cooking. He spends his days painting.

Harry's work, which he sells at outdoor exhibitions, is of dramatic scenes of the High Sierras and Rocky Mountains in oil. Asked if he paints from scenic photos he replied, "I've been shot at and killed on every hill and ravine and hanged from every kind of tree there is. I don't need a thing but my memory."

He is recognized today as much for his TV series, on which he played good guys, as for his many portrayals of heavies and louts, but his image of the screen villain is the one he cherishes. Once when his only child, Brooke, cried because the kids in her class teased her about her "mean" father he advised her, "Just bear in mind that if I were a hero type I'd be like most actors—out of work—and you wouldn't be going to a private school."

Lauter is seldom tempted to accept a part. Most of those he liked working with, like his old friend Roy Barcroft, are dead or retired. He considers the generation making films today to

Phil Boroff

Harry Lauter and his wife travel frequently throughout the Western states and Canada to sell their paintings at various exhibitions.

be less than professional. Then, too, after many years of smoking as many as five packs of cigarettes a day, he has emphysema and asthma and never goes into high smog areas like Los Angeles.

Harry Lauter, whose paternal grandparents were both trapeze artists, played a high-wire acrobat when he starred in *King of the Carnival* (1955), one of the last movie serials ever made. He owns 16-mm prints of all twelve chapters and runs them for friends and neighbors. "We boo the bad guy, who for once isn't me," he says, "and eat popcorn and have a hell of a time!"

He insists his largest following is among black males, but could never understand why until Sidney Poitier explained it: "He told me that they identified with me because I was always on the run. I was shot at, hunted, hanged, and put in jail. 'But,' said Sidney, 'you're always cool. We like that.'"

Barbara Lawrence was publicized during her six years under contract to Twentieth Century-Fox as "Hollywood's Most Beautiful Starlet."

Barbara Lawrence

The movie actress who specialized in playing the star's best friend was born on February 23, 1930, in Carnegie, Oklahoma. She won a kiddie beauty contest when she was three years old and began modeling two years later. When she was in fifth grade her mother, who produced radio programs, took her to Hollywood.

Barbara became a popular model for junior fashions and was chosen "Little Miss Hollywood of 1942." When at age fourteen she was pacted by Twentieth Century-Fox she thought it was a "wonderful dream come true." At that time she considered herself the "world's biggest fan of movies and movie stars." She had gone to the studio to audition for one of the showgirls in *Billy Rose's Diamond Horseshoe* (1945). By the conclusion of picture's filming she had been signed to a stock contract.

Barbara had her regular schooling on the Fox lot and took lessons in acting, singing, and dancing as well. She had been at the studio for eighteen months when she was cast in *Margie* (1946). The role, which was a real break for her, was also an omen. The part, originally intended for June Haver, was of Jeanne Crain's best friend. In most of her films afterward Barbara Lawrence played a secondary role. As in *Margie,* she often had sharp dialogue which she invariably delivered very well. In that picture with her was Conrad Janis, who became what she recently described as "my first big romance."

She made screen tests for two pictures, either of which would most probably have changed her career in different ways. Jean Hagen got an Oscar nomination for her work in *Singin' in the Rain,* a part that would have been well suited to Barbara's comedic talents. The part that brought Shelley Winters the Best Supporting Actress award in *A Place in the Sun* was the other.

In 1948 Barbara Lawrence played Jeanne Crain's friend again in *You Were Meant for Me,* was manhandled by Richard Widmark in *The Street with No Name,* played Dan Dailey's sister in *Give My Regards to Broadway,* had a supporting part in *Captain from Castile,* and was directed by Preston Sturges in *Unfaithfully Yours.*

In 1949 Jules Dassin directed her in *Thieves' Highway,* which was Valentina Cortesa's American debut. *Mother Is a Freshman* with Loretta Young[8] and Robert Arthur (who heads his own insurance agency in Los Angeles) was also that year. She had some good lines as Linda Darnell's sister in *Letter to Three Wives* (1949).

She was in *Peggy* (1950) as Diana Lynn's[8] sister and made two 3-D films, *Arena* (1953) with Lee Aaker (now a carpenter in Manhattan Beach, California) and *Jesse James vs. the Daltons* (1954). Some of her other credits are: the Bette Davis vehicle *The Star* (1953) in which she made a brief appearance playing herself; *Her 12 Men* (1954) with Tim Considine (now a photographer living in Beverly Hills); *Oklahoma* (1955); *Man with the Gun* (1955), and *Joe Dakota* (1957) with Luana Patten.

Her marriage to actor John Fontaine lasted one year. Her second husband was Johnny Murphy, centerfielder for the Tucson Cowboys. After they were divorced Barbara married a stockbroker. She has now been single since 1974. In between husbands she dated both Howard Hughes and Ronald Reagan.

Barbara Lawrence lost interest in her career when she was pregnant with the third of her four children. She has removed herself so completely from the film colony that she was completely unaware of *The Films of Barbara Lawrence* for two years after it had been published. When she did learn of the book's existence her reaction was, "Why would anyone write such a book and who on earth would buy it?"

Jim Janisch

Barbara Lawrence is a realtor at the Jon Douglas Company in Beverly Hills.

She says she does not miss acting and that it usually saddens her to see her contemporaries on television.

"Many of them were stars, not just promising people like myself," she said recently. "They made wonderful films in their heyday. Now I see them in what I think is just junk. Maybe they need the money, but I hate to see them destroy the images they created."

Ms. Lawrence, who now sells real estate in Beverly Hills, explained in a recent interview why she changed professions: "I realized that I wasn't getting anywhere. My parts were getting smaller or worse or both. It was no longer the fabulous life I first thought it was. It wasn't even an interesting one."

To Richen
Thanks for listening
to my SAG

Marc Lawrence has called his famous features "my terrible mask: the holes in my face, the black eyes staring through . . . I'm hate material."

Marc Lawrence

The screen's distinguished heavy was born on December 17, 1910, in New York City. His original surname was Goldsmith. Marc's uncle was Jechial Goldsmith, a star in the Yiddish theater, who encouraged Marc's interest in acting.

While earning a B.A. degree in literature at the City College of New York, Marc spent his summers working at a camp that specialized in drama. He was a member of the Provincetown Playhouse before being awarded a scholarship with Eva La Gallienne's repertory company. Lawrence joined the group in 1930 along with John Garfield. In 1932 after the La Gallienne company was disbanded, Lawrence hopped a freight train to Hollywood.

Shortly after he arrived in the film capital he fell in love with a beautiful young woman, but soon learned that she was a prostitute. Just at that time he heard that a little theater was holding auditions for *Waiting for Lefty*.

"My heart was broken," he said recently. "I got up on that stage and used all the pain I was feeling. I didn't know it but Will Geer had already been cast in the role I was trying out for, but he was so impressed with my reading he withdrew."

After making his screen debut in *White Woman* (1933) he was quickly established as a reliable character actor who specialized in portraying criminals. Whether it was small- or big-time crime that his character was involved with he never played just a "mug." Frequently he was cast as the head of the rival gang or the boss's "enforcer." Though playing scenes with some of the screen's most effective bad guys Marc somehow managed to look the most treacherous of all.

He has made more than one hundred features. Among them: *Little Big Shot* (1935); *Counterfeit* (1936); *Racketeers in Exile* (1937); *Penitentiary* (1938); *Dust Be My Destiny* (1939); *The Great Profile* (1940); *Blossoms in the Dust* (1941); *This Gun for Hire* (1942); *The Ox-Bow Incident* (1943); *Dillinger* (1945) with Lawrence Tierney; *My Favorite Spy* (1951), and *Johnny Cool* (1963).

For a while Lawrence was under contract to Columbia Pictures. He got along well with production head Harry Cohn, who felt Marc could be developed much beyond what he had been allowed to do on the screen. But, when he was denied a salary increase, he left to freelance.

"I don't fret about it," he insists. "In those days I didn't understand anything about how careers are brought along. I was a typical hotheaded actor."

One thing that does trouble him and that greatly affected his life was his appearance before the House Un-American Activities Committee in 1950. He was one of the first from Hollywood to be called and his testimony brought headlines. There were those who appreciated the comical aspects of Marc's performance as he responded to his inquisitors. Sounding like a Damon Runyon character, he claimed to have joined the Communist Party because he had been told by Lionel Stander that "it was a good way to get to know the dames."

He also named John Howard Lawson and Karen Morley, while dismissing the years he spent in association with the Reds as "a great unholy mistake."

"People today have no idea what the heat was like then," he said not long ago. "My other choices were to run away to Mexico or to go to jail. They ask me still if I think I did the right thing. There *was* no 'right thing' to do."

Shortly afterward Marc Lawrence moved to Europe, where he worked steadily, becoming a star in Italy. As early as 1953 right-wing activist Ward Bond told Marc that he was not blacklisted, but among the Left in filmdom he was. He said in 1984 that he is still persona non grata to many and felt "there will always be bad feelings about what I did. I realize that and even understand it. But that doesn't make it any easier to live with."

To those unconcerned with his political past the character actor is highly thought of for his work in *Key Largo* (1948) and *Asphalt Jungle* (1950). Many felt his offbeat characterization in *The Shepherd of the Hills* (1941) should have brought an Oscar nomination.

The highlight of his stage career was his performance in *A View from the Bridge*, which won raves in the English production of 1958.

During the sixties he directed dozens of TV shows. In 1963 he produced and directed the feature *Nightmare in the Sun*. He produced, directed, and starred in *Pigs* (1973), a picture about man-eating swine. He and his wife, Fanya Foss, wrote the script. They have also written a play together which had been optioned by Stanley Baker.

Marc Lawrence and his wife live in an apartment overlooking the Pacific Ocean in Marina del Rey, California.

Although he now lives in the U.S., he says that most of the roles he gets are in European films. He has been seen recently in *Marathon Man* (1976), *Foul Play* (1978), and *Super Fuzz* (1981), but the parts were small ones.

He sometimes watches his old pictures on TV but says, "It's like looking at someone I once knew a long time ago."

Lawrence has an impressive collection of ancient Greek and Etruscan artifacts and several watercolors by Henry Miller, who was his friend. His son Michael is a sculptor and his daughter is the actress Toni Lawrence.

The swarthy, pockmarked skin which is his trademark is the result of an extreme case of adolescent acne.

In the dramatization of *Are You Now or Have you Ever Been*, Alan Garfield, the son of his old friend, played Marc in his appearance before the HUAC. Asked if he had seen the play he replied, "No. I don't need to see it. I know what I did and what I said. It's all too clear in my memory."

Baron Leone

The wrestler who became a popular personality on early television was born on June 8, in Pettorano in the province of Abruzzi, Italy. He describes his father, a building contractor, as "small but very, very strong" and his mother as "a big woman."

He began to wrestle when he was young and, although his parents strongly disapproved, they did not forbid it. "It was a fad then," he explains. "All the boys did it, but I was the best. By fourteen I was the champion in my area. But my family no like. 'Too brutal,' they say!"

Michele Leone began to win cash prizes and invested some of his earnings in wrestling lessons. He was well known throughout Europe and in South America by the time he first came to the United States in 1938.

Leone was not drafted into service during World War II because he was still a citizen of Italy, a member of the Axis. Instead, he wrestled in many exhibition bouts at military installations.

Wrestling and the Baron came into their own with television. As early as 1941 he had wrestled on the new medium and was fully aware of how well the sport televised. In 1947, when TV first became available to the general public, most sets were in bars. Popular from the beginning, wrestling sustained its home audience much longer than any of the entertainment personalities of the early years.

The first genuine stars of wrestling were the late Gorgeous George and Baron Leone. Both had the builds and the flamboyance that drew a surprisingly mixed viewership. People who would never go to an auditorium to watch a wrestling match from a few rows away from the ring found themselves mesmerized by close-ups of thickly built men bending each other

None of Baron Leone's claims to wrestling championships were acknowledged by legitimate sports organizations, but, because of TV, he was much better known than most titleholders.

into what appeared to be painful positions.

Most big-time wrestlers had at least one hold that they were well known for. Leone's was his "Baron's stranglehold."

He was always referred to in his introductions to the crowds and in ringside interviews as a "continental nobleman." When he entered an arena he did so with an air of great arrogance. Once in the ring he would strut around under the lights with his hands on his hips and a sneer on his face conveying his aristocratic contempt for the audience of "peasants." When asked recently the source of his title of "Baron," Leone answered, "My ancestry, of course," with a perfectly straight face.

Throughout his television career he flaunted shoulder-length hair, usually worn in ropelike curls, a style that had not been seen even among European gentry in several centuries. Men were often enraged by his coiffure, which was made worse by the Baron's pompous manner. It intrigued a great many women who watched the matches with a degree of interest that they could not explain to their friends, their husbands, or themselves.

Today Baron Leone takes no interest in the sport that made him financially independent. He does not watch wrestling on television and has not appeared at a match in so long there are rumors that he retired because he was seriously injured in his last bout.

In 1954 Leone married a woman who was aware of his standing within his profession but was, in the words of the Baron, "no fan." They share an apartment in "The Baron's Castle," a building he owns in Santa Monica. It is a pink structure on several levels topped by a large cupola. Leone spends several hours every day swimming in the Pacific Ocean and jogging on the beach, which is about two blocks from his door. The Leones have no children and travel frequently.

When Baron Leone lost a highly publicized

Donna Schaeffer

A sign on the large pink apartment building where Baron Leone and his wife live proclaims it "The Baron's Castle."

bout to Lou Thesz on May 21, 1952, he had the consolation of knowing that the match broke all existing records. When the two met in the ring that night at Gilmore Stadium they drew 22,256 fans who paid $103,277.75 to see Leone, who always played the villain, defeated.

The Baron's explanation for his defeat was, "I beat Gorgeous George, Szandor Szabo, and Danny McShain, but that Lou Thesz, he was the toughest."

He continued to wrestle until 1955, when he and his wife made a return visit to his hometown, where he saw his mother for the last time. "She still worry that her boy get hurt," said Leone recently in his heavy Italian accent. "My wife and I love Italy so we stay a long time and I get lazy."

He never fought again.

The Lonesome Gal *was sponsored by breweries in many of the 265 communities in which she was heard. She had a huge following among males whom she called "sweetie," "muffin," and "baayybeee."*

"The Lonesome Gal" (Jean King)

The unique radio personality was born Myrtis Simmons on November 4 in Dallas, Texas. A calcium deficiency put her in and out of hospitals throughout her childhood.

Having been snubbed by girls in her school because of her leg braces, she was overjoyed to be rid of them when she turned sixteen years old. Her widowed mother gave her a "Sweet Sixteen" party and a boy who had a crush on her came with his band. She sang with the group that night and was so well received she became their vocalist. It was then she changed her name to Jean King.

"All ten of the musicians were boys," she said recently. "And most of them were real cute. All those girls who'd cut me just about died. That's when I got the show business bug."

When he appeared locally Rudy Vallee used her as vocalist for his band for one night and told her she had a real chance as a singer, but offered no help.

Shortly after that Jean King moved to Hollywood. The only person she knew when she arrived in Los Angeles was Fat Joe Cobb (single and living in Los Angeles) of *Our Gang* fame. Through him she got a walk-on in *Swiss Miss* (1938) with Laurel and Hardy. Jean worked steadily as an extra and bit player. She also acted on radio shows and did a lot of dubbing.

She made a close friend in Joan Crawford and had a torrid romance with Johnny Weissmuller. Jean was ambitious but not as an actress. She felt she wanted to write but didn't know quite how to begin.

In 1947 she went to Dayton, Ohio, for a few months to baby-sit with her sister's children. When she realized she was in need of money Jean applied for a job with radio station WING and was hired as a "girl disc jockey," a very unusual concept for the time.

"I was told that since my name meant nothing to listeners I had to come up with a title and a personality," she recalls. "It wasn't hard, because I was so lonesome for California all the time."

The Lonesome Gal was an immediate success. Within three months *Billboard* magazine placed her "number one" in her category on the air. She remained with WING until, on a sudden impulse she never understood, Jean resigned during a broadcast in the spring of 1949.

Within days of her return to Hollywood, actor Barton Yarborough introduced her to William P. Rousseau, the producer-director of *Dragnet* on radio. They were married three weeks later.

"He was everything I ever wanted," she says today. "I was barren and he had an adorable son and daughter whom I proudly raised. He took my 'Lonesome Gal' character, polished her, and then produced the shows which we syndicated."

Her salutation was always: "Sweetie [pause], no matter what anyone says [pause], I love YOU more than anyone in the whole world."

The records she played and her spiel, which she delivered in what soon became her famous come-hither voice, was directed at men—lonely men who needed a bit of cheering up and the make-believe company of a woman who cared about them. One listener mistook her for his wife who had deserted him. Claiming he recognized her voice, he wrote endless letters. When a threatening one was accompanied by a doll with a broken neck he was arrested.

Many women wrote in to say she made their ironing easier and to thank her for showing them how men liked to be talked to. The exception was the woman who wrote long passionate letters accompanied by bouquets of yellow roses. The police persuaded her to desist after she sent a detailed account of the lovemaking she expected them to share.

"I touched a lot of hearts," says Ms. King.

The Rousseaus bought a sixteen-room house with what M-G-M paid them for the rights to the "Lonesome Gal" movie which was never made.

A strong part of her appeal was mystique. Her real name was never given. Jean reasoned she could never have lived up to the expectations of her audience and wore a full mask at all personal appearances.

Her theme song, "The Lonesome Gal," was recorded by Dinah Shore, Ella Fitzgerald, and Margaret Whiting. It was her eventual undoing. *The Lonesome Gal* was the title of the album

RCA recorded with Lurlene Hunter. Within days of its release her stepdaughter came home in tears after a schoolmate asked her why her father had married a black woman. Listeners, feeling they had been deceived, complained to stations and overnight the Rousseaus were deluged with cancellations.

Jean sued and the album was withdrawn but, as she says, "We really lost—everything!" Being unmasked publicly stemmed the tide of the cancellations but by then her husband had had a heart attack. In October 1958 *The Lonesome Gal* left the air forever.

After Bill Rousseau died in 1972 she says she began to think more and more about the imaginary man she used to talk to over the radio. "I missed Bill and that other guy a whole lot," she said recently in her slight drawl.

In her first interview in more than twenty-five years Jean King spoke of her present life: "When I was doing *The Lonesome Gal* I drew on my childhood and the way I felt then as a little girl whom people thought of as a cripple. But off the air I never had time to be lonely or lonesome. Now I have. Life plays strange tricks because I've become her. That's me—a real lonesome gal."

Wayne Parks

Jean King lives with her housekeeper of thirty-five years and a Siamese cat in an apartment above the commercial property she owns in North Hollywood.

Donna Loren singing the hit song "Goldfinger" on the TV show Shindig. *She had just been signed to appear in* Beach Blanket Bingo *(1965).*

Donna Loren

The teenage songstress of the sixties was born in Boston, Massachusetts, on March 7, 1947. She began singing at a very early age and won an amateur contest when she was five years old.

Her father, then an animator for Walt Disney, eventually left the studio and devoted all his time to managing her.

Donna was not yet in her teens when she first guested on *The Mickey Mouse Club* and began recording. Her material at the time was still being slated for the children's market.

Her first recording was made under her original name, Donna Zukor. Then she worked as Barbie Ames and for a while was known as Donna Dee. She has performed as Donna Loren since 1962.

She first came to national prominence as the "Dr Pepper Girl," appearing on television commercials and in print advertising for the soft drink. The thinking was that Donna was the right age and type to promote the beverage that had its largest market among youth. Subsequent sales figures proved them correct.

A tie-in between Dr Pepper and American International Pictures led to Donna's appearance in *Bikini Beach* (1964), *Muscle Beach Party* (1964), *Pajama Party* (1964), and *Sergeant Deadhead* (1965).

Donna sang in her pictures, but more often than not her numbers are edited out of the prints that are shown on TV. In fact, she did little other than sing in those movies. Her image, carefully shaped by her parents and the Dr Pepper organization, precluded her wearing a bikini on the screen or playing a "beach bunny." Her role in each was very definitely a star turn.

Perhaps her greatest exposure came as a regular on the pop music show *Shindig,* which was on ABC-TV from September 1964 to January 1966.

She did nonsinging guest stints on such television programs as *Dr. Kildare*, *Gomer Pyle*, and *Batman*.

During the four months the *Milton Berle Show* was on the air in late 1966 Donna and Bobby Rydell were the featured vocalists.

There was a "Donna Loren's Young Hollywood" column in the fanzine *Movie Life* and a series of ads in which she appeared for Simplicity dress patterns.

The Zukors kept their daughter away from most of those she worked with. In her publicity she often dated Paul Peterson (owner of a limousine service in Hollywood) but Donna says he was "an escort, nothing more."

At age twenty-one, with two years still left to run on her contract with Dr Pepper, Donna asked for and received her release. By then she had married Lenny Waronker, who was a record producer. It was the last the public saw of her.

Donna Loren recently explained why she retired so early: "I'd been singing ever since I could remember. When I became pregnant I decided to call it quits. My mother and father had put away my money for me. I had a boy and then a girl and then another girl. I never missed working and with my husband in the business I heard all the news."

Donna's first single in many years, "Somewhere Down the Road," was released in March 1984 by Warner Brothers Records. She and her husband, who is president of that label, were divorced two months later.

Because of her feelings about the music business Donna Loren is not at all certain that she would ever want a full comeback as a singer. According to her, "almost all" of the executives in the recording industry are "either homosexuals or short, straight men with huge insecurities." Both groups, she says, are very chauvinistic. She thinks the only musicians living a natural existence are in country music.

Donna and her children live in Santa Monica.

Donna Loren produces the annual American Music Festival which is held in Sedona, Arizona.

Frank Banks as "Lumpy Rutherford" and Ken Osmond as "Eddie Haskell" caught in one of their frequent conspiracies on **Leave It to Beaver.**

"Lumpy Rutherford" Frank Banks

The child actor who gained fame as "Lumpy Rutherford" on the *Leave It to Beaver* television series was born in the entrance to Hollywood Presbyterian Hospital during an air raid alert. His birthday was April 12, 1942, and his real name is Frank Banks. He describes his background as "very middle class, Jewish." Frank often helped out in his father's butcher shop when he wasn't acting.

When he was nine years old Frank accompanied the boy next door on a casting call. His neighbor was a professional actor who had been called to Ben Hecht's office to audition. While waiting for his friend, Banks was noticed by the scenarist-producer and given a part in *Cargo to Capetown* (1950). "That was it," says Frank. "My mother just loved it. Her baby was in the movies!"

He caught on at once with casting directors and worked frequently. "There were a lot of cute kids around Hollywood," explains Frank, "but very few of them were fat."

Jack Benny cast Frank as the president of the "Beverly Hills Beavers," a boys' club that figured in the plots of his TV shows.

The part that made him a household word throughout North America was that of "Lumpy Rutherford," which he played from 1957 to 1963. He enjoyed making the half-hour shows and liked the rest of the cast. "We were all treated alike on the set," he said recently. "Of course, our paychecks differed quite a bit, but as a kid that didn't seem to mean very much." He feels that during the last two seasons the characters of "Lumpy" and "Eddie Haskell," the show's other heavy, were developed by the scripters until they were equal to those of "Beaver"[8] (Jerry Mathers) and his brother "Wally Cleaver"[8] (Tony Dow).

"Lumpy" was the loutish, fat son of a blowhard insurance man played by Richard Deacon. He always called his father "Daddy." Deacon usually referred to the boy as "my lad,

Clarence," and constantly browbeat him. "Mr. Rutherford" and the father of "Beaver" were in the same firm and "Lumpy's" father carried the competition over to the children. Whether it was sports or girls, "Lumpy" invariably lost to "Beaver's" older brother "Wally." He often bullied "Beaver," usually at the instigation of "Eddie Haskell" [8] (Ken Osmond).

Banks sees his years of playing "Lumpy" as a mixed blessing. He claims to have been the only member of his class at UCLA who drove a new Cadillac convertible, but found that the fans who recognized him then, as now, were nearly all overweight males. He has described them as "hostile as hell. Not towards me, but at the world in general." As to the reaction of the co-eds, he says, "Whether it was the fame or the Cadillac, I don't know which, but I got laid more than anyone else I knew."

Several years after production on *Beaver* had ceased, Frank took off twenty pounds and was cast in the title role of *Archie Andrews.* But after three episodes were filmed the series was canceled when TV station managers complained that viewers would not accept Banks as any character other than "Lumpy."

He has no regrets that he did not continue in the acting profession. Banks says he was "different from any of the kids I worked with. I was very intent on making money—big money." He feels that he has achieved his goal and satisfied his ego as well as a financial consultant. He has stars, directors, and producers among his clients, but is most proud of the widows who put their trust in him to handle their money. "I get off on the fact that these people, especially old ladies who live off the investments I make for them, believe me to be honest and capable of managing their affairs."

His two daughters by his first marriage live with him, his second wife, and her two girls in Rancho Mirage, California. Among their neigh-

Paul Schaeffer

Frank Banks is now a financial consultant living near Palm Springs, California.

bors are Priscilla Presley, Don Drysdale, and Spiro Agnew.

When *Still the Beaver,* the ninety-minute special that reassembled the original cast, was shown on CBS-TV in 1983 there was serious talk of renewing the series. "Had that happened," says Frank, "I'd have had to decide whether or not I would want to act again. The other consideration would have been the pay. They were talking about $2,000 a week. I just can't afford to work for that kind of money."

The man still known to millions as "Lumpy" thinks he is the antithesis of the character. He describes himself as "a very boring person who is never bored. I love my work but it is a stressful profession. My kids and wife are great. My only real concern is my health. I'm a heavy smoker and I'm still overweight. But you're looking at a happy man."

The license plate on one of his cars, a De-Lorean, reads: "IMLUMPY."

John Lupton played the role in Broken Arrow *on TV that James Stewart had originated in the 1950 movie. He was married at the time to Nina Foch.*

John Lupton

The movie actor and star of the television series *Broken Arrow* was born in Highland Park, Illinois, on August 22, 1928.

John decided on acting as a career after appearing in high school plays in Milwaukee, where he was raised. During the summers he apprenticed in a local stock company. After graduation he spent two years appearing in children's plays. When his parents realized how serious he was, he was allowed to study at the American Academy of Dramatic Arts.

John made his Broadway debut in a small part in the Mae West vehicle *Diamond Lil* and had one scene with her until she noticed how young he looked. "Who's the little boy in that scene?" the star demanded to know. Looking younger than his age restricted his range of parts for much of his career.

After touring with Susan Peters in *The Glass Menagerie* Lupton was engaged to go on the road in *As You Like It.* The company's star, Katharine Hepburn, brought him to the attention of Metro-Goldwyn-Mayer.

John had planned to join one of the country's leading repertory companies when his play closed. Although he had not aspired to acting in movies, he chose instead to go with M-G-M when that studio offered a stock contract. He felt the money and living in California, which he loved, would more than compensate for whatever he might miss in the theater. Recently he admitted that acting before a camera has never been as fulfilling as acting on the stage.

He found life as a contract player to be frustrating. "There would be a good role for a young man in an upcoming movie, but it would go to someone like Robert Taylor who was into his forties. I asked to play 'Octavius Caesar' in *Julius Caesar,* but I ended up as a spear carrier. I talked my way into playing a village idiot in *Scandal at Scourie,* but I was still thought of as the boy next door, not a young character actor."

After two years under contract his option was not picked up, but he was soon brought back on a freelance basis for *All the Brothers Were Valiant* (1953) and *Escape from Fort Bravo* (1954).

In *Battle Cry* (1955), one of his favorites, Lupton was cast as a soldier who is killed in action just after learning that the girl he has fallen in love with, Anne Francis, is a prostitute.

Among his other features are: *Shadow in the Sky* (1951) with Nancy Davis; *Rogue's March* (1952); *Prisoner of War* (1954) with Ronald Reagan; *The Man with the Gun* (1955); *The Great Locomotive Chase* (1956) with Fess Parker (living in Santa Barbara); *Drango* (1957) with Donald Crisp[8]; *Taming of Sutton's Gal* (1957); *The Man in the Net* (1959); *The Greatest Story Ever Told* (1965), and *Jesse James Meets Frankenstein's Daughter* (1966).

John thinks he gave his best performances in the many live dramatic shows he did on TV in the fifties. He was seen frequently on such programs as *Robert Montgomery Presents, Playhouse 90,* and *Studio One.*

He is best known for the seventy-two half-hour episodes of *Broken Arrow.* He played the lead, "Tom Jeffords," a U.S. government agent who helped keep peace by making friends with Chief Cochise. The black-and-white shows were on ABC from 1956 until 1958 and remained popular in reruns for several more years.

John was married to the former wife of the son of silent stars Milton Sills and Doris Kenyon. They have a daughter and are divorced.

For ten years Lupton played "Dr. Mark Brown" on the TV soap opera *Days of Our Lives.* He appeared frequently on commercials into the seventies.

At the time *TV Guide* did a profile on him, his picture was on the cover, his series had just been renewed, and his fan mail was about 1,000 letters a day. Yet the interview ended with John wondering aloud what the future held for him and whether he would eventually "make it." That was 1957.

In 1984 he gave *Charlie's Angels* as his last credit. He had a full-time job with a computer firm that allowed him to take time off for acting jobs or auditions.

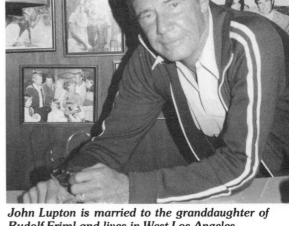

Diana Keyt

John Lupton is married to the granddaughter of Rudolf Friml and lives in West Los Angeles.

His problem as an actor, he believes, is that he is often confused with other actors—most frequently with Marshall Thompson. "I guess I just don't stand out as a distinct personality," he told *TV Guide.* Twenty-seven years later he said the title of his book, if he were ever to write one, would be "Whatever Became of What's His Name?"

He plays tennis, sometimes in celebrity tournaments, and frequently with his close friend James Franciscus.

A stranger recently approached him in a market and asked, "Didn't you used to be an actor?"

"I'm still an actor," he explains. "I'm what I call a blue-collar actor. I take parts that some might think are of no consequence. There's no way to be noticed or look good in these jobs. But I don't believe there are ever small parts. Only small actors."

"Irrepressible" was the word most frequently used by RKO publicists to describe Marcie McGuire, "The Female Mickey Rooney."

Marcie McGuire

"The Female Mickey Rooney" was born Marilyn Jeanne McGuire on February 22, 1926, in Kansas City, Kansas. Marcie was five years old when she and her divorced mother moved to Des Moines, Iowa.

Mrs. McGuire could play the piano and loved music but had never attempted a career. When her daughter showed an interest in singing she did everything she could to encourage her. By 1939 the teenager had won a talent contest and began to get jobs as an entertainer. In 1941 the two moved to Chicago.

Marcie, billed as "The Mick of Rhythm," was on the same bill with Danny Thomas at Chicago's 5100 Club. From there she moved to the Rhumba Casino where producer-director Tim Whelan caught her act. He gave her a 16-mm screen test in the diner of the *Santa Fe Chief* and left for Hollywood with the film. Marcie started out on a tour with the Camel Caravan, a traveling show sent by Camel Cigarettes to U.S. troop installations.

When Marcie and her troop reached the Army camp, a telegram was waiting. Whelan had gotten the okay from his studio to cast her in his next picture, *Seven Days' Leave.*

There was some talk when Marcie was signed to a contract that she would be presented as RKO's answer to Judy Garland. They were both belters, close in age and neither offered much in the way of sex appeal. Instead, the studio played up her hoydenish quality and gave her the title "The Female Mickey Rooney," which still embarrasses her.

The moviegoing public first saw Marcie McGuire in *Seven Days' Leave* (1942) with Victor Mature (divorced and living in Rancho Santa Fe, California). Her big song in the picture, "A Touch of Texas," became quite popular.

At a time when most teenage girls wanted to appear more mature and sophisticated than they were, Marcie was being publicized and often cast as a "jitterbug" or a snoopy kid sister. It was thought that young males found high school girls boring and annoying. Marcie was playing characters who were recognizable but neither enviable nor sexy.

She made *Around the World* (1943) with Kay Kyser,[8] *Seven Days Ashore* (1944), *Ding Dong Williams* (1946), *It Happened in Brooklyn* (1947), *You Gotta Stay Happy* (1948) with Willard Parker (married to Virginia Field and living in Palm Springs), and *Jumping Jacks* (1952) with Mona Freeman[8]. Her best-known film was *Higher and Higher* (1944), Frank Sinatra's screen debut. Her last was Disney's *Summer Magic* (1963) with Una Merkel.[8]

Her energy and big voice came over very well at the many personal appearances she made in presentation houses and USO shows. In her act she always sang "I'll Buy That Dream" which was from her movie *Sing Your Way Home* (1945), and "I Get the Neck of the Chicken," which Marcie had introduced in her first movie. Another of her numbers was "Chickery Chick (Cha La Cha La)," a hit of the forties.

In 1947 she became the wife of M-G-M contract player Wally Cassell. Both drifted away from acting after their children were born. Their daughter is an attorney and their son is a businessman.

Marcie was offered featured roles in *Finian's Rainbow* and *Lend an Ear* on Broadway but preferred to remain with her family.

She still sings and has begun to compose. Currently she is working with her grandson who, Marcie believes, has inherited musical talent.

The Cassells own and operate a large specialty printing business that was founded by her father. Their modern home in the Hollywood Knolls overlooks Lake Hollywood. They also have a house at Lake Arrowhead and a condominium in Palm Springs. On their front doors

Richard Lamparski

Marcie McGuire and her husband, former actor Wally Cassell, live near Lake Hollywood in Hollywood.

and in several rooms of all their residences are THANK YOU FOR NOT SMOKING signs. Both Marcie and Wally are ex-cigarette smokers.

Occasionally they see some of those they worked with in pictures, such as Esther Williams, Adele Mara, Ann Blyth, and Mickey Rooney, who was the best man at their wedding.

Speaking recently of her early years in Hollywood Marcie said, "I was such a dumb kid. One of the first VIPs I met when I came here was Lew Wasserman. Then he was the head of MCA, the big talent agency. Now, of course, he runs Universal. I'll never forget the look on his face when I told him how impressed I was to meet the man who had discovered the test for syphilis."

Trudy Marshall was one of Harry Conover's top models before being contracted to Twentieth Century-Fox.

Trudy Marshall

The leading lady of B films was born in Brooklyn, New York, on Valentine's Day.

Her father predicted throughout her childhood that his daughter would go into show business. She was still in high school when he entered her photo in a beauty contest sponsored by the Brooklyn *Daily Eagle.* Trudy came in second.

After graduation she was represented by Harry Conover, one of the nation's leading agents for fashion models. Trudy's face appeared everywhere in the United States on billboards and in print advertising. Very quickly she became a "cover girl," the highest-paying category in her profession.

She was twenty years old when *Look* magazine chose her for a feature story entitled "A Typical American Girl Visits a Movie Studio." The lot she toured was Twentieth Century-Fox and its production head, Darryl F. Zanuck, offered her a screen test before she left.

Forty years later she commented: "I'd been doing very well as a model, so I was much less impressed with the offer of a contract than most girls would have been. But when Zanuck told me that I had bedroom eyes I felt I might really go places in pictures. Yet he never cast me in sexy roles or even in very interesting ones. I was picked as one of Fox's 'Stars of Tomorrow,' which was exciting, but then I became engaged and the studio seemed to completely lose interest in me."

The pattern that began during her three and a half years at Fox never changed. Trudy was used as a supporting player in big-budget features such as *Orchestra Wives* (1942), *Heaven Can Wait* (1943), *The Purple Heart* (1944), *The Dolly Sisters* (1945), *Sentimental Journey* (1946), *Dragonwyck* (1946), *The Fuller Brush Man* (1948), *The President's Lady* (1953), and *Full of Life* (1957).

When she played leads it was always in programmers: *Roger Touhy—Gangster* (1944);

Circumstantial Evidence (1945) with Lloyd Nolan (living in West Los Angeles); *Boston Blackie and the Law* (1946); *Joe Palooka in The Knockout* (1947), and a "Jungle Jim" feature, *Mark of the Gorilla* (1950).

Laurel and Hardy fans known her for her appearance in *The Dancing Masters* (1943).

She is probably best remembered for *The Sullivans* (1944), which was based on the true story of five members of the same family who were killed while serving on a U.S. naval vessel during World War II. Two of the Sullivans were played by James Cardwell and George Offerman, Jr., who are deceased. She has lost touch with two others, John Campbell and Edward Ryan. A fifth brother was John Alvin, who is a character actor.

Trudy drifted away from acting while she was raising her son and two daughters. Occasionally she made an appearance on TV shows such as *Starsky and Hutch* and *McMillan and Wife.* She was seen briefly in *Shampoo* (1975).

She says that whatever resentment she might have felt over her own career has been completely wiped away by the success of her daughter, Deborah Raffin. Trudy, who helped train her in modeling and acting, has been in *The Dove* (1974) and Jacqueline Susann's *Once Is Not Enough* in support of Deborah Raffin.

Trudy Marshall produced *The Family Hour,* a play by Gene Stone that received excellent notices when it was presented in Hollywood in 1978.

For many years Ms. Marshall has devoted much of her time to various charities. For a while she was the president of the Screen

Francie Neiman

Jordon Winter and his grandmother, Trudy Marshall.

Smart Set which benefits members of the movie and TV industry. Since the recent death of her husband, a meat wholesaler, she has become even more active.

Trudy drives a silver Rolls-Royce and lives in a condominium in Century City.

Mary Anderson, the former actress and widow of cinematographer Leon Shamroy, and Coleen Gray have remained her close friends. Trudy and her best friend, Anne Gwynne,[8] toured Europe together in 1984.

Lori Martin as "Velvet Brown" wearing the floral wreath won by her chestnut thoroughbred named "King." Her series National Velvet *began on NBC in September 1960 and lasted for two years.*

Lori Martin

The star of the television series *National Velvet* was born Dawn Menzer in Glendale, California. Her birth date was April 18, 1947. Her father was an art director at Warner Brothers.

From a very early age she seemed set on drawing attention to herself. Her parents felt it was because she was so much smaller than her twin sister. When she was six years old her mother took her to an agent who specialized in children, thinking that performing might be a healthy outlet for her. "I started getting parts immediately," recalls Lori. "My little brother was signed by the same agent, but he lacked my interest in acting. I just loved it."

She took to interviews so well that as soon as she was thought old enough her parents allowed her to go on most of them by herself.

She appeared on a national TV commercial for Milky Way. Then she did a segment of *Whirlybirds* and was featured on *On Trial* and *Leave It to Beaver.* Tony Dow,[8] one of the stars of the latter, took Lori out on one of her first dates. She was escorted by John Gavin on several occasions.

In *National Velvet* Lori played "Velvet Brown," a twelve-year-old girl living on a dairy farm in the Midwest. Her dream was to run her horse "King" in the Grand National Steeplechase. The series was based on the 1944 feature film that brought Elizabeth Taylor to prominence in the same part. Lori was chosen for the role because many felt she bore a striking resemblance to the star at that age.

"We filmed *National Velvet* on the M-G-M lot," remembers Lori. "One day someone told me that Elizabeth Taylor was going to be in the Thalberg Building. I ran right over hoping to see her and caught a glimpse just as she left. She was just so beautiful! I guess I was pretty at that age, but never anything like her!"

Lori liked acting and all the people she worked with except Abner Biberman. She especially enjoyed making *National Velvet* because of her love of horses.

Some of her guest appearances were on *Please Don't Eat the Daisies, Family, I Spy,* and *Wagon Train.* Her feature film credits include: *Machine Gun Kelly* (1958); *The F.B.I. Story* (1959); *Cash McCall* (1959); *The Chase* (1966), and *The Angry Breed* (1968).

Lori Martin was in *Cape Fear* (1962) which has become a cult film. In it she plays a very nubile teenager whom Robert Mitchum is bent on seducing. She thinks she did her best work in that role. Polly Bergen, who played her mother in the picture, is the only person Lori has stayed in touch with after she abandoned her career in her late teens.

"I'd been in the business long enough to know I'd been stereotyped," says Lori. "My mother was in poor health and I felt I had worked from such an early age I could take some time off and get a college education." A few years later she tried to reactivate her career but became discouraged by the many changes in casting people and techniques.

As a child Lori was not allowed to watch herself on the screen, nor does she now when one of her pictures plays on television.

She was working for a firm that sells medical supplies when she met and married her husband, who is almost twenty years her senior. They, their young son, and three toy poodles share an apartment in Westlake Village, California.

In April 1961 *TV Guide* did a cover story on Lori Martin, whose series was then being seen on NBC on Sunday nights. In the article she is quoted as saying that what she wanted to be when she grew up was "normal." "It was probably an accurate quote," she admitted recently. "Because that's what I wanted and as it turns out that's what I am."

Asked about the money she was paid during those years Lori responds with a shrug, "My mother spent every last dollar."

Amaryllis Bierne-Keyt

Lori Martin with her son, Brett Breitenbucher.

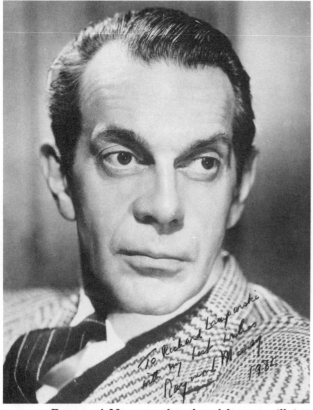

Raymond Massey, who played heroes, villains, and character parts on stage and screen for nearly six decades, is best remembered for his portrayal of "Dr. Gillespie" in the Dr. Kildare TV series.

Raymond Massey

The star of TV, stage, and screen was born on August 30, 1896, in Toronto, Canada. The scion of one of that country's leading industrial families, his ancestors had come to North America in 1629.

Massey never considered acting as a profession until he was stationed in Siberia as an officer in the Field Artillery during World War I. In order to amuse his bored troops he organized a show and played one of the parts. After the armistice he studied at Oxford University in England and became part of the drama society. So many, including John Drew, told him he had exceptional stage presence that he decided to pursue a theatrical career.

His West End debut came in Eugene O'Neill's *In the Zone* in 1922. In England he functioned with much success as a producer, an actor, and a director. He was thought of primarily as the latter after having directed about thirty plays in London. When he signed a contract with Universal in 1931 the studio asked him to direct, but he only acted in pictures.

Raymond Massey played *Hamlet* (1931), starred in *The Shining Hour* (1934), *Ethan Frome* (1936), and *Idiot's Delight* (1938) on Broadway, but his *Abe Lincoln in Illinois* (1938) was such a success the other hits were almost completely eclipsed. The long run of the play, followed by his appearance in the 1940 screen version, made him both a household name and the brunt of much good-natured humor within his profession and by radio comedians. He claimed the jokes never bothered him and frequently delivered the Gettysburg Address at patriotic functions. In *How the West Was Won* (1963) he played the Great Emancipator again. He also portrayed John Brown twice on the screen: *Santa Fe Trail* (1940) and *Seven Angry Men* (1955).

The Massey screen debut was as "Sherlock Holmes" in *The Speckled Band* (1931). Among those that followed were: *The Old Dark House* (1932); *Things to Come* (1936); *Prisoner of Zenda* (1937); *The Hurricane* (1937); *Reap the Wild Wind* (1942); *Action in the North Atlantic* (1943); *Arsenic and Old Lace* (1944); *The Fountainhead* (1949); *Prince of Players* (1955); and *The Great Imposter* (1961). Two of his favorite screen roles were in *The Scarlet Pimpernel* (1935) and *East of Eden*

(1955). Of James Dean, his co-star in the latter, Massey once said, "He was an example of The Method at its worst. No discipline, whatever. I don't think he ever came on the set knowing his lines. And yet, to be fair, I can't fault the performance that emerged."

He returned to Broadway many times, producing five plays, including *Grand Hotel* (1931). *The Silver Tassie* (1929) and *The Father* (1949) are among the plays he directed. His one venture into playwriting, *Hanging Judge,* was presented on Broadway in 1952 and later on TV's *Climax.* After appearing in *The Doctor's Dilemma* (1941), he co-starred with Katherine Cornell in *Candida* (1942). After that came *Pygmalion* (1945) opposite Gertrude Lawrence, *Julius Caesar* (1955), and *The Tempest* (1955). In *John Brown's Body* (1952) he was with Tyrone Power and Judith Anderson. He was last seen on Broadway in *J.B.* (1958) playing the part of God.

"King Lear" was the one role that he wanted very much to play, but which eluded him.

The fact that Raymond's elder brother, Vincent, became Canada's first native-born Governor General brought him greater prestige. Both in England and in the U.S. Massey was among the elite of the theater and international society. It was at one of their parties that Mrs. Massey introduced Wallis Warfield Simpson to Thelma Furness, thus beginning the chain of events that eventually led to the abdication of Edward VIII.

From 1961 to 1966 Raymond Massey was the gruff but warmhearted "Dr. Leonard Gillespie" on the *Dr. Kildare* TV series. The part had been played by Lionel Barrymore in fifteen feature films. Ironically, he did not watch himself on television and felt he was "basically a stage actor." He was bemused by the knowledge that after his long, diverse career it was the "Gillespie" part for which he was best remembered. He was fond of his co-star, Richard

Phil Boroff

The distinguished actor in the den of his Beverly Hills mansion less than a year before his death.

Chamberlain, and gave his last performance with him on stage in Los Angeles in the 1976 production of *Night of the Iguana.*

There were two well-received autobiographies—*When I Was Young* and *A Hundred Different Lives.*

His oldest son, an architect, is by his first marriage. The actor Daniel Massey and actress Anna Massey are by his second marriage to the English actress Adrianne Allen. Both marriages ended in divorce.

Raymond Massey's final years were spent in constant pain from a severe arthritic condition. He shared a Beverly Hills mansion with his third wife of over forty years. Mrs. Massey died in July, 1982. He survived her by a year and several days.

Before playing Danny Thomas's stubby sidekick on television Sid Melton made quite a few low-budget features, including Girls in Chains *(1943) and* Suspense *(1946).*

Sid Melton

The comedian best known for his role on television as Danny Thomas's sidekick was born in Brooklyn on May 23. His father was I. Meltzer, a comedic actor who was featured in vaudeville and the Yiddish theater. Sid gravitated to show business and comedy because of his father and never seriously considered another profession or specialty.

In 1942 he made his stage debut in a tour of *See My Lawyer.* Next was a road show of *The Man Who Came to Dinner* with Laird Cregar in the title role. He was part of the *Three Men on a Horse* company that starred Sam Levene and entertained U.S. troops throughout the British Isles during World War II. His one appearance on Broadway was *The Magic Touch* in 1947.

Melton made his film debut in *Shadow of the Thin Man* (1941). After that came: *Blondie Goes to College* (1942) with Arthur Lake;[8] *Suspense* (1946) with Belita (the proprietress of a nursery in London); *Tough Assignment* (1949) with Marjorie Steele (living in New York City); *Holiday Rhythm* (1950) with Mary Beth Hughes (a beautician living in Canoga Park, California); *Mask of the Dragon* (1951) with Richard Travis (a realtor in West Los Angeles); *Treasure of Monte Cristo* (1949) with Glen Langan and Adele Jergens (married to each other and living in Camarillo, California); *Three Desperate Men* (1951) with Virginia Grey (single and living in Sherman Oaks); *Thundering Jets* (1958) with Audrey Dalton (married and living in Sherman Oaks), and *The Atomic Submarine* (1959) with the late Dick Foran.

His movies, with a few exceptions such as *Knock on Any Door* (1949) and *The Lemon Drop Kid* (1951), were low-budget productions. Among the Bs he starred in are *Leave It to the Marines* (1951), *Sky High* (1951) and *Stop That Cab!* (1951) with Iris Adrian.[8]

Sid thinks his best-known movie role was in *The Lost Continent* (1951). The role that is his personal favorite is the nightclub owner who is pivotal in the career of Diana Ross in *Lady Sings the Blues* (1972).

He is recognized "almost every day" for his part on *The Danny Thomas Show* from 1959 to 1971. He played the fretful bachelor, "Uncle Charlie Halper," owner of the Copa Club where Danny often performed, and his manager. He would frequently be seen taking pills to calm his nerves. After several seasons Pat Carroll was written into the scripts as his wife "Bunny." His character worried as much after the marriage as before and possibly more after he became a father. During the long run of the series Sid frequently told interviewers that he got the part because he was the only actor Thomas could find who was uglier than he was.

Sid was considered for the role of the neighbor on *Bewitched* and "Alf Monroe" on *Green Acres*. He got the latter part, which he played from 1965 to 1971, but would have preferred the former, which went to the late George Tobias.

From the many people he has worked with throughout his career he has retained only Richard Webb as a friend. The two became close when Sid played "Ichabod Mudd" on the television series *Captain Midnight*. Melton was supposed to be his aide but usually provided more laughs for the viewers than help for the hero. His only other close contact with show business is his brother, screenwriter Lewis Meltzer.

Asked recently why he is no longer seen on television, he replied, "For years I auditioned for producers and directors who would fall on the floor laughing, but then I'd never hear from them again. Go ask them why I'm not working. Believe me, there's a lot more to working steadily than being a name and delivering the laughs. There's a certain—let's call it kowtowing—that I'm not prepared to do. I guess their egos need it. And then, too, I'm outspoken, which does not go over in this town."

He does not rule out acting in the future, although he has turned down a number of parts in what he describes as "raunchy" feature films and does not feel up to working again in live theater.

Walter Alexander

Sid Melton today with his companion "Piper."

Melton devotes all of his time and energies now to getting his situation comedy about a health club, *Rub-A-Dub,* on the air. He is the show's creator and director but does not appear on camera. Sid produced the program with a nonunion cast and crew expecting to sell it to a cable TV network.

As to playing a similar part throughout his career, he says, "How can I complain? That's the guy I am—a little man with big anxieties. I worry all the time about everything and everybody."

Sid's one marriage ended in divorce. He has no children. His companions for the last thirty years have been a series of wirehair terriers. He shares his Van Nuys home with a male named "Piper."

Paramount Pictures brought Isa Miranda from Italy in the late thirties. The studio intended to use her as a replacement for Marlene Dietrich, who had been named "Box Office Poison" by a group of theater owners.

Isa Miranda

The star of European films was born in Milan, Italy, on July 5, 1909. Her original name was Ines Isabella Sampietro.

Her family was so poor she began working in a dressmaker's shop after school as a "piccinina" when she was seven years old. Her duties were to pick up small pieces of fabric from the floor. She was twelve when she began evening classes in shorthand and typing after daytime classes and her job. At that point her goal was secretarial work, but once Isa began modeling she dropped her other studies to become an evening student at the Milan Academy of Dramatic Art.

She had some stage experience before making movies, but only in small parts. Max Ophuls chose her from among hundreds of actresses when she auditioned for the central character in *La Signora di Tutti* (1936). Upon its release in Europe she became a star. *Come le Foglie* (1938) was another great success.

Although still virtually unknown in the United States, she was being hailed as the "new Garbo" and "young Dietrich" on the Continent. American audiences saw very few foreign language pictures prior to the end of World War II.

Isa Miranda's arrival in Hollywood was well publicized by Paramount Pictures, the studio that had successfully launched the American careers of two other continental beauties, Pola Negri and Marlene Dietrich.

In 1937, Harry Brandt, President of the Independent Theatre Owners Association, sent shock waves throughout Hollywood when he released a list of major stars whose very presence in any movie was, in his opinion, a liability. Marlene Dietrich was one of those mentioned on what became known as the "Box Office Poison" list.

Filming of *Hotel Imperial* (1939), a big-budget remake of the Pola Negri silent vehicle, had begun with Dietrich in the starring role. Isa Miranda replaced her, but there was trouble with the script and a change of directors. The completed film was a disaster and Paramount released it as a programmer.

Her second and last Hollywood movie was *Adventure in Diamonds* (1940) which was much less pretentious and did quite well. But by then her country was at war and Isa chose to return home.

In Europe Ms. Miranda continued to act on stage and in many pictures. Some of her credits are: *Malombra* (1942); *The Flesh Is Weak* (1950) opposite Vittoria De Sica; *The Seven Deadly Sins* (1953); *La Ronde* (1954); *What Price Murder* (1958); *The Yellow Rolls-Royce* (1965), and *The Night Porter* (1974). She was seen frequently in dramatizations on Italian television and for the BBC.

The zenith of her career was the role opposite Jean Gabin in *The Walls of Malapaga,* which the academy of Motion Picture Arts and Sciences awarded an Oscar as the most outstanding foreign language film of 1950. She received the Golden Palm for her performance at the Cannes Film Festival.

A problem she had in both of her Paramount pictures was one she never overcame. Isa's heavy accent, though often extremely effective, could not be understood by English-speaking audiences. As late as 1955 when she played the *pensione* owner in *Summertime,* her dialogue had to be dubbed.

She made an *easy* transition into character acting, appearing on the London stage in Tennessee Williams's *Orpheus Descending* and in two films directed by Vittorio De Sica. Her work in *The Empty Canvas* (1964) won the Gold Caravelle award from the Italian film critics.

Isa was married to Alfredo Guarini, who had directed her in two films in World War II. In later years he produced movies. The childless

The late Isa Miranda photographed in her London flat by the author.

couple lived in London. Guarini died in 1981.

While working on a film in 1978 she fractured her right hip, the same one she had broken twenty-six years before. According to her obituary in weekly *Variety* Isa remained in a Rome hospital after that, "practically neglected by colleagues and public, until her death" on July 8, 1982.

To Isa Miranda her experience in Hollywood was nothing more than two pictures which she described as "one pretty awful and the other not so bad." She professed to have no regrets and maintained that even if she had achieved stardom in America, the outbreak of the war would have necessitated her return to Italy. The film capital, she would sometimes admit, was not to her liking. Although she acted in Hollywood films after 1940, all of them were made abroad.

Jackie Moran usually played sympathetic roles in movies. Even as the mischievous "Huckleberry Finn" in The Adventures of Tom Sawyer *(1938) he was basically a good kid.*

Jackie Moran

The child actor of the movies was born on January 26, 1923, in Mattoon, Illinois. His father was a special prosecutor for the state. Mrs. Moran played the piano and before her marriage appeared locally in concerts as a contralto. Having trained Jackie, the younger of her two boys, she was extremely proud when he became a soloist in their church choir.

Mrs. Moran took Jackie on the rounds of Chicago advertising agencies where his all-American-boy looks met with immediate acceptance. His winning smile was seen in national advertisements for Coca-Cola and the Nash automobile.

He remembers "never liking any part of it. From the very beginning I was always afraid that they wouldn't like me. When they did and I'd get the job, the work made me very self-conscious. I wanted my parents' approval and for people to like me, but what I was being asked to do embarrassed me a lot."

When Mary Pickford came to Chicago in the play *The Church Mouse* Mr. Moran obtained a letter of introduction for Jackie from the mayor. After hearing the boy sing several Roman Catholic hymns she promised to get him a screen test if he ever came to Hollywood. Shortly after that the Morans moved to Los Angeles.

Jackie made a screen test, but while he came over very well, he was unable to cry on cue. Failing to get a contract he went into a play, *The King Sleeps,* which was presented at the Vine Street Theater. By then he had learned to cry whenever the part called for it. The youngster was singled out for praise by most of the reviewers and received offers from three studios. The Morans chose to contract their boy to Paramount Pictures.

The classic tearjerker *Valiant Is the Word for Carrie* (1936), one of his first screen appearances, was a hit at the box office and brought Jackie a rave from columnist Ed Sullivan. It is the one and only time he liked his own performance. He remembers the film's star, Gladys George, as "just as kind and warmhearted as she was in that part."

Herbert Marshall made *Mad About Music* (1938) an enjoyable experience and the late Buster Crabbe and Jackie became friends when they made the serial *Buck Rogers* (1939). Most adult actors, however, seemed to him "only interested in how well we looked and played together in the scenes we shared."

"That was the worst part of the Hollywood experience," he admitted recently. "You could never believe anyone was your friend. Most people were so damn ambitious and competitive!"

About his contemporaries he has said, "I wouldn't want to name the ones I didn't like for fear of leaving one of them out. But the Mauch Twins [Bob is a film editor at Universal Pictures, Bill is retired and lives in Big Bear, California] were great to play sports with and I liked Gene Reynolds a lot. I realize now about the others that it probably wasn't their fault that they came over to me as such pains in the ass. Look at the life they were in. It's so unnatural!"

Among the more than thirty features he made were: *Mother Carey's Chickens* (1938); *Gone With the Wind* (1939); *Anne of Windy Poplars* (1940) with Anne Shirley (widowed and living in West Hollywood); *Song of the Open Road* (1944); *Since You Went Away* (1944); *Spectre of the Rose* (1946), and *Betty Co-Ed* (1947), his last.

Jackie was co-starred with Marsha Mae Jones (single and living in Los Angeles) in three films and had supporting roles in "Dr. Christian," "Henry Aldrich," and "Andy Hardy" movies.

He developed crushes on June Preisser, Deanna Durbin, and Olympe Bradna, but was not allowed to date until he was a senior in high school. After he eloped at age seventeen the Morans insisted his wife stay upstairs when anyone came to their home. Marriage, they felt, would ruin his career. After six weeks there was an annulment but not before Louella O. Parsons ran a blind item about "a child actor who keeps his bride hidden away."

"If ever anyone went Hollywood we did," he has said. "My dad never practiced law again. He was my personal manager, although he queered more deals than he made. We had servants and big houses, which he always rented, and gave big parties. We lived always off my future earnings. As soon as a contract was signed we'd borrow against it from the bank."

Readings for parts always terrified him and since he knew he was his family's sole support, the more important the role, the more traumatic it was. On the morning he was to read for David O. Selznick he shook so he couldn't stand, but his parents felt he was merely "highly strung."

Today he is known as "Jack." Almost no

Jerry Bierne

Jack Moran and his wife of seventeen years are separated. He lives in a small beach town near San Diego.

one he knows is aware of his screen career and he usually denies it when a fan recognizes him. He has not seen his older brother, who worked as his stand-in, in fifteen years. His only connection with films since he left Hollywood in the late forties is the seven movies he has written for Russ Meyer under noms de plume.

He made his living in the wholesale and retail liquor business until in 1982 he was forced to face the fact that he was alcoholic. Since then he has sold newspapers, hot dogs, taken bets for a bookie, and worked at a detoxification center.

He concluded his first interview in more than thirty-five years by saying, "My life is all backwards. I'll never make the kind of money I did as a kid which makes me appear to myself as a failure as an adult."

*In 1919 when producer Hal Roach (left) pacted "Sunshine Sammy" Morrison,
he became the first black contract player in the history of motion pictures. Shortly
afterward, his father (right) opened Morrison & Co., a chain of grocery stores,
and then a wholesale candy firm, the first such black-owned businesses in California.*

"Sunshine Sammy" Morrison

The first black child movie star was born Ernest Morrison in New Orleans on December 20, 1912.

His father, a chef to a wealthy family, was hired away when a couple, visiting from California, tasted his cuisine. Shortly after moving to Los Angeles with his new employers Mr. Morrison learned that a very young black boy was needed to play a part in a feature starring Baby Marie Osborne (a retired movie costumer living in San Clemente, California). For reasons that he never really explained, he took the little boy who lived next door, not his own son, to the studio.

The boy whined all day and proved ineffective in the role. When the director asked Morrison for another boy, but "with a better disposition," he returned with his son.

"I liked it right from the start," recalls "Sammy." "Right away I got named, because they couldn't get over that I smiled all the time. It's because I was so happy to be there and doing all those things."

Hal Roach heard about him and was impressed with how quickly "Sammy" caught on to comedy routines. He used him frequently in shorts with Snub Pollard, Paul Parrot, and Harold Lloyd.

"Sunshine Sammy" Morrison is considered by some to be the inspiration for *Our Gang* because Roach first attempted to star him in his own series. But when theater owners in many parts of the country showed no interest in the first and only one made, *The Pickaninny,* he abandoned the idea—but not completely.

Determined to make movies only with children, Roach conceived *Our Gang,* which was also the title of the first of the famous shorts.

"Sammy" was not only the first member but also worked with all the children during their auditions.

"I'm not saying I had the final word," he says, "but if I thought they didn't have a sense of what we were trying to do they weren't hired."

"Sunshine Sammy" was featured in twenty-eight *Our Gang* comedies, all silents. By the time he left the series after *Cradle Robbers* (1924), the late Allen "Farina" Hoskins was well established as another black "Gang" member. "Farina" was a discovery of "Sunshine's" father, who had him under personal contract and subcontracted his services to Hal Roach.

The senior Morrison and his son then made an extensive personal appearance tour. He was a good draw in vaudeville houses everywhere, but when he played black theaters the Morrisons were able to negotiate a 60 percent share of the gross receipts.

By the age of fifteen he was producing his own act in which he was billed as "Sunshine Sammy, The Sepia Star of Our Gang Comedies."

When he played the Palace Theater in New York "Sammy's" spot on the bill was supposed to be next to closing the first half.

"But it didn't matter what my contract read," explains Morrison today. "I'd often stop the show and the next act would scream 'You're not going to put that nigger in front of me!' So I got moved around a lot."

After a tour of Australia he came back to the U.S. with an eight-piece band called "Sunshine Sammy and His Hollywood Syncopators."

During World War II he replaced one of the Step Brothers who had been drafted and appeared with them in *Shine On, Harvest Moon* (1944) and *Greenwich Village* (1944).

He also played the part of "Scruno," a jive-talking, street-wise member of the *East Side*

Richard Lamparski

"Sunshine Sammy" was the first one on his feet, leading what became a standing ovation for Hal Roach, when he received a special Oscar at the Academy Awards ceremony in 1984.

Kids, a series of low-budget features produced by Sam Katzman.

In the mid-fifties Morrison took a job in the aerospace industry. When he retired, twenty-seven years later, almost none of his co-workers knew of his show business background. Not one member of his lodge, which he had been in for fifteen years, was aware of his career until some caught a glimpse of him at the 1984 Oscar show on TV.

"Sunshine Sammy" is a widower and lives in an apartment near the Los Angeles home of his sister, who worked as "Farina's" double. His daughter is in charge of cultural affairs for the Ivory Coast, where her husband is a government official.

In 1984 "Sammy," as his friends and family call him, told an interviewer: "I was the first black movie personality to be featured in fan magazines and the first black to be a millionaire because of the movies. My family is close and very loving with each other. I have good health and I drive a Continental Mark IV. I fall asleep every night of my life counting my many, many blessings."

Mae Murray was the most popular female star in the world when The Merry Widow *was released in 1925. Her famous bee-stung lips, frizzy blond hair, and butterfly gestures were copied by women everywhere.*

Mae Murray

The superstar of the twenties was born on May 10, 1889, in Portsmouth, Virginia. Her original name was probably Marie Adrienne Koenig. At a very young age she left the home of her grandmother, who raised her, to dance on the stage.

Always vague about her early years, she is thought to have graduated from a Gus Edwards kiddie review to a featured spot in *The Ziegfeld Follies of 1908*. She appeared again in the *Follies of 1909*.

The dance craze that had begun in Europe was sweeping the United States. After spending a short time in Paris Ms. Murray returned to dazzle New York with all the new steps. She went from a nightclub engagement into an Irving Berlin musical in which she took over for the most famous female ballroom dancer in the world, Irene Castle.

When Adolph Zukor saw her in *The Ziegfeld Follies of 1915* he convinced her to come to Hollywood. While Mae did not at first take to the movies or picture making, the camera and the public liked her, especially her dancing. By 1917 her own unit at Universal was producing Mae Murray features. Rudolph Valentino played opposite her in two of them.

Mae Murray seems the quintessential movie star of the silents. Her salary of $7,500 a week was one of the highest in Hollywood in the mid-twenties. She was the first Ziegfeld girl to star in motion pictures and the first dancing star of the screen. She was the first of her contemporaries to marry a socialite, although she soon divorced him so she could marry Robert Z. Leonard, one of Hollywood's most prominent directors. When she married a bogus Russian "prince," one of the "marrying Mdivanis," his best man was Valentino and her maid of honor was Pola Negri. She lived lavishly, made outrageous demands, threw legendary tantrums, and dealt with everyone in the most imperious manner.

When a merger brought about the formation of Metro-Goldwyn-Mayer in 1924 Mae Murray was considered the new company's most valuable asset. After *The Merry Widow* (1925), her first film for the studio, she proved to be their biggest and most expensive problem. Even during the making of that picture she repeatedly clashed with its director, Erich Von Stroheim, until he was taken off the film. Although he was eventually reinstated, the release print of *The Merry Widow* was the one that had been edited to her satisfaction. It was a box-office blockbuster and the zenith of her career, but she made only six more movies. Three were mediocre silents. All of her talkies were disastrous.

M-G-M fired her and Louis B. Mayer black-balled her. David Mdivani had spent or taken all of the millions she had earned before they separated. Her only child was given over to a couple who raised him as their own and whose name he chose to use throughout his life.

Mae was seen during the thirties in a vaude-ville act and heard on radio. In 1941 she briefly headlined the show at New York's Diamond Horseshoe but producer Billy Rose found her impossible and fired her.

Mae Murray once spoke of how as a teen-ager she caught the attention of Florenz Zieg-feld: "I could dance since I could stand on my feet, and when everyone else was doing what they were told to do in a show I would be doing a little bit extra."

To the end of her life she danced and danced beautifully, usually the "Merry Widow Waltz." She stood out in any group, if not always for the most desirable reasons. She usu-ally had far more than "a bit extra" of every-thing. "Too much!" was how most people described her whether she was being recog-nized while shopping at a supermarket or at-tending an opening night.

In 1964 Mae Murray was again on the front pages when she was found wandering the streets of St. Louis, penniless and ill. She had suffered a stroke and for a while didn't even know her name, an ignorance shared by then with most people.

The Motion Picture Relief Fund took care of her basic needs and old friends and fans pro-vided a few extras during the last years of her life. But near-poverty seemingly did not dimin-ish the high esteem in which she held herself. "Haughty" or "condescending" were words

Mae Murray in her later years often said, "You don't have to keep making movies to be a star. Once you're a star, you're always a star!"

frequently used to describe her until the end, which came on March 23, 1965.

Her long-estranged son sent flowers, as did Mary Pickford. Silent stars Ramon Novarro, Claire Windsor, and Vivian Duncan attended her Christian Science funeral service. As her casket was taken for burial in North Holly-wood's Valhalla Memorial Park Cemetery the chapel's organist played the "Merry Widow Waltz."

Lori Nelson in a 1953 publicity still.

Lori Nelson

The movie actress and television star was born Dixie Kay Nelson in Santa Fe, New Mexico. Her birthday is August 15. Lori's parents took her to Hollywood when she was five years old. It was her mother's idea that Lori would eventually go into the movies and she saw to it that her only child was trained in dance and dramatics from the age of two years.

She did a lot of modeling before she was tested for the role of "Cassandra" in *King's Row* and would have played the part had the twelve-year-old not come down with rheumatic fever.

She was in high school when a friend brought her to the attention of an agent who interested an M-G-M executive in auditioning the young blonde. Minutes before they arrived at his office the man was rushed to the hospital with an appendicitis attack. Her agent immediately phoned Rufus LeMaire at Universal Pictures, who made an appointment for Lori to meet with Sophie Rosenstein, the drama coach at that studio. The two took an immediate liking to each other and Lori was used whenever producers or directors wanted to have scripts read aloud by actors. It wasn't long before she was pacted by Universal.

Lori says that she enjoyed being under contract to a major studio and got on well with all of those she worked with, but she never developed a real ambition for her career. She accepted every role she was assigned and wasn't aggressive about getting better or larger roles. Although she appeared in *Walking My Baby Back Home* (1954), Janet Leigh played the part that Lori wanted. She was considered for the title role in *The Story of Esther Costello* that went to Heather Sears.

Ms. Nelson feels she did her best movie work in *All I Desire* (1953) with Barbara Stanwyck and Lyle Bettger (living on Maui, Hawaii). From television she was happiest with the role she had with the late Raymond Massey on a

Climax dramatization entitled *Strange Hostage.*

Some of her other screen appearances were: *Bend in the River* (1952) with James Stewart and Arthur Kennedy; *Francis Goes to West Point* (1952); *Underwater!* (1955) with Jane Russell; *Pardners* (1956) with Dean Martin and Jerry Lewis, and *Untamed Youth* (1957) with Mamie Van Doren (living in Newport Beach, California). She was in two "Ma and Pa Kettle" features and in *I Died a Thousand Times* (1955), a remake of *High Sierra,* she played the part that Joan Leslie had originated. It was her appearance in *Revenge of the Creature* (1955) that has made Lori popular among science-fiction movie buffs. In it she plays an ichthyologist to whom the creature is attracted.

On TV Lori Nelson was "Greta," the breezy manhunter on *How to Marry a Millionaire.* She took the part that Betty Grable had played in the 1953 feature of the same title. Although the series lasted from 1957 to 1959 Lori left after the first season. The publicity at the time had it that she was unhappy with the size of her part. It was about the last the public saw of her until the two plays she did in Los Angeles in 1979 and 1980.

Fanzines of the period often carried photos of Lori out on dates with other contract players, such as Hugh O'Brien, Jack Kelly, and Race Gentry. "But those were all set up by the studio's publicity department," she explains. "The only one I was serious about was Burt Reynolds. We almost got married. A couple of years ago my two daughters and I had lunch with him at the Universal commisary. My kids aren't over it yet."

Tab Hunter was not only a frequent escort but also a close friend, as were Rock Hudson and Debbie Reynolds.

After she married Johnny Mann in 1961 she decided to retire. She says she has not had any film or TV offers since then. Lori and the choral director have been divorced since 1971.

James Cury

Lori Nelson in her home in Northridge, California.

The videotapes she makes of her own movies are about the only connection she has with her former career. Barbara Eden is the only one of the co-stars of her TV show she still hears from. Asked if she completely rules out a comeback, she responded, "It would be almost impossible, because my business is a very personal one. A few days would be the very most I could be away from it." She owns Lori Cosmetics, located near her home in Northridge, California. The firm manufactures semipermanent eyelashes.

In 1983 Lori Nelson married an officer of the Los Angeles Police Department.

Tommy Nolan with Sallie Brophy, his co-star on the TV series Buckskin.

Tommy Nolan

The star of the TV series *Buckskin* was born of French-Canadian parentage in Montreal, Canada, on January 15. His original name was Bernard Girouard.

When he moved with his family to Los Angeles he had already had almost two years of dance classes, having begun at three years of age. His mother took him to agents and casting directors for about a year before he got his first part.

He made his debut with Sarah Churchill in a *Hallmark Hall of Fame* dramatization in which Tommy played the Prince of Wales, son of Henry VIII. After that he was a pathetic refugee on *Lux Video Theater*. Then he guested as a crippled boy who makes friends with "Flicka" on the series of the same name that starred

Johnny Washbrook (married and living in Canoga Park, California). On *Medic* he played a rich asthmatic youngster. By then Tommy Nolan was a familiar face to television viewers and he had a reputation within his profession as an accomplished boy actor who was especially effective in scenes where crying was called for. His dream at that point was to star in his own series.

The only time he recalls being disappointed was when the title role in *Circus Boy,* which he very much wanted to play, went to Mickey Dolenz.

He appeared in the recently restored "lost" footage of *A Star Is Born* (1954) and *The Seven Year Itch* (1955).

Nolan was ten years old when he was chosen to play "Jody McConnell," the central figure on the television program *Buckskin.* The shows were set in the 1880s in the frontier town of Buckskin, Montana, where his widowed mother, played by Sallie Brophy, ran a boardinghouse. Publicized as "a human interest western," the thirty-nine half-hour episodes contained very little violence and provided Tom with opportunities of working with guest stars such as Jane Darwell, Shirley Knight, and Warren Oates. It began on July 3, 1958, as a summer replacement for Tennessee Ernie Ford's show, but drew such good ratings NBC kept it on the network until the end of August 1959. The shows, which were all in black and white, were rerun in the summer of 1965. There were "Buckskin" comic books with Tommy on the cover, fans writing to him from all over the country and stopping him on the street for his autograph. He rode in parades and guest-starred on other TV shows. The experience was all its star had expected it would be. What he had not imagined was what it would be like when it came to an end.

"They teach you to succeed, but you're unprepared for failure," Nolan has remarked.

"You're led to expect fame, but no one tells you about the rejection waiting at the end of the trip. Something fantastic had been given to me, then taken away, leaving a big hollow place at the center of my twelve-year-old life."

He continued acting on such shows as *Lassie, Rawhide,* and *Wagon Train,* but was acutely aware of his change in status. Adults who had formerly made a great fuss over him seemed much less friendly. Some, including the man who had always done his makeup during *Buckskin,* appeared to be embarrassed when they encountered him. "I was yesterday's series," he says. "It was like starting all over again and some part of my heart wasn't in it."

Nolan did continue acting, however, until what he describes as "the routine of interviews and agency politics and daily rejection" made him decide to quit completely. His swan song was in *The Moonshine War* (1970).

Tommy lost touch with Sallie Brophy shortly after their series went off the air. Bobby Diamond,[8] star of *Fury,* and he were friends as kids but have lost touch. Occasionally he sees Johnny Crawford, another friend from the old days.

One of the numerous articles that were done on Tommy Nolan when he had his own series was in *TV Guide.* In it he was quoted as saying that when he grew up he hoped to be a writer. For the last eighteen years he has supported himself with articles for such publications as *New West, Playboy,* the *Los Angeles Times* and the *Village Voice.* He has authored books on Jimmie Hendrix and the Allman Brothers. *Los Angeles* magazine carries his column "On the Town with Mr. L.A." in every issue.

Recently he described his feelings about how his life has evolved: "There were two categories of little boys who acted then—the ones who were just terribly cute and those who could really bring something to a part. I knew

David Strick

Tom Nolan's writings have been published in the Village Voice, TV Guide, *and* Rolling Stone.

that I was as good an actor as the best of my contemporaries, so there was no insecurity there and I took pride in my work. But it seemed very easy to me. I get a sense of accomplishment from writing that acting never provided. Even the attention you get as a writer is, to me, more gratifying."

As to a possible comeback: "A very challenging character part might tempt me. Whether or not I'd take it would depend on what writing assignments I had at the time."

Tom Nolan lives in the San Fernando Valley and is engaged to be married.

In the early fifties Edmond O'Brien was the star of the coast-to-coast radio program, Yours Truly, Johnny Dollar. *The Young Women's League of America had just chosen him as having "more male magnetism than any of the other sixty million American males."*

Edmond O'Brien

The Oscar-winning actor was born in the Bronx on September 10, 1915. He grew up in Harlem, learning magic from Harry Houdini, who was a neighbor. For a brief time as a teenager Edmond had an act, "The Great Neirbo," but completely lost his interest in that particular form of illusion when he saw his first Broadway play. Upon leaving the theater that day he firmly decided to become an actor.

O'Brien got his training at the Neighborhood Playhouse and in summer stock. *Daughters of Atreus* (1936) was the first Broadway play he appeared in. Then he was "Marc Anthony" in the Orson Welles production of *Julius Caesar* (1937) and was with Katherine Cornell in *The Star-Wagon* (1937). He was playing "Prince Hal" to Maurice Evans's "Henry IV" in 1939 when RKO signed him for his first screen role.

Edmond has said that at that point he had no interest in films, so he was surprised at how much he enjoyed making *The Hunchback of Notre Dame* (1939).

After his Hollywood debut he became essentially a motion picture and television actor. He did, however, make a few more Broadway appearances, all of them prestigious. In 1940 he was in *Leave Her to Heaven,* which starred Ruth Chatterton, who had been known in the early thirties as the "First Lady of the Talkies." The same season when Laurence Olivier and Vivien Leigh were teamed in *Romeo and Juliet* O'Brien played "Mercutio." He appeared in New York and on the road in *Winged Victory* during World War II and returned to Broadway in 1952 in *I Got Sixpence.*

Edmond O'Brien's style and abilities lent themselves very well to screen acting and he worked constantly. Sometimes he played the lead, sometimes he took the part of the hero's best friend. As he matured his voice became much deeper and his weight greatly increased, making him very effective as a heavy.

Among his many features are: *The Killers* (1946); *Another Part of the Forest* (1948); *White Heat* (1949); *Julius Caesar* (1953); *Pete Kelly's Blues* (1955); *1984* (1956); *The Girl Can't Help It* (1957); *Up Periscope* (1959); *The Man Who Shot Liberty Valance* (1962); *The Birdman of Alcatraz* (1962); *The Longest Day* (1962), and *Fantastic Voyage* (1966).

At times he acted as producer, as director and, for the film *Man Trap* (1961), he starred, produced, and directed. He was star and director of *The Town That Slept with Its Lights On,* a teleplay written by his brother Liam O'Brien, which was seen in 1958 on the Schlitz Playhouse of Stars.

He had two TV series, *Sam Benedict,* on which he played a colorful trial lawyer during the 1962–63 season, and *The Long Hot Summer,* which ran from September 1965 to July 1966.

Edmond O'Brien won the Academy Award as Best Supporting Actor of 1954 for his performance in *The Barefoot Contessa.* He was nominated in the same category again in 1964 when he played in *Seven Days in May.* He received the Golden Globe award for both pictures.

Nancy Kelly, who co-starred with him in *Parachute Battalion* in 1941, became his wife the same year. They were divorced in 1942. His two daughters and one son are by Olga San Juan, whom he married in 1948.

O'Brien suffered his first heart seizure on location while making *Lawrence of Arabia* and was replaced by Arthur Kennedy. Although his health continued to deteriorate, he acted until the early seventies when it was no longer possible for him to remember lines. In recent years he has been diagnosed as having Alzheimer's disease, which results in premature senility. Since the Motion Picture and Television Hospital does not accept patients with mental disor-

Courtesy Bridgit O'Brien

Although they were divorced in 1976, Edmond O'Brien is visited frequently by Olga San Juan.

ders Edmond lives in a rest home in Santa Monica.

Edmond O'Brien once spoke of the advantages and disadvantages of being a top character actor, as opposed to a star in motion pictures: "Versatility is a dangerous thing. It's very satisfying to portray many types of roles, but often your own identity gets lost. Seldom does a producer say, 'This is an Eddie O'Brien part.' On the other hand, while the rewards might be great in fame and financially for stars, the work becomes monotonous. No actor who plays himself is a happy person."

His awareness varies from day to day, but the letter he received recently from President Ronald Reagan was a great boost to his spirits.

Walter O'Keefe was a humorist, lyricist, raconteur, and author, but he was probably best known as the quizmaster on radio's Double or Nothing.

Walter O'Keefe

The show business jack-of-all-trades was born on August 18, 1900, in Hartford, Connecticut. Part of his early schooling was acquired in England, where he lived with his uncle, a Roman Catholic priest. When Walter returned to the U.S. he entered a seminary, but soon decided he did not have the vocation. He enlisted in the Marine Corps in World War I, but was discharged because of poor health.

During his freshman year at Notre Dame he rented a room in the home of the legendary football coach Knute Rockne. One of his classmates was George "The Gipper" Gipp. "I never dreamed he was helping write the script for the life story of the future President of the United States," he once quipped.

O'Keefe knew from an early age that he wanted to be an entertainer. As a little boy he had witnessed his father telling stories and jokes and vowed to be like him. Walter worked his way through Notre Dame as a toastmaster and emcee, graduating cum laude in 1921. After Rockne became nationally known O'Keefe often accompanied him at speaking engagements where he would introduce the sports hero.

He spent a year in vaudeville as a monologist before going to New York, where he was an immediate hit at Texas Guinan's El Fey Club. When he attempted to accept an offer from a rival nitery the hoodlum backers of the El Fey had him severely beaten.

In 1931 he was featured along with Bea Lillie in *The Third Little Show.* He wrote the lyrics of the song "When Yuba Plays the Rhumba on the Tuba," which he performed in the revue. It was a hit, as was his other song, "Henry's Made a Lady out of Lizzie." He had his biggest success, however, with a song that was written in 1868. Walter changed the tempo and a few of the lyrics and reintroduced America to "The Man on the Flying Trapeze."

Walter O'Keefe's delivery and timing were

perfect for radio. As early as 1932 he hosted the network show *Lucky Strike Magic Carpet.* He starred on the *Camel Caravan* from 1934 to 1936 and later emceed *The Packard Hour.* When Fred Allen and Don McNeill went on vacation from their shows Walter took over for them. The program that he made very much his own was *Double or Nothing.* He was its quick-witted quizmaster for seven seasons.

Walter appeared in only a few films, but wrote lyrics for many songs that were performed in movies. Broadway audiences saw him in *Casino Varieties* (1934), *Spring Tonic* (1936), and *Top-Notchers* (1942).

His Irish Catholic background was very evident in his humor, whether he was headlining in a nightclub, which he did frequently, or writing in the nationally syndicated column he did for United Features.

Walter was the lyricist for the musical *Just a Minute* (1928), which ran on Broadway for six months. He wrote special material for Ina Claire (widowed and living in San Francisco) and Eddie Cantor. Oscar Hammerstein II and he spent ten days attempting to work together, but were unsuccessful. "It was a terrible disappointment at the time," he said many years later. "But now I only feel honored that he even considered me."

When Sylvester "Pat" Weaver attempted to bring pay television to the state of California in the sixties he hired O'Keefe, who videotaped ten programs before voters rejected the proposal.

A series of heart attacks greatly curtailed his activities, if not his wit, in later years. His last radio appearances were for *Monitor* in the late fifties. The PBS special of Walter doing his songs and patter for a live audience of senior citizens was telecast shortly after he died in the summer of 1983.

Richard Lamparski

Walter O'Keefe in his Palos Verdes, California, home not long before he died in June 1983.

He used to say that his coat of arms was "broken bottles over dropped options." It was a line that went over especially well at the meetings of Alcoholics Anonymous, where he spoke frequently and with much success.

In an interview he explained why the public had in recent years heard so little of and from Walter O'Keefe: "I reached the point where I was doing things that weren't especially fun only for the money—which I knew damn well I didn't need anymore. And, let's be frank, I was a drunk and had been one for a long time."

"Thy Will Be Done," his last composition, was sung at his funeral mass.

Luana Patten made films for Walt Disney as a little girl and as an adult.

Luana Patten

The Disney heroine was born in Long Beach, California, on July 6, 1938. Her first name, which is Hawaiian, was originally spelled Lu Ana. Her father was a career naval officer. She was an only child until she was fifteen.

When she was not quite three years old her mother was stopped one day on the street by a photographer who wanted Luana to pose for him. She caught on immediately as a commercial model.

In 1945 Walt Disney was conducting a well-publicized search for a little girl to play opposite Bobby Driscoll in *Song of the South* (1946). Shortly after he saw Luana on the cover of the magazine *Woman's Home Companion* she was signed for a prominent part in the picture, which was the Disney studio's first cartoon and live-action feature.

Luana was pretty, dimpled, and appeared quite natural in all of her screen roles. She was especially cute in scenes with "Charlie McCarthy" and "Mortimer Snerd" in *Fun and Fancy Free* (1947).

She enjoyed the six years she spent under contract to Walt Disney and particularly liked Bobby Driscoll. Their studio paired them again in *So Dear to My Heart* (1948) which is one of her favorite pictures. "He was like a brother to me," she said recently. Commenting on the serious drug problems he had later in life she said, "Bobby was always looking for someone to show him the way. He was a follower, not a leader."

In one of her first pictures, *Little Mr. Jim* (1946), she was teamed with Jackie "Butch" Jenkins (heads a large real estate firm in Fairview, North Carolina), a child actor she remembers as "a really awful little boy."

Luana was off the screen for a few years during adolescence. While in high school she was married but soon got a divorce.

In 1956 she made *Rock, Pretty Baby* with the late Sal Mineo and Fay Wray (married to a physician and living in Century City). Then she returned to Disney for *Johnny Tremain* (1957) with Hal Stalmaster (a prominent Hollywood casting director) and Richard Beymer. Next she made *Joe Dakota* (1957) with Jock Mahoney (married to the mother of Sally Field and living in Sherman Oaks, California).

Among her other movies are: *The Restless Years* (1958) with the late Margaret Lindsay; the underrated western *A Thunder of Drums* (1961), and *Little Shepherd of Kingdom Come* (1961) with the late Neil Hamilton. Luana agrees with fans who think the love scene she did with George Hamilton in *Home from the Hill* (1960) is the best work she did as an adult. Her last, again for Disney, was *Follow Me, Boys* (1966).

Luana Patten and John Smith met when she guested on his TV series *Cimarron City*. They were married in 1960 but divorced four years later. They have, however, remained friends.

Recently the former actress explained why she walked away from her career at such a young age: "I think I started too young and it came too easily. I'd been in front of a camera ever since I could remember. What I really wanted was to be a wife and mother."

She has never attempted a comeback because "it's such a different business today. I know I could never cope with what goes into starting over again and, frankly, I've never missed any of it."

The only aspect of picture making she didn't like was going out on dates which had been set up by the studio with boys she didn't know. The one role she wanted and didn't get was in *Sweet Smell of Success,* playing Burt Lancaster's sister.

That disappointment, however, she considers quite minor. Her real regret in life is not having had any children.

Richard Lamparski

Luana Patten recently in her Arleta, California, home with "Fuzzy," one of her companions.

She remained friendly with Peggy Ann Garner until Peggy's death in October 1984. Her ex-husband is now her only link with the past. She hears from fans occasionally and is very appreciative of their continued interest.

In February 1984 as she was recuperating from her third major operation, she said to one loyal admirer: "Please say a prayer that I'll soon regain my health. I've been ill for such a very long time."

Jean Peters played Anne Baxter's sister in **The Last Leaf** *segment of* O'Henry's Full House *(1952).*

Jean Peters

The movie star of the late forties and fifties was born on October 15, 1926, in Canton, Ohio.

Jean was still quite young when her father died after a long illness. Her mother brought up her two daughters on a small chicken farm.

She was in college when she was voted Miss Ohio State. Along with the title Jean won a screen test at Twentieth Century-Fox. The studio executives, however, were unimpressed with her footage and she boarded a train back to Ohio. But at one of the stops along the way she received a wire offering a contract. There had been some second thoughts after her test was shown to one of Fox's major stockholders, Howard Hughes.

The public first saw her playing opposite Tyrone Power in *Captain from Castile* (1947). Such an auspicious debut with her studio's most important male star immediately established the twenty-one-year-old as one of the screen's most promising young actresses.

She never played anything less than a leading role in films and was cast opposite such stars as Paul Douglas in *Love That Brute* (1950), Marlon Brando in *Viva Zapata!* (1952), Joseph Cotten in *Niagara* (1953), Robert Wagner in *Broken Lance* (1954), and Burt Lancaster in *Apache* (1954). Her best performance was in *Pickup on South Street* (1953). Her best picture was her last, *A Man Called Peter* (1955).

The one time in which Jean was truly "the star" in a picture was *Anne of the Indies* (1951) in which she was quite fetching as a pirate. The picture has achieved a minor cult status.

Her other credits include *Deep Waters* (1948) with Anne Revere (living in Locust Valley, New York), *Take Care of My Little Girl* (1951), and *Three Coins in the Fountain* (1954).

Jean Peters achieved stardom without plan or preparation and then proceeded to behave quite contrary to the usual ways of Hollywood in those days. She very seldom gave interviews even to promote the big-budget films in which she often appeared. When she did talk with the press it was usually to extol the values she was brought up with and give more details on the rural, impoverished life she lived as a child. She had a long, unpublicized romance with Howard Hughes, but then in 1945, suddenly married a wealthy businessman, Stuart Cramer III.* When they were divorced after two years she became the wife of the reclusive billionaire Howard Hughes.

During the years they were husband and wife Jean almost completely disappeared from social and professional life in the film colony, although she continued to live there. She shopped and even attended classes at UCLA incognito and always under guard.

Under the terms of their 1971 divorce Jean would receive $70,000 annually for twenty years. This amount could double, depending on the consumer price index. Although the agreement mentioned nothing about her talking or writing about the mysterious Hughes, Jean has said nothing beyond the statement that she would never discuss him. Publishers offering huge advances for her biography are turned away politely, but very firmly.

A few months after divorcing Hughes she married the widower producer Stanley Hough, whom she had met when he worked as assistant director on her first picture. Childless herself, she helped raise his three children. The Houghs live in Beverly Hills.

Ms. Peters is only slightly more public now than she was as Mrs. Howard Hughes. She devotes some spare time to working at the Screen Smart Shop, which sells used articles for the

Allan J. Studley

Jean Peters modeling at a recent charity luncheon to benefit the Motion Picture and Television Country House and Hospital.

benefit of the Motion Picture and Television Country House and Hospital.

She has acted only twice since 1955. She received good notices for her portrayal as a neurotic, middle-aged woman in the PBS production of *Winesburg, Ohio,* in 1973. Three years later she had a small role in the four-part TV special *The Moneychangers.*

In spite of the wealth of her husbands and her own personal fortune Jean Peters always made many of her own clothes and still does.

Someone who has known her since she was working her way through college said of her recently, "Jean's values haven't changed in the slightest. She always knew who she was so fame had no effect on her personality. Nor has money. She was never owned by her possessions. If Jean were broke she'd still be rich."

*Jean's first husband was later married to and divorced from Terry Moore who, after Hughes's death, claimed that she, too, had been his wife. She has received an out-of-court settlement of eight figures.

Poncie Ponce as "Kazuo Kim" on **Hawaiian Eye.**

Poncie Ponce

The actor who became famous as "Kazuo Kim" on the TV series *Hawaiian Eye* was born on Maui, Hawaii, on April 10, 1933. His original name was Ponciano Ponce.

Poncie was working at Ben Blue's in the late fifties when he was "discovered." He was a bus boy–entertainer at the Santa Monica nitery when a producer at Warner Brothers took note of him. Bill Orr, the son-in-law of Jack Warner and executive in charge of production, then caught Poncie's act in which he did impressions of Louis Armstrong, Johnny Ray, and Elvis Presley.

Ponce had always liked to entertain and amuse people but he had never considered an acting career. The day after Orr saw him Poncie got a call to come to Warner Brothers studio for an interview. Thinking someone was playing a joke on him, he failed to respond. The following day he was made to understand that there was serious interest in him. Within a week he was signed to a contract and remained on the lot for five years.

He was cast as "Kazuo Kim," the operator of a one-man taxi service, on *Hawaiian Eye*. The half-hour series was very popular, especially among teenage girls, from its debut in October 1959. For years after it went off the ABC network in late 1963 it was seen in syndication.

The plots of the shows revolved around the adventures of the four young "swinging" bachelors. Robert Conrad, Anthony Eisley, and Guy Williams played private detectives operating out of a poolside office at the Hawaiian Village Hotel. Troy Donahue joined the show later in its run as the hotel's social director. Connie Stevens rose to national fame as "Cricket," the somewhat dizzy photographer who from time to time sang on the program.

Poncie's character was an integral part of most of the plots, providing transportation in his cab and invaluable informational services through his many relatives spread among the islands. His corny jokes were the comic relief on a show that concentrated on crime and pretty young women, more often than not in bathing suits.

Even while *Hawaiian Eye* was a hit network show Ponce found time to make personal appearances. His exchanges with those live audiences and on talk shows proved an excellent experience for him when he toured the U.S. and the Orient in nightclubs after the series was canceled.

Poncie enjoyed making *Hawaiian Eye* and still feels close to the other members of the cast. He sees all of them at least once a year because they all attend Robert Conrad's New Year's Eve party. "We were family," he says. "When we see each other it's like no time has passed."

He considers himself a "bit actor," usually playing gardeners and porters. He has been seen on U.S. television commercials for Oldsmobile and United Airlines. On Mexican TV he was a spokesman for Bacardi Rum. Satori hired him to pitch their whiskey to the Japanese.

His three daughters dance the hula in his nightclub act, which he takes to Japan every year. He also works on many cruise ships and is especially popular on the "condo circuit," a tour of senior citizen housing projects in Florida.

Not long ago Poncie had an engagement in El Salvador where *Hawaiian Eye* at the time was one of that nation's most popular shows. "It was like old times," said Ponce. "Everybody recognized me. But now I don't need to work so hard which is even better than everyone knowing who you are. A series means long hours and lots of travel. I'm a family man. Now are the years when I can really have fun with my kids."

Richard Schaeffer

Poncie Ponce today in his San Fernando Valley home with the hat that became his trademark.

Poncie and one of his daughters run Poncie's Place, a fast-food restaurant two blocks from his home.

"We open late and close early," says Ponce. "And never on weekends. That's when I go fishing or to the racetrack. We have a saying where I come from—'Life is meant to be enjoyed.' That's my motto!"

Ponce and his Chinese wife live with their daughters in a home in Van Nuys, which is decorated inside and out with a Hawaiian theme.

Cool, sleek, and gorgeous Ella Raines was the personification of the Hollywood movie star of the forties.

Ella Raines

The emerald-eyed screen siren was born in Snoqualmie Falls, Washington, on August 6, 1921.

Her father, an engineer, taught his only child archery, swimming, skiing, and horseback riding. She excelled at all of them, earned good marks at school, and was considered one of the most popular co-eds at the University of Washington.

She had been in plays in college and almost immediately got a part in *Away We Go*. By the time it opened under the title *Oklahoma*, Ella, who had been "discovered" for the movies, had left the cast.

David O. Selznick gave her a screen test. When it was shown, agent Charles Feldman, who was in the projection room, went immediately to her hotel and signed Ella for representation. Subsequently, Selznick was outbid for her services by Charles Boyer and Howard Hawks, who formed a corporation with her as the sole asset.

She made her screen debut as Randolph Scott's leading lady in *Corvette K-225* (1943), which Hawks produced. Then he and Boyer loaned her to M-G-M for *Cry Havoc* (1943).

Phantom Lady (1944), her own favorite, was one of the few times she was used to advantage. Although not a big-budget picture, it was *her* picture and the star quality was very much in evidence. To most of her large cult following it is the definitive Ella Raines movie.

Her contract was then sold to Universal. The studio was aware of her talent and special appeal but she was much too classy and sophisticated for the films Universal was then producing. The best thing they did was to have Travis Banton design her clothes.

Ella Raines was never considered a major star, made no really important films, and was not a great actress. What she had was a throaty voice, a flair for wearing the fashions of the day, and exceptional beauty. Her green eyes seemed to suggest an intelligence as well as a sense of humor.

Among her motion pictures are: Preston Sturges's *Hail the Conquering Hero* (1944); *Tall in the Saddle* (1944) with John Wayne; *The Strange Affair of Uncle Harry* (1945); *The Web* (1947); *Brute Force* (1947); *The Senator Was Indiscreet* (1947); *Time Out of Mind* (1947) with Phyllis Calvert; *The Second Face* (1950), and *The Man in the Road* (1957).

She starred on TV in the title role of *Janet Dean, Registered Nurse,* a series that dealt rather intelligently with themes that were considered quite mature in the mid-fifties.

In 1955 she played in *The Wisteria Trees* on Broadway with Helen Hayes.

If Ella Raines's career never really took off as most thought it should have, all the other aspects of her life in Hollywood appeared extremely glamorous. Both Louella O. Parsons and Hedda Hopper had only good things to say about her. She made the cover of *Life* magazine's issue of February 28, 1944, and again on August 11, 1947. After meeting Henry Ford II over lunch he allowed her, for a token gratuity, to buy his own custom-made paneled convertible, the prototype for the Ford Sportsman. She had dates with Clark Gable.

The three features she made for Republic Pictures were all poor quality, but she enjoyed making them. It took Ella and the late Rod Cameron an entire afternoon to shoot one scene of her last film for that studio, *Ride the Man Down* (1952). Both cast and crew broke up every time Cameron spoke his line to Ella, "As soon as you left town my business fell off." They were having a romance at the time.

When she became the wife of Major Robin Olds in 1947 the couple seemed, even to other movie stars, like a pair out of a fairy tale. As Audrey Totter said recently, "This town is full of men who *look* the handsome hero type, but they're only actors. This guy that Ella landed was the real thing. Talk about good-looking and dashing!"

Olds, who had shot down twenty-four German planes in World War II, went on to be a much-decorated air ace of the Korean and Vietnam wars. He eventually rose to the rank of brigadier general and ended his colorful career as the head of the Air Force Academy.

Gary Daum

Ella Raines shares a laugh with the audience during her personal appearance at the Vagabond Theater in March 1984.

In 1984 Ms. Raines spoke of the marriage that had looked ideal to so many: "The travel was wonderful. I got to see the Orient and live in places like England and Tripoli. But the man had no heart. I think they program hearts out of them at West Point. So macho all the time, but when he testified at our divorce he had to admit that he'd had a free ride financially on me all the years we were together."

She does not rule out acting again, but is presently concentrating on writing her autobiography, which she insists is not a sad story. "I spent over thirty years of my life with a man whom I must admit I dislike. But my two daughters and my granddaughter more than compensate for him."

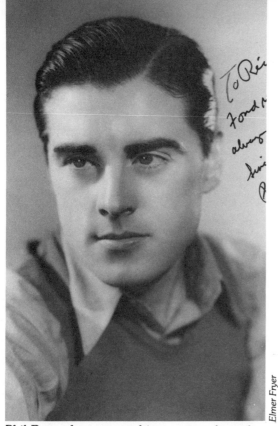

Elmer Fryer

Phil Regan has appeared in over two dozen features, including Manhattan Merry-Go-Round (1937), Sweet Rosie O'Grady (1943), and Three Little Words (1950).

Phil Regan

"The Singing Cop" of movies and nightclubs was born in Brooklyn, New York, on May 28.

In pre-World War I America boy sopranos were the rage. Phil was a soloist with Father Finn's Choir, a well-known group of the day, and often sang between prizefights in and around New York City. He was thirteen when he went on a year's tour in vaudeville as part of a Gus Edwards kiddie review.

Orphaned at age fifteen, Regan left school and went to work as an office boy for an oil company. When a soft-drink bottle broke in his hand he was so badly cut that the bottler settled his claim for $10,000. Seventeen-year-old Phil and his sixteen-year-old girl friend used the money to get married and set up house-keeping.

Regan was an officer with the New York City police force when he attended a large theatrical party in plain clothes. He was there to arrest one of the expected guests. While waiting for the suspect to arrive Phil sang a few songs. Afterward the president of CBS radio gave him his card and told him to contact him.

He dropped by CBS while Guy Lombardo was auditioning vocalists for the network show he was doing with George Burns and Gracie Allen. Phil was hired on the spot at $125 a week and a short time later got a three-times-a-week show of his own as well.

At Christmastime 1933, he left for Hollywood, where he planned to spend a maximum of one month trying to get into pictures. The first night there he attended Lombardo's opening at the Coconut Grove. Before the evening was over the director Clarence Brown had asked him to test for the lead in a Joan Crawford film, a top agent had offered to represent him, and he had met Charlie Chaplin.

The test he made didn't get him the part but it was shown to Warner Brothers and Regan was placed under contract.

One of his first pictures was *Student Tour* (1934) with Betty Grable. *Dames* (1934), *Sweet Adeline* (1935), *Laughing Irish Eyes* (1936), and *Las Vegas Night* (1941) followed.

When he wasn't making movies Regan sang in niteries, presentation houses, and gambling clubs. He began then to build a large and loyal following among the most wealthy and powerful men in the nation.

"I always played to the men in any audience," he once said. "The ladies might bring the guys in to see you the first time around, but if men don't like you they won't be back. I was always careful about remembering names and letting them know I knew they were in my audience."

He might have gone a bit further than he did if he had not been forced to leave the cast of *DuBarry Was a Lady* before it got to New York. His number stopped the show, which made the remainder of the scene awkward for its star, Ethel Merman. Buddy DeSylva deeply resented having to buy out Phil's contract and told him so. Regan believes it was DeSylva who later kept him off the screen when he headed Paramount Pictures. He would neither use him in a movie nor release him from his contract.

Not since 1948 has he needed to work at anything. On Easter Sunday that year an oil field in which he was partnered with Bob Hope and Bing Crosby brought in its first of many gushers. It is still producing.

Within a short time Regan's personal fortune, important contacts, and considerable charm made him one of the country's most influential political catalysts. Harry Truman, who once seriously considered appointing his friend ambassador to Ireland, was Phil's houseguest at his three-acre Palm Springs estate. Newark's mayor publicly credited him for settling a potentially bloody dock strike. There were whispers that it was Phil Regan who brought the support of big labor behind John F. Kennedy early in his Presidential campaign.

To many he was "Mr. Democrat," so when he endorsed Ronald Reagan when he first ran for the governorship of California it was quite a surprise. Old friends like Chicago's Mayor Daly refused to speak to him after he became a Republican.

An even bigger shock was his conviction in

When it was pointed out to Phil Regan that many of the signed photos on the wall of his den were crooked he replied, "Of course, they're all politicians."

1973 of the attempted bribery of a public official. Although the amount was a relatively small one he was sent to prison.

The Regans live part of the time in their luxury duplex in Pasadena. They moved there many years ago so their four children would not absorb what they considered to be the false values of the movie colony. Their other home is a suite at the Santa Barbara Biltmore Hotel.

Phil, a Roman Catholic, is a daily communicant. He has twenty grandchildren and twenty-two great-grandchildren.

Gene Reynolds's soulful quality was especially effective as one of Father Flanagan's charges in Boys Town *(1938). His other movies with Spencer Tracy were* Captains Courageous *(1937) and* Edison the Man *(1940).*

Gene Reynolds

The child actor was born in Cleveland, Ohio, on April 4. His original name was Eugene Reynolds Blumenthal.

Gene's career was his mother's doing. Mr. Blumenthal was less enthusiastic about his only child becoming an actor but he had been all but wiped out by the Depression and did not object.

The Blumenthals lived in Detroit, where Gene began doing commercial modeling when he was two years old and appeared on stage for the first time when he was six. He gained valuable experience acting in industrial films and on some of the many radio dramas that emanated from that city.

Encouraged by some of the professionals who worked with their boy, his parents took him to Hollywood when he was ten years old.

By the late thirties Gene had become one of the most active child character actors in Hollywood and an exceptionally gifted one. He had a poignant quality and was pretty without seeming delicate.

He was perfectly cast as the young Tyrone Power in *In Old Chicago* (1938) and very moving in *Of Human Hearts* (1938), playing James Stewart as a boy. He supported Shirley Temple in two of her pictures and Mickey Rooney in a couple of his "Andy Hardy" series. Gene and the late Virginia Weidler were co-starred in *Bad Little Angel* (1939) with Cora Sue Collins (married with residences in Beverly Hills and Phoenix). His performance added much to *The Mortal Storm* (1940)

His most prominent part was in *They Shall Have Music* (1939) which introduced the violinist Jascha Heifetz to the moviegoing public.

Reynolds appeared with Frances Farmer in *Too Many Parents* (1936) and Gladys George in *Madame X* (1937). Both have since become cult figures. He also supported Errol Flynn and Ronald Reagan in *Santa Fe Trail* (1940).

He was under contract to M-G-M from 1938

until he went into the Navy in World War II. Ensign Reynolds served on the minesweeper that inspired his shipmate Herman Wouk to write *The Caine Mutiny.*

He acted in many early TV dramas and appeared in the features *The Big Cat* (1949) with Lon McCallister (single and living in Little River, California), *The Bridges at Toko-Ri* (1954), and *Diane* (1956). But by then he had begun to write and direct, work much more to his liking.

Reynolds became casting director for TV's *Matinee Theater* and then on the *Peter Gunn* series.

When Jackie Cooper sold *Hennesey* to CBS he hired Reynolds as the show's director. The last time Gene acted was on that series. He and Cooper had been friends since making *Gallant Sons* (1940).

Next Gene directed and produced the pilot for *The Ghost and Mrs. Muir.* That led to *Room 222* and then to *M.A.S.H.* After directing and producing both of those hit series he brought *Lou Grant* to the air, while remaining a creative consultant on *M.A.S.H.* during its last seasons on the air.

Recently Reynolds directed two episodes of the *Duck Factory* and produced and directed the TV movie *In Defense of Kids.* He is currently developing several projects for M.T.M. Productions where he is under contract.

His first marriage was to the novelist Bonnie Reynolds and lasted nine years. In 1979, three years after they were divorced, he married the actress Ann Sweeny. He beams at any reference to their son Andrew, his only child. The Reynoldses have their home in The Outpost, a quiet, exclusive area of Hollywood.

Sybil Jason,[8] who has known him since they made *The Blue Bird* in 1940, said of Gene Reynolds in 1984, "Gene is even more of a success than he appears to people who don't know him personally, because he's become a

Gene Reynolds beside dummy copies of the newspaper that Ed Asner edited on **Lou Grant.** *Gene produced and directed the series on the lot that was once Republic Pictures.*

top producer-director without losing any of the sensitivity to others that he always had as a boy. He is such a rarity in his profession!"

Reynolds says the sole motivation throughout his acting career was "a sense of obligation to please my mother. It was very important to her that I be successful, yet I never felt like a success. I felt pressure and anxiety."

Recently the man who has won four Emmys and been nominated for nineteen others was asked if he now felt successful and responded, "I guess so. Sometimes, anyway."

Erik Rhodes played in pictures during the thirties, often using a foreign accent.

Erik Rhodes

The suave comedian–character actor of movies and stage was born in El Reno, Oklahoma, on February 10, 1906.

He studied law at the University of Oklahoma but by the time he graduated Phi Beta Kappa he had decided to be an entertainer.

He debuted on the old Chautauqua circuit as a lecturer on Prohibition. Then his singing won the musical scholarship established by the late Marion Talley and he went to New York City to study.

He was first seen as a Spanish playboy in *A Most Immoral Lady* (1928) in support of Alice Brady. *The Little Show* (1929) with Clifton Webb and Libby Holman followed.

He then went through a period when, in order to support himself, he played in small-time vaudeville and sang off-color songs in Greenwich Village clubs and speakeasies. Recently he recalled the lyrics of one of his numbers after almost fifty years: "Perversion, I love you. Just a twist of the wrist and I become a masochist."

Being cast as the gigolo in *The Gay Divorcee* (1932) changed his luck and started a friendship with the show's composer, Cole Porter, that lasted Porter's lifetime. The musical was a huge hit and he played "Tonetti" in it both on Broadway and in the West End of London. He repeated his role in the screen version, which was called *The Gay Divorce* (1934) and starred Fred Astaire and Ginger Rogers.

After playing a similar role, "Alberto Benddini" the dress designer, in *Top Hat* (1935), again with Rogers and Astaire, Erik began to find it a real struggle to be cast as anything other than a flamboyant European with an arched eyebrow.

"At first it seemed easy," recalls Rhodes. "I speak five languages and it was no trouble to give them what they wanted, but I soon realized what harm it would do to my career if I continued. Even when I was offered the part of a heavy they'd insist I do it with a thick accent."

He says he felt "artistically strangled" and missed the cultural life and conversation he had known among theater people in New York. He made a dozen pictures before joining Army Intelligence at the outbreak of World War II. He returned only once when he acted in an episode of *Perry Mason.*

Among his screen credits are: *Give Her a Ring* (1935); *Chatterbox* (1936) with Anne Shirley; *Woman Chases Man* (1937); *Meet the Girls* (1938) with June Lang (sharing her North Hollywood home with her daughter); *Mysterious Mr. Moto* (1938); *Say It in French* (1938) with Olympe Bradna (married and living in Carmel, California); *Dramatic School* (1938) with Luise Rainer (married and living in Switzerland), and *On Your Toes* (1939).

Rhodes was seen on Broadway in *The Great Campaign* (1947), *Dance Me a Song* (1950), and *Collector's Item* (1952) before his second Cole Porter musical, *Can-Can* (1953). When it was revived in 1959 he repeated his performance and has since then done it in summer theater several times.

Right You Are (1957), *Shinbone Alley* (1957), *Jamaica* (1957), *My Fair Lady* (1968), *The Madwoman of Chaillot* (1970), and *Colette* (1970) are among his other New York stage credits. He had the lead in the *Song of Norway* production at Jones Beach in the summer of 1958. His favorite part (and the one for which he got his best notices) was the title role of the King of Siam in *The King and I.*

When the late Greta Keller was unable to appear for her engagement at the Waldorf-Astoria in 1962 Erik filled in for his friend with an act in which he was billed as "The Sophisticate of Song."

In her autobiography, *Swanson on Swanson,* the late star wrote of her association with him: "We worked like a charm together." He co-hosted her early TV show and worked

Howard W. Hays

Erik Rhodes and his wife share a luxury apartment on the East Side of Manhattan furnished in fine antiques and mementos from their extensive travels.

closely with her in preparing the programs.

Mrs. Rhodes, a widow of a socialite-sportsman, was a close friend of Edna St. Vincent Millay.

Although he acts occasionally in TV commercials, he considers himself retired. He reads a great deal, sees a lot of theater, and sings and plays at the baby grand piano in his living room.

It is for his movies, especially the Rogers-Astaire musicals, that he is recognized.

"When I was making movies I tried to do a good job," he mused recently. "But I didn't really take pictures seriously. Now they serve as my family album. It's an awfully good feeling to know that what you did so many years ago is still entertaining people."

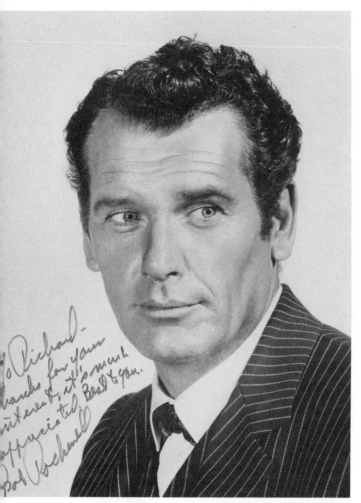

Robert Rockwell played "Mr. Boynton" on the Our Miss Brooks *radio series, all 127 of the television shows, and the feature film made in 1956.*

Robert Rockwell

The actor who played "Mr. Boynton" on *Our Miss Brooks* was born on October 5. He grew up in a small Illinois town forty miles north of Chicago, the city where he was born. His mother, who was widowed when he was four years old, was the principal of the local grade school.

Rockwell enrolled at the University of Illinois but after three years as a business major came to realize that his real interest was in acting and had been since he played the hero in a fourth grade skit. He spent the next three and a half years studying at the Pasadena Playhouse.

His first break came in the José Ferrer Broadway production of *Cyrano de Bergerac* (1947). Robert then moved to Hollywood, where he made *You Gotta Stay Happy* (1948) with James Stewart. He was put under contract to Republic Pictures where he turned out such B features as *Alias the Champ* (1949) with the late "Gorgeous George," *Belle of Old Mexico* (1949) with the late Estrellita, and *Federal Agent at Large* (1950) with Kent Taylor.

Our Miss Brooks originated as a weekly radio show in 1948. It was simulcast for two seasons after the TV version premiered on October 3, 1952. The character of "Philip Boynton" was originated on radio by Jeff Chandler. Rockwell took over the part of the impossibly shy biology teacher on both the radio and television shows when the latter began, and played it through the last segment which aired September 21, 1956. Although the program's format had been changed during the last season, the relationship between the bachelor and "Miss Brooks," who was always played by Eve Arden, remained the same. When Warner Brothers made the feature *Our Miss Brooks* (1956), he was again cast as "Philip Boynton."

When complimented on the convincing performance he gave in the role Rockwell responds, "I must have made people believe me in the part because it was over a year before I could get another job. As far as this town was concerned I *was* 'Mr. Boynton.'"

After playing the husband of Loretta Young on a few of her TV shows Robert asked her why she didn't let him try another role. "Nope," was the star's answer. "I can find hundreds of actors to be romantic, but I can find very few who are believable as my husband." He was cast many more times after that—always as her husband.

From October 1959 to September 1960, Rockwell starred on his own series, *The Man from Blackhawk,* playing the title role. His character, "Sam Logan," was an insurance investigator who traveled about the Western states in the latter part of the nineteenth century.

While working on *Our Miss Brooks* Rockwell built a home in Pacific Palisades, where he lives with his wife. They are the parents of three sons and two daughters. Their four grandchildren are all girls. For a time Robert was the honorary mayor of his community. Among his neighbors are Walter Matthau, Mel Blanc, Ed "Captain Midnight" Prentiss,[8] and Bert Convy.

Robert Rockwell and Eve Arden still see each other frequently. He says of her, "She is a pleasure to work with and I'm proud to say we've remained good friends over the years."

To trivia fans Robert is remembered not as "Mr. Boynton," but as "Jor-El," father of "Superman" on the first episode of *The Adventures of Superman,* the television series that starred George Reeves.

Rockwell has been seen in commercials for margarine, detergent, several banks, and insur-

Donna Schaeffer

For a while Robert Rockwell was the honorary mayor of Pacific Palisades, where he and his wife have lived since 1956.

ance companies. In the late seventies he had a running part on the daytime soap opera *Search for Tomorrow.* He has appeared on stage with Ginger Rogers and in Ireland as the lead in *I Do, I Do.* Some of his recent parts on TV have been in *Dallas, Dynasty,* and *Private Benjamin.* He is recognized often and, as he admitted recently, always by someone who remembers him as "Mr. Boynton."

In 1946 when Andy Russell began the first of two seasons as the featured male vocalist on **Your Hit Parade** *he had three hundred fan clubs throughout the United States calling themselves the "Russell Sprouts."*

Andy Russell

The popular singer of the forties and fifties was born Andres Rabago on September 16 in East Los Angeles. One of his earliest memories is of hiding behind the family radio and pretending to be his favorite singer, Dick Powell.

He began singing professionally for Don Ramon. Andy mastered the drums and stayed with the group until the summer prior to his senior year in high school when he got a job drumming and singing with Gus Arnheim's orchestra. It was Arnheim who started Russell singing part of each song in Spanish. The bilingual rendition became Andy Russell's trademark.

In 1943 he recorded "Besame Mucho." Latin America was having a strong influence on tastes in fashion and music at the time in the U.S. The style was thought different and romantic. Andy's record sold more than one million copies and skyrocketed him to national prominence. His recordings of "I Dream of You," "The Anniversary Waltz," and "I Can't Begin to Tell You," which followed, all made *Billboard*'s Top Ten list.

Russell was vocalist on Joan Davis's radio series and, for a while, had his own network program.

When Frank Sinatra left radio's *Your Hit Parade* he was replaced by Metropolitan star Lawrence Tibbett. When Andy Russell took over from the baritone in 1946 two of his singles, "They Say That Falling in Love Is Wonderful" and "I'm laughing on the Outside and Crying on the Inside," were among the hottest records in the nation. He was heard on the Saturday evening broadcasts for two seasons.

In his opinion he was "terrible" in all three of his screen appearances. He accuses Betty Hutton of seeing to it that he came off poorly in *The Stork Club* (1945) because she was envious of him. He did not make a strong impression in *Breakfast in Hollywood* (1946) either. He played what could be described as a "Dennis Day part'' with the Marx Brothers in *Copacabana* (1947).

While it lasted, the marriage of Andy and Della Russell was as much publicized as their act. Fanzines carried pictures of the two nuzzling and they were always mentioned on any list of ''Hollywood's Happiest Couples.'' On the *Andy and Della Russell Show,* which was on ABC-TV in 1951–52, they sang together—often cheek to cheek.

When their separation was announced in the mid-fifties both began to receive hate mail from disappointed fans. Andy heard directly from Roman Catholic clergy reminding him that, as a well-known member of the church, his divorce was a mortal sin and would cause public scandal. He was accused of ''setting a bad example.''

Partially to avoid such pressure he went to Mexico. His early hit ''Amor'' was still a favorite throughout the Spanish-speaking countries and he was welcomed as ''one of our own.'' For nine years he hosted the very popular *El Show De Andy Russell* which emanated from Argentina. He starred in movies made in Mexico and on Spanish television specials. The recordings he made received little exposure in the U.S. but were hits all over Latin America and in Spain. One brought him the ''Disco de Oro,'' Spain's equivalent to a gold record.

But the gimmick that brought him fame in his native country was unwanted south of the U.S. border. He felt negative responses from audiences when he sang in English.

He felt he was losing his professional identity and also being subtly pressured into becoming a citizen of Mexico. Almost twenty years after he left, Andy Russell returned to the U.S.

In 1967 he married Ginny Pace, a talk-show hostess who was a former ''Mrs. Houston.'' Describing himself as ''a real family man,'' he spends as much time as possible with his own six children and two grandchildren.

Lucy Lane-Harrison

Andy Russell today in his Encino condominium beside a citation given to him by the late Pope Paul VI.

Andy thinks he sings better today than ever in his career and has made several albums recently. But to audiences under forty his name is not recognizable, except among Latinos. For years he was the spokesman for a large savings and loan company in their commercials heard on Spanish-language radio stations.

As Russell sees his situation: ''My parents were born in Mexico, but I hate the word 'Chicano.' I am an American. Part of the reason I changed my name—as did many Jewish entertainers—was that I did not want to be stereotyped. But now I'm hard to sell in my own country—except to those who already know me.''

The former Della Russell lives most of the year in Mexico. She is the widow of one of that country's wealthiest men.

GIs of World War II voted Ann Savage "the savage we'd most like to meet in a jungle."

Ann Savage

The B movie actress whom film historian Doug McClelland has called the "Perfect Vixen" was born on February 19, 1921, in Columbia, South Carolina. Her original name was Bernice Lyon. She and her mother moved about with her father, a U.S. Army officer who was transferred from Dallas to New Orleans and finally to Jacksonville, Florida, where he died when she was four years old.

Ann's mother, who worked as a jewelry buyer, brought her only child up in Los Angeles, where she acted in a little theater production when she was ten years old. By her teens she had become such an expert bowler that she was giving lessons professionally.

It was at a sports center that she became acquainted with an acting student at the Max Reinhardt Theater Workshop. He introduced her to the school's manager, Bert D'Armand, who was also an agent. D'Armand agreed that she could attend classes in exchange for secretarial services, in spite of the fact that she lacked knowledge of typing and stenography.

When Ann played in the workshop's production of *Golden Boy,* Twentieth Century-Fox and Columbia Pictures offered her stock contracts. D'Armand, who by then was representing her, reasoned that she would have less competition among the blondes at Columbia than Fox.

She was first seen in *One Dangerous Night* (1943). A "Blondie" movie, *Footlight Glamour* (1943), *Two Senoritas from Chicago* (1943), and *The Unwritten Code* (1944) followed. She appeared only in programmers with the exception of *The More the Merrier* (1943) with Jean Arthur (single and living in Carmel-by-the-Sea, California).

Ms. Savage gladly accepted any role she was assigned and never questioned anyone's judgment at the studio, whether it was publicist, director, or costumer. She immediately stopped dating young western actor Russell Hayden when a Columbia executive told her the relationship could harm her career.

After two years it was decided that Marguerite Chapman had more star potential than Ann and Ann was dropped by Columbia.

In 1945 she married Bert D'Armand, who was eighteen years her senior. But, in spite of all his efforts, she could not be sold for parts in A pictures.

Freelancing, she made *Scared Stiff* (1945), *One Exciting Night* (1945) with Don Beddoe (married to Joyce Mathews[8] and living in Mission Viejo, California), *The Spider* (1945), *The*

Dark Horse (1946) with Philip Terry (married and living in Montecito, California), and *Renegade Girl* (1946) with John King (proprietor of a pancake house in La Jolla, California). All were B Films.

She worked frequently into the mid-fifties on such TV shows as *Ford Theater, Death Valley Days,* and *Starlight Theater.* Then she and her husband moved to New York City. He had by then left agenting and become a professional trader in securities.

Because of *Detour* (1945) Ann Savage is undoubtedly of more interest now to cinema buffs than when she was active. She made the picture in four days under the direction of Edgar G. Ulmer at cheapie studio PRC. Although the production values are low the performances and sordid story are riveting. Film critic Andrew Sarris, the late Don Miller, author of *"B" Movies,* and François Truffaut are among the many who consider the picture to be one of the best low-budget movies ever made. Ann as "Ver," the hard-bitten, consumptive woman of the road was described in the L.A. *Reader* in 1983 as the "most metaphysically grotesque actress ever to grace an American film."

Although *Detour* was acknowledged by many reviewers as an exceptional film when it first came out, it played only on the second half of double bills and was not promoted or advertised.

After she was widowed in 1969 Ann moved back to Los Angeles and has worked ever since for a large law firm.

In late 1983 Ann Savage spoke about *Detour* and her career: "No one would wish to be remembered for things like *Two-Man Subma-*rine or *Saddles and Sagebrush,* which were typical of the kind of pictures I did. The part in *Detour* seemed like the opportunity every actress longs for. When I first read the script by Martin Goldsmith I knew that I was going to be part of something very exciting. And had John Garfield played the lead, as Mr. Ulmer had hoped, we would have gotten a better release. Not that Tom Neal wasn't excellent, because he was, but distribution is so very important and without Garfield's name we were just another B to exhibitors. Knowing that the good work we did in *Detour* all those years ago is finally receiving some recognition is very gratifying. Better late than never, I guess. It's the good luck that I always seemed to lack back then."

Jerry Bierne

Ann Savage has been flying airplanes since the early seventies. The license plates on her Mercedes Benz 280SL read: "PILOT99."

Bidu Sayao's voice was a light soprano, flaw-lessly even from top to bottom.

Bidu Sayao

"Brazil's greatest treasure," as she was known in operatic circles, was born in Rio de Janeiro on May 11, 1906. Her full name is Balduina de Oliveira Sayao.

Her early ambition was to become an actress, a profession that was considered unthinkable for the daughter of a wealthy, socially prominent family. Her uncle suggested an operatic career and she was allowed to take vocal lessons, but for a young woman of her background even grand opera was considered *déclassée.*

Finally she was permitted to study abroad and went to France for lessons from the internationally renowned Jean de Reszke.

Bidu Sayao's first concert in her country's capital in 1925 was a triumph. The next year she made her operatic debut in Rome in *The Barber of Seville.* She became such a favorite in Italy that the crown prince presented her with a diamond pin. Parisian critics dubbed her the "Brazilian nightingale." The French government honored her with a diamond-encrusted Palmes Académiques. Queen Marie of Romania made her an honorary colonel in the queen's regiment.

It was Arturo Toscanini who brought her to the attention of the American public. The conductor insisted she sing Debussy's *Blessed Damozel* with the New York Philharmonic under his baton in 1936. Olin Downes, then the dean of American music critics, led the raves. Danton Walker noted the "exquisitely sensuous quality of her voice."

Mme. Sayao was applauded for more than her superb voice. American audiences were taken as well by her beauty and dramatic skills. She debuted in *Manon* at the Metropolitan Opera House on February 13, 1937, and remained a critical and box-office favorite until her last performance there, as "Mimi" on February 26, 1952. She was heard in concerts in all of the major cities and throughout North America in radio broadcasts.

About the U.S. she says, "I was at first regarded as strange. I understand, of course, because I spoke not one word of English when I arrived. Many thought I was Oriental because of my name,* which people could not pro-

*Pronounced "Bee-du Sigh-ow."

nounce. But soon we fell in love, this country and I.''

In 1958, after three concerts in Carnegie Hall, where she had debuted, she decided to retire. No announcement was made, but she was determined never to perform again.

For one year she did not sing a note. Then Heitor Villa-Lobos, her friend and countryman, talked her into recording ''The Forest of the Amazon.'' ''Bachianas Brasileiras #5,'' another of his compositions, had been one of her biggest selling records. It had taken her exactly six minutes to record it. Her ''swansing,'' as she calls it, took her until 3:00 A.M. to complete and left her physically and emotionally drained. ''But then it was clearly over,'' she says today.

In the winter she lives in a Manhattan hotel suite acting as judge at various vocal contests and giving master classes in voice.

The woman who grew up on an estate that stretched for two miles along the sea near Rio spends most of each year in her home on the coast of Maine. It faces the ocean and has a private beach. It was purchased in 1947 as a summer house, but after the deaths of her husband and her mother she made it her main residence.

When in Maine ''Biddy,'' as her friends call her, occupies herself with fishing and gardening.

''I feed the many birds that come to me,'' she says. ''And I see lots of the lovely people who have made me so welcome here. Many of them are very young and I think that keeps me youthful. I read a great deal—everything—because there is nothing that does not interest me.''

She lives and travels with her large cat named ''Big Bidina.''

She considers the highlight of her career to have been her appearance at the Metropolitan as ''Susanna'' in *The Marriage of Figaro*, an all-star production of 1940. Ezio Pinza, John Brownlee, Elisabeth Rethberg, and Rise Stevens were the others in the legendary performance.

About her career she has said, ''I very much regret that of Puccini's works I could sing only *La Bohème,* but most of his music is too heavy for my voice. I would love to have been ''Desdemona'' and to have performed in Germany and Austria. But *Otello* was beyond me and those countries and I somehow missed each other. But those years before the public were so happy that I shouldn't complain about these things.''

Asked if the life of a prima donna was as satisfying as her original choice of professions might have been, she responded, ''While it lasted, yes. But an actress at my age would not only still be able to practice her art, she would be or should be even better at it.''

Mme. Sayao lives in a house on the coast of Maine, except during the winter, which she spends in Manhattan.

Hazel Scott on stage had wit, sex appeal, and a total command of her audience. Although primarily a pianist, her singing has been described as "lush," "earthy," and "haunting."

Hazel Scott

The innovative pianist-singer was born on June 11, 1920, in Port of Spain, Trinidad. She was the only one of five children who survived infancy. "All my life I tried to be a superduper kid to make up," she once said.

On her fourth birthday her mother, a saxophonist in Lil Armstrong's all-girl band, took her to New York City.

Hazel began private lessons at the Juilliard School when she was eight years old. But practicing the piano bored her and she began to improvise. "Swinging the classics," as her style was sometimes called, became her trademark.

She played for a while in her mother's group and then began working as a single.

At age fifteen she had her own radio show and appeared regularly in jazz clubs such as the Hickory House. When Billie Holiday ended her engagement at Café Society in Greenwich Village she recommended that Hazel take over. The teenager was such a sensation that the club's owner opened a place uptown where Hazel played on and off for more than seven years.

The general public first became aware of her when she debuted on Broadway in *Sing Out the News* (1938). Her big number in the musical, "Franklin Roosevelt Jones," was a show stopper. Her other Broadway appearance was in *Priorities of 1942*.

"Dazzling bravura" and "saucy showmanship" were phrases used to describe her in performance. Hazel Scott was, however, equally spirited offstage, a factor of her personality that was seldom appreciated. Cole Porter, who wanted her to introduce "You'd Be So Nice to Come Home To" in the picture *Something to Shout About* (1942), was less than pleased when she passed up the opportunity with the explanation that she had no feeling for the lyrics.

I Dood It (1943), *Broadway Rhythm* (1944), and *Rhapsody in Blue* (1945) are among her few screen appearances. She performed in her pictures but had little opportunity to act. Her parts were written so that they could be edited out when the features played in Southern states. When she held up production on *The Heat's On* (1943), because of what she considered to be a racial slur, Harry Cohn vowed to end her Hollywood career, and did.

Hazel Scott was among the first to speak out on the matter of civil rights. When she found that her audience at the University of Texas would be segregated she refused to play, resulting in 7,500 admissions being refunded. The year was 1948. When a Seattle restaurant in 1949 refused her service she sued. Hazel won her case, but earned an even greater reputation for troublemaking.

No one contested critics who praised her keyboard artistry with words like "genius" and "brilliant." She could solo with the New York Philharmonic and concertize at Carnegie Hall. But troubles began for her when it became obvious that this black woman believed she had all the rights and privileges of a white male.

In 1945 she married the controversial and volatile clergyman-politician Adam Clayton Powell, who came to her defense in Congress when she was blacklisted during the McCarthy era. Hazel spoke her mind before the House Un-American Activities Committee and her daily television show, probably the first sponsored program on the medium held by a black artist, was canceled.

In 1957, after separating from her husband, she went into self-imposed exile in Paris. She acted on stage, made a few European films, and divorced Powell by proxy. Her second marriage was to a Swiss-Italian entertainer who was fifteen years her junior. When they parted twenty-two months later he remarked, "Hazel is a Maserati and I can only handle a Fiat."

She was as frank with militant young blacks when she returned to the U.S. in 1971 as she had always been with whites: "I don't need to be an 'instant African.' I've always known I belong to the Yoruba tribe. I know who I am and I have nothing to prove. Sometimes I wear my hair natural—but when it suits me. I happen to look too good in a turban!"

After her death in 1981 musicologist Leonard Feather wrote: "What is saddest about the loss of Hazel Scott is that for all her talent and all her beauty and all the vitality of her unique presence through the years, her era never really began . . . the most notable element of her career was what could have been."

Michael Knowles

The late Hazel Scott during an interview with author Richard Lamparski in the New York apartment of her only child, attorney Adam Clayton Powell III.

Bobby Sherman's recordings of "Hey, Little Woman," "Easy Come, Easy Go," "Cried Like a Baby," and "Julie, Do You Love Me?" were all hits.

Bobby Sherman

The teen idol of the sixties and early seventies was born Robert Cabot Sherman, Jr., on July 18, 1943, in Santa Monica, California. He began playing various musical instruments while he was still in elementary school.

Sherman says he had no thoughts of a career in show business, but admits he was star-struck. At a party to celebrate the conclusion of the filming of *The Greatest Story Ever Told* he found the band was made up of boys he had known in high school. After some coaxing Bobby sang with them.

At that point Sherman's college major was child psychology. He intended to specialize in gifted children. They were the subject of his thesis at Pierce College.

Bobby had a good time that night with his former classmates and felt he had been well received. One of those who congratulated him on his performance was Natalie Wood. But when he had a call several days later from an agent he was astounded. He had no hesitation when the man offered him a chance to audition for a pilot being made for a musical TV series that would be geared to a youthful audience.

The show, *Shindig*, made him a recognizable name nationwide within a few weeks of its premiere on the ABC network on September 16, 1964. The program became so popular it was telecast twice a week during its second season.

Sherman's publicity claimed that he was the "first personality in history to star in three television series before age thirty." Actually, Bobby was only featured, not "starred," on *Shindig*, although it could be argued that the show made him a star. To the editors of such teenybopper publications as *Sixteen* and *Tiger Beat* he was cover material, issue after issue.

He was very popular, even with older audiences, when *Here Come the Brides* went on the air in September 1968. Bobby played the stuttering younger brother on the sitcom, which was set in Seattle in the 1870s. It lasted for two years and was a huge boost to his record sales and in attendance at personal appearances.

He was definitely the star of *Getting Together,* but the half-hour shows were seen for only four months after the premiere on ABC-TV in September 1971.

Bobby Sherman had a pleasant voice, an engaging smile, and obviously enjoyed performing. During his heyday he played as many as 113 concerts a year. His audience was primarily girls between eleven and sixteen, placing him in the "bubble gum" category of music. He also had a great many adult fans, but they were drawn to his looks, not his music.

His most recent album, *Remembering You,* is sold only through the mail by TV ads. Bobby produced it in the twenty-four-track studio he has constructed in his home. He frequently rents out the facility to other musicians.

He has made a few guest appearances on TV shows, directed some commercials, and co-produced the ABC *Movie of the Week, The Day the Earth Moved,* in 1974. In 1983 he hosted *The Video Game Challenge,* a syndicated TV show.

The young woman he married had not been one of his fans. In fact, according to Sherman, she disliked his profession and most of the people he worked with.

"She always wanted to live in the country," says Bobby. "And that's where she is—without me."

When the marriage ended in divorce after eight years he retained their Encino home. In its backyard Sherman has built a replica of Disneyland's Main Street. He spent almost three years and over $15,000 constructing the buildings which are one-fifth the size of the original. His two sons play there when they come to spend weekends with him, his two bloodhounds, and the young woman he lives with.

Bobby Sherman is single and lives in Encino, California.

Arnold Stang became well known to TV viewers for his frequent appearances on Milton Berle's show and on the series Broadside.

Arnold Stang

The character actor was born in Chelsea, Massachusetts, on September 28. His response to those who ask his original name is, "Do you really think anyone would change his name to Arnold Stang?"

From a very early age Arnold listened a great deal to the radio. When he was nine years old he sent a postcard to his favorite show, *Let's Pretend.* The program aired Saturday mornings, presenting child actors in plays for children. Stang wrote asking if he, too, could be on. He was sent a form letter stating that the producers would be interested in auditioning him the next time he was in New York City. Using money he had been saving for an anniversary present for his parents, he traveled to Manhattan on a bus and presented himself.

"I recited Edgar Allan Poe's 'The Raven' but with gestures because I was going to be a *serious* actor," he recalls. "They were very kind. No one embarrassed me. But they must have left the room and fallen on the floor. Anyway, I was on their very next show and played a part and from that I got on *Horn and Hardart's Children's Hour.* I've never really been out of work since."

On Broadway he was cast opposite Elliott Nugent in *All in Favor* (1942). He made his movie debut in *Seven Days' Leave* (1942).

Stang's nasal, high-pitched voice was heard on radio frequently in the forties and fifties. He guested with Al Jolson, Frank Sinatra, and Tallulah Bankhead on their programs and was a regular with Milton Berle's radio show.

During the years Milton Berle was considered "Mr. Television" Stang played "Francis," the NBC stagehand who pestered the star and was the secret crush of "Max," Berle's secretary. On *Broadside,* the naval TV series of the mid-sixties, he played the ship's cook.

Although he has played a wide variety of roles, the two that have forged the strongest impressions are the nebbish character for which he is best known and "Sparrow," the pathetic junkie in the film *The Man with the Golden Arm* (1955). According to Stang, Nelson Algren wrote "Sparrow" with him in mind. He expected the portrayal to bring him an Academy Award and was deeply disappointed when he was not nominated. For years after the picture's release he received scripts offering him the opportunity to play what he considered to be other "Sparrow" types.

In *The Wonderful World of the Brothers Grimm* (1962) he was "Rumpelstiltskin." He was part of the all-star cast of *It's a Mad Mad Mad Mad World* (1963). His last Broadway appearance was in *The Front Page* (1969).

On one of his frequent guestings on the *Tonight* show, Johnny Carson remarked, "You can see Arnold Stang any time you turn on anything but the hot water." Realizing that he was nearing the point of overexposure, Stang decided then to withdraw from all on-camera work unless the part presented a real challenge. He had also been aware for some time that the constant travel and hectic schedules of television had begun to affect his performing skills.

He still wears his trademarks, horn-rimmed glasses and bow ties, and does even better financially than when he was being seen so often on TV. Stang's voice is heard on radio and television commercials, recordings, and in the many motion pictures he dubs. He frequently turns down offers of parts on TV situation comedies because "it's always the same role. The one I've played repeatedly. I don't think of myself as a comedian. I am an actor who can do comedy."

He appears in several plays a year, usually for regional theaters. In 1983 he did *Harvey* and *The Diary of Anne Frank*.

Arnold and his wife, Joanne, met when she interviewed him for the *New York Times*. Since their marriage she has written several mystery novels and *Marathan Mom,* a book on running. Neither their son nor daughter has any interest in show business.

He prefers radio to television both as a listener and a performer. At the twenty-fifth anniversary of the National Academy of Television Arts in 1981 he toasted the season of 1956— "When everything was 'live from New York.' Now it's dead from California."

Two years later he told journalist Dolores Barclay, "Radio depends on your intelligence. TV dinners really describe what television is."

Arnold Stang, his wife, and their two children live in New Canaan, Connecticut.

Eddie Brandt

Bob Steele was listed by Motion Picture Herald *in 1938 as being the seventh biggest money-maker among the western stars. Thirty years later he was a regular on the TV series* F Troop.

Bob Steele

The star of more than 180 western movies was born Robert Bradbury, Jr., on January 23, in Pendleton, Oregon. His family moved to Glendale, California, when he was five years old.

Bob and his brother, Bill, were boys when their father took films of them on a hunting and trapping expedition. Sold to Pathé, they were released beginning in 1921 as a series of shorts entitled *The Adventures of Bill and Bob.*

Bob's father was well established as a writer-director-producer of westerns when he signed with FBO as a supervisor. That studio planned a series of pictures and was looking for a young actor to play "Bob Steele." Bradbury, Sr., showed the executives photos of Bob without revealing that it was his son who had just graduated from high school. Borrowing a horse and gear from cowboy star Fred Humes Bob made a test and was signed to a contract. He starred in his first feature as *The Mojave Kid* (1927) under the billing of "Bob Steele" and has used that name ever since. Many of his early efforts were directed by his father.

Steele never became as popular as Tom Mix or Gene Autry,[8] but he had a longer career than either and established a firm hold on the loyalty of western fans who still hold him in high esteem. At the beginning he was considerably younger than his contemporaries.

There was never a lack of action in a Bob Steele picture, and usually the brawls were much more believable than in other horse operas. The late film historian Don Miller, in his book *Hollywood Corral,* described the fight scenes in Steele oaters as "the best of the day, practically unchallenged in the flying fists department."

Perhaps what provided the strongest point of audience identification was the fact that Bob was short of stature. No trick camera work was used to minimize that this hero was usually smaller than the villains he faced. Wrote Miller, "He gave every little kid hope in a world that seemed at times peopled with big bullies."

Steele had a good speaking voice and made the transition to talkies with ease. His first sound picture was *Near the Rainbow's End* (1930).

What probably limited Bob's career was that he moved back and forth among the studios and independents. His pictures were produced at various times by Tiffany, Republic, Monogram, Supreme, and PRC. Seldom was much care taken on production values. In one period of less than five years during the thirties Steele starred in thirty-two westerns.

Among his many starrers were: *Ridin' Fool* (1931); *Hidden Valley* (1932); *Galloping Ro-*

meo (1933); *Border Phantom* (1936); *The Red Rope* (1937), and *Durango Valley Raiders* (1938). In most of his movies he rode a horse named "Raider."

Bob Steele played the title role of "Billy the Kid" in six features before becoming one of the "Three Mesquiteers," a popular western series. After that he was a "Trail Blazer" in a series of the same name.

His leading ladies, such as Adrian Booth (married to David Brian and living in Sherman Oaks) and Linda Stirling (married to screenwriter Sloan Nibley and living in North Hollywood) found him a considerate and uncomplicated actor to work with. The fact that he was one of the best-looking of the cowboy stars drew more females to his features than were usually found in audiences for westerns. Ms. Stirling, who played with him at Republic, was struck by his acting. "He wasn't just going through the motions in another western," she recalled recently. "He cared about his performances and worked on them." As early as 1939 moviegoers were aware of Bob Steele as more than just a cowboy hero. He was excellent as the mean-tempered "Curly" in the filmed version of John Steinbeck's *Of Mice and Men*. The man who had played the good guy so many times was even more effective as the sadistic fighter in *City for Conquest* (1940) with James Cagney and the hoodlum who kills Elisha Cook, Jr. (single and living in Bishop, California), in *The Big Sleep* (1946).

When it was thought that he had begun to slip at the box office he took supporting roles in the films of other western stars, such as Johnny Mack Brown and Roy Rogers. Two of his last starring vehicles were *Northwest Trail* (1945) with Joan Woodbury (director of the Valley Guild Players in Palm Springs) and *Thunder Town* (1946).

Steele worked as a character actor in features and on television, often unrecognized by

Robby Robertson

In 1983 Bob Steele was given a tribute at the Masquers Club in Hollywood. It was the first the public had seen him in some time.

adults who, as kids, had cheered his exploits at Saturday matinees. He supported Mickey Rooney in *Killer McCoy* (1947) and Dennis Morgan[8] in *Cheyenne* (1947). John Wayne, who had been his friend since the early thirties, saw to it that Bob had parts in his pictures *Rio Bravo* (1959) and *The Comancheros* (1961). He played "Trooper Duffy" on the military farce *F Troop* from 1965 to 1967. Some of his other credits are: *South of St. Louis* (1940); *The Enforcer* (1951); *The Steel Jungle* (1956) with Walter Able (widowed and living in New York City); *Band of Angels* (1957); *Pork Chop Hill* (1959); *Six Black Horses* (1962); *Town Tamer* (1965), and *Something Big* (1971) with Dean Martin.

Bob Steele rarely makes personal appearances and does not enjoy interviews. When asked once about the direction his career took after the star years, he replied, "Well, things got a little quiet for me for a while, but I've always worked. I never went in for all this hoop-de-do about demanding top billing and huge salaries. When a lot of 'em were starring I was content to do bit parts just to be active, to add a little something. Why disintegrate because of pride?"

Before going into pictures Venetia Stevenson appeared on the covers of many national magazines and was chosen "The Most Photogenic Girl in the World" by a photography publication.

Venetia Stevenson

The starlet of the late fifties was born on March 10 in London, England. Her mother is Anna Lee, who was then a star of the English cinema. Her father is Robert Stevenson, director of such films as *Jane Eyre* (1944) and *Mary Poppins* (1964).

The Stevensons went to Hollywood just before World War II started in Europe. By 1944 they were divorced.

When she was fourteen years old Venetia was noticed on the beach by a fashion photographer who offered to launch her on a modeling career. She found the work agreeable and lucrative. Her youth and fine features soon made her one of the most popular junior models in the country.

Her parents neither encouraged nor discouraged her concerning a movie career. But being their daughter kept her, both professionally and socially, from ever being just another pretty actress in Hollywood. Shortly after she signed with RKO Venetia complained to a writer for a fanzine that her mother's moviemaking schedule often made her unavailable when she needed her. Ms. Lee gave an interview to the same publication in a subsequent issue in which she described her daughter as a girl who was exceptionally self-involved.

She made her acting debut as a corpse on *Matinee Theater.* Had she felt adequate to the part the show's producer was agreeable to presenting her in *Romeo and Juliet,* but Venetia declined.

The only things she did during her six months at RKO was to take various lessons and pose for publicity stills.

Warner Brothers, where she went next, used her on all of their TV series and loaned her out for guest appearances as Ricky Nelson's girl friend on *The Adventures of Ozzie and Harriet.* She had a featured role in the movie *Darby's Rangers* (1958).

Anyone interested in Hollywood's younger set at that time was well aware of Venetia Stevenson. Many girls identified with her while others merely envied her dates with Tab Hunter, Elvis Presley, and Tony Perkins. Some were set up by publicists and served as good opportunities for photo layouts. But her romance with Russ Tamblyn was very real and led to marriage in 1956. When the gorgeous daughter of filmdom royalty became the wife of one of the cutest boys on the screen it played in the media like a modern-day fairy tale. It lasted, however, less than one year.

Twenty-five years later Venetia commented to reporter Donald Chase for the *Los Angeles Times:* "I don't think Russ and I would have thought of marriage had we not been so much in the public eye and getting so much encouragement from everyone around us."

She appeared on TV with Art Carney in *Charley's Aunt* and at the Phoenix Playhouse in *Liliom* with Fernando Lamas and Arlene Dahl. But she considered herself to be a very poor actress and when Don Everly, whom she married in 1962, asked her to retire she was more than willing. Venetia bore two daughters and a son during the eight years she and the singer were together. Neither she nor their children have seen him since the divorce. Stacy, the oldest, acts in commercials and wants to direct. Erin Everly is an aspiring actress. Edan, who is sixteen and lives with his mother in Studio City, plans a career in music.

She has never viewed any of her movies all the way through and has not seen any of *Studs Lonigan* (1960). Ms. Stevenson feels that *Seven Ways from Sundown* (1960) contains her best performance—"if I ever had a 'best.'"

Some of her other screen appearances were in *Island of Lost Women* (1959), *The Big Night* (1960) with Randy Sparks (married to Diane Jergens and living on a ranch in Mokelumne Hill, California), and *Horror Hotel* (1963).

She missed movies and the people who made them. Remembering that her father once told her that she had a good story sense, Venetia became a script reader for Burt Reynolds's production company. She laughs now about her recommendation that he not do *Smokey and the Bandit.*

Richard Lamparski

Venetia Stevenson is vice-president of Cinema Group, the company that made Take This Job and Shove It (1981), Southern Comfort (1981), and The Philadelphia Experiment (1984).

She is adamant about never acting again.

Venetia, who has described herself as "very unmarried," admitted in a 1983 interview that she has never dated anyone who was not directly connected with show business. She will not, however, go out with actors.

"I've never really known anything but Hollywood," she says. "I don't think I could relate to a physician or an accountant. What would we talk about? I guess, when I really stop and think about it, I have lived a very narrow existence because movies are all I know."

Alan Sues appeared weekly on Laugh-In *during its first four seasons on the air, 1968–72. The character he did most frequently was "Big Al," a somewhat nellie sportscaster.*

Alan Sues

The actor-comedian who became famous for his appearances on *Laugh-In* was born in Ross, California, on March 7. Alan and his younger brother were brought up in and around San Francisco by parents who moved fifty-two times while the boys were growing up.

A class wit throughout school, Sues attended the Pasadena Playhouse before making his Broadway debut in the original production of *Tea and Sympathy* (1953). In it he played one of the boys who harassed John Kerr (now a criminal attorney in Los Angeles), a student suspected of being homosexual.

Sues began making his reputation at small swanky Manhattan nightclubs such as the Reuben Bleu and Blue Angel. He worked off and on as a solo act and with other performers, such as Julius Monk.

Sues was featured in *The Mad Show* (1966) and it was from his work in that off-Broadway hit that he was signed for *Laugh-In*. During the lengthy period it took to put the TV show on the air, Alan spent six months at the Interlude, a nightclub on the Sunset Strip, doing improvisational comedy to prepare for what he eventually did so well on *Laugh-In*.

He then accepted a part in a play with Elaine May which she also wrote. *A Matter of Position*, which was directed by Arthur Penn, opened in Stockbridge, Massachusetts, to mixed notices. Most reviewers, however, singled Sues out and praised his portrayal of an extremely insecure telephone repairman. Had he been able to get out of his commitment to Rowan and Martin at that point he would have, but was soon relieved that he hadn't. The play never reached Broadway.

Alan had done a comedy act on the premiere of *Shindig* in 1966 and was a regular on the musical-variety show thereafter, but it was on *Laugh-In* that he became a familiar face all over the country.

Sues credits the show's writers as having had the original idea for the character that brought him the most success, "Big Al," the fey sportscaster. Originally, it was to be "Bruce Sues and the Sports Scene," but Alan resisted.

"They let me do it my way," he explained recently. "In my mind 'Big Al' was a drama critic, a Rex Reed type, who had been reassigned to the sports desk which he obviously hated. Had I made him real swishy he'd have worn thin quickly."

"Big Al" used to award "ding-dongs," as he called them, on his bell to the athletes who had excelled that week, and often complimented sports figures on their uniforms as part of his "report." That character and the other work he did on *Laugh-In* have made him one of the most popular regulars on the shows once again now that they are seen in reruns.

Sues chose to do the lead in a Broadway-bound revival of *Good News* rather than remain with *Laugh-In* for its last season. Audiences seemed delighted that he could also sing and act, but the show closed on the road.

He was married for five years to Phyllis Sues, who has in recent years become one of California's leading designers of women's apparel.

He is recognized frequently as much for his many appearances on the *Merv Griffin Show* as for his exposure on *Laugh-In*. He is also remembered as the campy "Peter Pan" on the TV commercials for the peanut butter of the same name.

Sues thoroughly enjoyed his years on *Laugh-In* and cherishes some of the relationships he made then, but one negative aspect of the shows was the two-day-a-week, 9:00 A.M. to 4:00 A.M. shooting schedules. Another, which he still lives with, is that his image has been so firmly set as a comedian among Hollywood casting people. Even after playing the archvillain "Dr. Moriarty" in *Sherlock Holmes* (1974) on Broadway and then on tour, he has not been cast in serious roles on TV. The one exception was when he played a menace on *Chips*.

Alan Sues is currently preparing a one-man show in which he will portray Dr. Franz Mesmer, the father of mesmerism.

Richard Lamparski

Alan Sues and his companion "Lois Lane" live in their Manhattan apartment.

John Cameron Swayze was nominated for an Emmy as Best News Reporter/Commentator in 1954 and again in 1955. An estimated 15 million people watched his newscasts nightly on NBC-TV. On his 7:00 P.M. news he always wore a boutonniere. His sign-off throughout his years as a newscaster was always "This is John Cameron Swayze. I'm glad we could get together."

John Cameron Swayze

NBC-Television's first network anchorman was born in Wichita and brought up in Atchison and Kansas City, Kansas. His birth date is April 4, 1906. Cameron was his mother's maiden name.

John's father, a wholesale drug salesman, felt his lifelong inability to communicate with groups of people had limited him socially and professionally. The elocution lessons that his son received led John to an interest in acting.

After military school and some time at the University of Kansas, Swayze went to New York City to study drama. Before giving up his theatrical ambitions and returning home in 1929 he met and married another acting student, his wife Beulah.

When John Cameron Swayze went to work as a cub reporter at the Kansas City *Journal*

Post his salary was $15 a week. Part of his job was to read the news as it came off the wire-service teletype. He did three ten-minute broadcasts each day from a cubbyhole in the corner of the newsroom. "I was the new kid," he says. "So I got any assignments the more experienced reporters felt were beneath them. Radio itself wasn't taken seriously by newspaper people then and radio news was considered beneath contempt. But the paper had an agreement with a local station and I was told to read the bulletins. I rather liked broadcasting right from the start. Must have been the actor part of me."

Even after John was promoted, eventually to feature editor, he continued to do newscasts. Later he spent five years as the newsman on the NBC affiliate in Kansas City.

When Walter Winchell, who was then nearing the peak of his influence, passed through Kansas City, he met and took a liking to Swayze. When the columnist encountered John's boss shortly thereafter he praised the young reporter. "For Winchell to single out a reporter like that was almost unheard of," says John. "It was worth more than an award would be today." Because of it he was assigned his own by-lined column.

In 1947 John began doing the night *World News Roundup* on NBC radio. He was assigned to cover the Democratic, GOP, and Progressive Party conventions of 1948 for NBC-TV and the following year became the host of the *Camel News Caravan,* the network's first regular evening newscast.

As early as 1948 Swayze began appearing on TV shows other than newscasts. He was a panelist on *Who Said That?,* an early quiz program. John, his son, and daughter appeared on *Watch the World* in 1950, a weekly current events show for young people. He hosted the dramatic anthology *Armstrong Circle Theater* from 1955 to 1957 and later had the syndicated series *Sightseeing with the Swayzes,* which featured his family of four.

Throughout his career John was known for his natty appearance. He made the Best Dressed list several years and was well known for his wide variety of neckties. For a few years a national manufacturer marketed a John Cameron Swayze line of neckwear.

John hosted the NBC evening news from 1949 until he was replaced in 1956 with the Chet Huntley–David Brinkley combination. Then he signed a contract with Timex and remained their TV spokesman for more than twenty years. He still occasionally appears in their commercials.

Swayze is remembered among his colleagues for his professionalism. One of TV's most memorable bloopers came about when a

Peter Schaeffer

John Cameron Swayze in the den of his Connecticut home. He says he has been "a very lucky man all my life."

Timex watch that had been fastened to the propeller of an outboard motor disappeared during a live commercial. The audience, as well as the show's host, Steve Allen, was convulsed at each attempt to find the timepiece, but John remained unflappable throughout. The watch was never found.

John Swayze, his son, is a newscaster on the NBC radio network.

The Swayzes take long cruises during the cold weather. He is still recognized by Americans wherever they go both for his Timex appearances and his newscasts.

They live in a modern house set on five and a half acres in the Glenville section of Greenwich, Connecticut. Several of their rooms have a panoramic view of the countryside.

Sometime ago the Swayzes switched from watching the network evening news shows in favor of the stock market reports on PBS.

M-G-M publicists likened Ralph Taeger to Clark Gable. When he starred on TV in Hondo *he was called the "new John Wayne." Warner Brothers, because of his voice, thought he might replace Humphrey Bogart.*

Ralph Taeger

Hollywood's "hot property" of the sixties was born on July 30, 1936, in Richmond Hill, New York.

In an attempt to overcome his extreme shyness Ralph became involved in public speaking and then acting. One of his high school teachers had made the suggestion and it was so effective Taeger continued to act in plays while attending college and apprenticed at a summer stock theater.

Up until this time he had intended to play baseball professionally and spent some time on a Dodger farm team. But he had hurt both knees several times and had been warned that further injuries might result in permanent damage. He decided to pursue an acting career instead but still refers to baseball as "my first love."

In the late fifties Taeger enrolled at the American Academy of Dramatic Arts in New York City. For about a year he attended classes and worked as a model. His type—close-cropped hair and strong-silent pose—was in vogue and he caught on immediately.

Within six months of his arrival in Hollywood he was appearing in a prominent role at the Beverly Hills Playhouse. It brought him to the attention of M-G-M where he was placed under contract.

He made his debut on a segment of *Northwest Passage* and then did a small part in *It Started with a Kiss* (1959). After six months he was dropped.

While making a *Manhunt* episode Ralph so impressed Victor Jory that he recommended him to Columbia Pictures as potential star material. He was offered another stock contract but chose instead to go with Ziv Television, where he was used frequently on such programs as *Highway Patrol, Tombstone Territory,* and *Sea Hunt.*

Taeger's first series was *Klondike,* which ran from October 1960 to February 1961. It has appeared on at least one published list of the worst programs ever on TV. After eighteen thirty-minute episodes were filmed, Ralph and his co-star James Coburn were abruptly shifted from Alaska during the Gold Rush to present-day Mexico. Telly Savalas was added to the cast and the title was changed to *Acapulco.* When this second attempt went off the air after eight shows he was being paid $2,500 a week.

Taeger's German-born parents were at first

baffled by his choice of profession but were very supportive once they saw he was serious. When he began to appear frequently on television they were delighted, a sidelight that he found to be one of the most satisfying aspects of his success.

Ralph Taeger had received enough exposure to be a recognizable name to much of the public. He had movie star looks and a manner that often passed for self-assurance. Twentieth Century-Fox placed him under contract, but when they failed to find a property for him he signed with Paramount Pictures. M-G-M, thinking he would be right for their series *The Rounders,* bought his contract from Paramount. Instead, he made a pilot for a series in which he would have starred as a hardboiled detective, but it did not sell.

His last real chance at stardom came with the title role of *Hondo,* which ran on ABC-TV from September through December 1967.

Taeger was in the features *X-15* (1961) with Mary Tyler Moore, *Stagecoach to Thunder Rock* (1964), *A House Is Not a Home* (1964), *The Carpetbaggers* (1964), and *The Delta Factor* (1970).

Recently he described what he believes went wrong: "I loved the money I was paid, but I never saved or invested any of it. I lived most of the time at a country club and never went near the studio unless I had to. The checks came in all the same. I didn't work at acting or making contacts. Then, all at once, it seemed to be over except for an occasional small part."

George Eells met Taeger at the height of the actor's career. The biographer, who was then the entertainment editor of *Look* magazine, remembers him as being "very opinionated with a swaggering manner. He already had the reputation for being difficult which is equated in some circles with talent."

Soon after Stephanie Zimbalist announced their engagement they broke up and Ralph married a young woman who was not in show business. According to him, she has no understanding of his profession or interest it it. To support them he has sold automobiles and worked as a tennis pro.

In 1983, with the money he inherited from his parents, Taeger bought a recently built house on six wooded acres in north-central California. He earns his living as a wholesaler of firewood and his wife works as a secretary. They have a teenage son.

From time to time he appears in productions at the playhouse in the nearest town, a community of nine hundred.

James Cury

Ralph Taeger is a wholesaler of firewood living near Camino, California.

Russ Tamblyn was nominated for an Oscar as Best Supporting Actor of 1957 for his performance in Peyton Place.

Russ Tamblyn

The actor-singer was born on December 30, 1934, in Los Angeles.

He was the sort of boy who would now be described as "hyperactive." A proficient gymnast, he got up on stage during intermissions at his local movie theater and did what amounted to an act of skilled tumbling.

He was chosen from the cast of a children's play for a bit part in *The Boy with Green Hair* (1949) which starred Dean Stockwell. Then he did *The Black Book* (1949) with Bob Cummings and *The Kid from Cleveland* (1949) with Tommy Cook (a tennis pro living in Los Angeles). His next, which he considers his first big break, was *Samson and Delilah* (1949) under Cecil B. DeMille's direction. He also played John Dall as a boy in the cult film *Gun Crazy* (1949).

When he made *Captain Carey, U.S.A.* with Wanda Hendrix,[8] *Father of the Bride* (1950), and its sequel, *Father's Little Dividend* (1951), he was still being billed as Rusty Tamblyn. He was also in *The Winning Team* (1952) with Tom Brown (single and living in Sherman Oaks) and *Retreat, Hell!* (1952).

Tamblyn's image in the minds of most moviegoers, as well as professionals, is that of a dancer. Yet he never danced a step on the screen until *Seven Brides for Seven Brothers* (1954) and, according to his count, "in no more than five" films after that. He is somewhat resentful of this, feeling that it has worked against him in later years when acting parts for men his age are being cast. At the same time he is proud of what he brought to the dancing in *Tom Thumb* (1958) and *Hit the Deck* (1955).

"A lot of the steps I did in movies were my own," he told writer Julie Wheelock. "And some of them I've never seen duplicated, like my back flip with a full twist."

During the fifties Russ Tamblyn was very much part of the "young Hollywood" set that was featured frequently in fanzines. His studio,

M-G-M, used him frequently and usually to good advantage, in such features as *Take the High Ground* (1953), *Many Rivers to Cross* (1955), *The Fastest Gun Alive* (1956), *Don't Go Near the Water* (1957), and *High School Confidential* (1958).

His marriage to Venetia Stevenson on Valentine's Day 1956 was front page news. They separated the following year.

By 1964 Russ had been married for four years to a young Englishwoman who had been a dancer in Las Vegas. He decided to "diversify my interests." He turned down any number of acting jobs, including the part that Bob Denver eventually played on *Gilligan's Island,* to concentrate on his art. "I was bored with the parts I was being offered," he explains. "I felt I could express myself more fully and freely in painting than I could in acting, which then was very limiting."

By 1980 his marriage had ended in divorce and he was again seeking employment as an actor. In the intervening years he had worked on his collages and made an occasional picture, the most notable of which was *The Last Movie* (1971). *Satan's Sadists* (1970) and *Dracula vs. Frankenstein* (1971) were two others.

In recent years he has been seen in *Cabaret* in Chicago, *George M* in Atlanta, and *Bye Bye Birdie* in Missouri. He very much wanted to head the road company of *Barnum,* but lost out to Tony Orlando.

Says Russ, "I'd just like to work more. I'd do any kind of parts now."

He describes his present wife, Bonnie Murray, as a "songwriter, singer, and graphic artist" and their baby, Amber Rose, his first child, as "just about the greatest thing that *ever* happened to me—or anyone my age." Their Santa Monica apartment contains no evidence of his movie career.

His brother, Larry Tamblyn, is the songwriter and keyboard player for The Standells.

The man who has worked under the direction of Michael Kidd, Hermes Pan, and Jerome Robbins had his first exposure as a choreographer in *Human Highway* (1982), a low-budget feature he made with his longtime friend Dean Stockwell.

"Life is strange," he said recently. *"West Side Story* was one of the high points of my career. Yet when I first saw it I was really disappointed in how I came off. Since then Fred Astaire has told me how much he admired my dancing in it. Now I see it very differently."

Michael Knowles

Russ Tamblyn's Santa Monica apartment is decorated with his collages.

Dion McGregor

Frankie Thomas played "Tim Tyler" and then "Ted Nickerson," the boy friend of "Nancy Drew" in the movies. On TV he played the title role in Tom Corbett, Space Cadet *for five years.*

Frankie Thomas

The child actor of stage and screen who starred on TV as "Tom Corbett" was born in New York City on April 9, 1921. He was the only child of the actress Mona Bruns and Frank M. Thomas, who acted, directed, and produced in the theater.

Frankie, Mildred Natwick, and Jimmy Stewart made their Broadway debuts together in *Carrie Nation* (1932), which also featured Frank M. Thomas. The following year he was seen in *Little Ol' Boy* and *Thunder on the Left.* In *Remember the Day* (1935) he played again with his father. *Seen But Not Heard* (1936) and *Your Loving Son* (1941) were among his other Broadway credits.

It was *Wednesday's Child* (1934) that took Frankie to Hollywood, where he repeated his performance in the screen version for RKO in 1934. Some of his other movie parts were in *Boys Town* (1938), *Little Tough Guys in Society* (1939), *Dress Parade* (1939) with Huntz Hall (married and living in North Hollywood), *One Foot in Heaven* (1941) with Beulah Bondi,[8] and *Always in My Heart* (1942) with Kay Francis.

In the late thirties he developed a large following among children slightly younger than himself. Boys identified with him in the title role of *Tim Tyler's Luck,* a series he made for Universal in 1937. The twelve chapters were later edited and released as a feature that became quite popular on television in the fifties. Young girls developed crushes on him when he played "Ted Nickerson," boy friend of "Nancy Drew," in the four features about the teenage sleuth by Warner Brothers.

Probably the role that brought him the most fame was "Tom Corbett." The science-fiction series was done live on television beginning in 1950. Frankie played the character on radio simultaneously for several seasons. The show was inspired by the success of *Captain Video* but was much more realistic and better produced because Willie Ley, a space scientist of some renown, was technical adviser and worked closely with the writers, one of whom was Frankie Thomas.

"When our viewers watched the first space walk and moon landing they must have thought of 'Tom Corbett,'" said the star recently. "Because we were the first program to deal with antimatter and weightlessness. And the gear the astronauts wore looked almost identical to our costumes."

The programs have recently been revived on cable TV.

After the show ceased production he wrote for television's *My True Story* and radio's *Theater Five*. He then spent some time producing the *Four Star Theater*, but no longer pursued an acting career. "I just didn't feel there was any place for me to go," he once explained. "And there were other things I was very interested in."

During the fifties when there was much live dramatic programming on TV the Thomases appeared so frequently on the medium that the magazine *TV-Radio Mirror* referred to them as the "First Family of Television." Frankie and his parents reside in Toluca Lake, California. He has remained single.

For over twenty years Frank Thomas, Jr., as he is now known, has taught bridge, edited magazines on the game, and written books on the subject. *From Average to Expert* is one that he co-authored with Charles Gooden. *The Sherlock Holmes Bridge Book* was the first of a series he has written.

It has been speculated that Frankie might have achieved greater success in movies had he played the title role in *David Copperfield*. Recently he told what happened:

"RKO suspended shooting on *Dog of Flanders* in 1935 when M-G-M asked to test me for the part. Thalberg had seen me on Broadway playing a crippled kid in *The First Legion* and felt I was right for 'David.' But Louis B. Mayer took one look at me and decided I was wrong. Mayer was right. I was much too husky for the role which Freddie Bartholomew subsequently

Jon Virzi

Frankie Thomas at a recent convention of science-fiction fans. He is an expert on bridge and lives in Toluca Lake, California.

did so beautifully. He even had the accent which I'd have found very difficult to master.

"I have no regrets about that or any other part. I got all the breaks I had coming. I consider myself to have been very lucky during my career, especially in knowing when to leave it. I smile when I think of those years but I've never missed any part of acting."

Lawrence Tierney was publicized as the "handsome badman of the screen" when he played the title role in Dillinger *(1945). Since then he has been arrested many more times than the real-life John Dillinger, who had been Public Enemy Number One.*

Lawrence Tierney

The actor whose life became confused with his movie roles was born on March 15, 1919, in Brooklyn. He attended Manhattan College for a while on the athletic scholarship he had won in a parochial high school.

One account of his "discovery" has Law-rence being spotted in a little theater production by a movie talent scout. In another he was a model keeping a friend company on an interview at the New York offices of RKO Pictures.

He was brought to Hollywood in 1942 with an RKO contract and made most of his early films at that studio. The one exception was *Dillinger* (1945).

In playing the famous gunman, Lawrence Tierney had about him an aura of sexuality and violence. It was a big money-maker for Monogram Pictures and made him a star.

When an almost unknown becomes a name overnight in a sensational role there is always a danger that the public will confuse the performance with the actor. In the case of Larry Tierney it would seem that he took on the tough-guy persona. As one tabloid put it, "The real Tierney and the 'reel' one seem the same."

Dillinger was still in release when his troubles with liquor and the law began making the news.

He has been arrested for breaking the jaw of a college student, tearing a public phone off the wall, shoplifting, trespassing, assaulting actress Jean Wallace, striking a nightclub pianist, hitting a waiter in the face with a sugar bowl, tearing off a friend's neck brace and then throwing a drink in his face, drunk driving, contempt of court, attempting to choke a cabdriver, breaking and entering, punching a security guard who attempted to prevent him from crashing the party Elizabeth Taylor was giving for the Moiseyev dancers, attacking a TV cameraman, kicking a collie and its owner, assault with a deadly weapon, and fighting with a professional boxer at Fifty-third Street and Broadway.

At one time a disheveled, barefoot, and belligerent Larry sought sanctuary in a Roman Catholic church and had to be removed in a straitjacket.

Some of his convictions brought jail sentences. He was ordered to stay out of Beverly Hills after a fistfight there with his younger brother, actor Scott Brady. Authorities on Fire Island told him he was persona non grata.

In 1960, on the morning of the day his mother died suddenly, he was released on bail after a drunken rampage. Hours after he learned of her death he was jailed again. Louella O. Parsons, who often commiserated with Mrs. Tierney, wrote that she had "spent her life praying for her boy."

The sober Lawrence Tierney seems a totally different person from the mean-spirited drunken one. He was not known as a problem actor on the sets of his pictures and several of the women he has dated remember him as a well-mannered, thoughtful escort. Another, whom he was seeing in 1975, either fell or jumped to her death from the window of her apartment while they were having a drink together.

Tierney did not always play criminals. He was in the comedy *Mama Loves Papa* (1945) and had the hero's role in *Step by Step* (1946). He was also in *Singing in the Dark* (1956), a low-budget musical. But it was as a villain that he registered strongly. The titles of his pictures tell the story of his career: *Youth Runs Wild* (1944); *San Quentin* (1947); *The Devil Thumbs a Ride* (1947); *Born to Kill* (1947); *Bodyguard* (1948); *Kill or Be Killed* (1950); *Shakedown* (1950); *Hoodlum* (1951), and *The Steel Cage* (1954). He played Jesse James in *Badman's Territory* (1946) and again in *Best of the Badmen* (1951).

He has supported himself over the years by construction work and bit parts like the doorman role in *Such Good Friends* (1971) and the newscaster in *Abduction* (1974). For a while he drove one of the hansom cabs that are for hire near the Plaza Hotel in Manhattan. In 1984 he played an over-the-hill boxer in *Terrible Joe*

Allan J. Studley

Tierney photographed in the spring of 1984 at a show business communion breakfast that followed a mass said by the Cardinal of Los Angeles.

Moran, a TV play that starred James Cagney.

Perhaps the most dramatic of all his arrests was in 1956 when he was taken into custody after a barroom brawl. A photo of Tierney surrounded by police with blood streaming down his face broke nationwide bearing the caption "Face of a Cop Hater."

Lawrence Tierney's father, who died in 1964, had worked at New York City's Board of Water Supply as chief of security.

Mary Treen's comedic skills lightened scenes in many films made in the thirties and forties. On television she was a regular on Willy *and* The Joey Bishop Show.

Mary Treen

The screen comedienne was born in St. Louis, Missouri, on March 27, 1909. Mary Louise was still a baby when her father died. Her mother, who had acted under the name Helene Sullivan, married a physician. She was raised in Los Angeles and educated at the Westlake School for Girls and then in a convent school. She appeared in class plays at both.

Just as soon as she graduated from high school the teenager became one of the "Hollywood Beauties" who appeared in vaudeville houses up and down the West Coast under the auspices of Fanchon and Marco. She thought of herself as a dancer and, being 5 feet 9 inches tall, soon worked out a comedy routine in which Mary would kick one of her legs over the head of another girl.

At first they were called "The Short and the Tall of It," her partner being 5 feet 3 inches. Then they went out on a national vaudeville circuit billed as "Treen and Barnett, Two Unsophisticated Vassar Co-eds." The act broke up when Marjorie Barnett retired to marry Jackie Klein, one of Paul Whiteman's musicians.

When Mary Treen appeared in a comedy in Hollywood, talent scout Max Arnow saw her in the play and took her to Warner Brothers. She signed a contract with the studio in July 1934, and remained on the lot for three years. She has freelanced ever since.

Whether she played the plain girl friend of the heroine or the bemused nurse/secretary, etc., her character never varied much. She can think of only one time during her long career that she was asked to be anything other than the lanky, wisecracking lady. On a *Wagon Train* episode she portrayed a pioneer woman who bawled out the other wives for complaining. She enjoyed the experience but has never sought out others.

Mary supported Jimmy Cagney in *G-Men* (1935), Marion Davies in *Page Miss Glory* (1935), Ruby Keeler[8] in *Coleen* (1936), Loretta Young[8] in *Second Honeymoon* (1937), Ginger Rogers in *Kitty Foyle* (1941), Barbara Stanwyck in *The Great Man's Lady* (1942), Joan Crawford in *They All Kissed the Bride* (1942), Claudette Colbert in *So Proudly*

We Hail (1943), Gary Cooper in *Casanova Brown* (1944), Bob Hope in *They Got Me Covered* (1943), and Jane Wyman in *Let's Do It Again* (1953). She was featured in two films with Martin and Lewis, three with Jerry Lewis, and three in which Elvis Presley starred.

She says she has never had any difficulty with a star or a director. She did not, however, become close to any of those she worked with, including June Havoc and Joey Bishop, who used her as a regular on their TV series.

"I think those who've employed me have also enjoyed me," Ms. Treen explained recently. "I like people and always go out of my way to get along with everyone. And I don't seem to threaten anyone—even the glamour girls, and they're the toughest to please."

She never asked for a specific role, nor did she want larger ones. The part that pleased her most was in *I Love a Soldier* (1944) because it was written especially for her. She claims to have no favorite screen appearance, but when pressed will admit that "Sugar Hatfield" in the Ritz Brothers[8] starrer *Kentucky Moonshine* (1938) was the one most fun to play.

About stardom Mary Treen has said, "I'm very proud to be able to work with stars, but I've never wanted to be one. They are nearly always driven, ruthless people and, I suspect, terribly unhappy basically."

She was married rather late in life to a wholesale liquor dealer. They had no children. Soon after he died in 1965 she moved to a house a few hundred yards away from the beach in Balboa, California.

Her well-known voice and chipmunk cheeks are still frequently recognized. On her last trip to Europe she was waved through customs by Spanish officials who were her fans.

Richard Lamparski

Mary Treen shares her home in Balboa, California, with her former vaudeville partner.

"Treen," as her friends call her, still makes an occasional appearance on TV shows such as *The Dukes of Hazzard* and *Fall Guy*. But she rules out a running part because it would mean moving back to Los Angeles.

After Marjorie Barnett-Klein was widowed she moved in with her close friend. They are now partnered again as members of a group that gives shows at rehabilitation centers and senior citizen projects. Mary emcees the program, which has a Hawaiian-Polynesian theme, and is very successful in getting oldsters to join in the dancing.

She is a practicing Roman Catholic.

Mr. I. Magination featuring Paul Tripp as "the man with the magic reputation" was telecast live for three seasons beginning in 1949.

Paul Tripp

The man known to millions as television's "Mr. I. Magination" was born on the Lower East Side of New York City on February 20. His father, who was an immigrant from Austria, supported his family as a sweatshop worker after trying unsuccessfully to establish himself as an actor-singer in the Yiddish theater.

Paul taught himself English, since his parents did not master the language until he was a young man. He spent most of his childhood reading books. Mark Twain was then his favorite writer.

Although he has written, composed, acted, narrated, and directed he feels his two major artistic achievements were authoring the children's story *Tubby the Tuba* and creating the TV show *Mr. I. Magination.* Although both were done for children, "Tubby" and the television programs have been enjoyed by some adults as pure entertainment and used by many educators.

Since Paul wrote the kiddie classic in 1942 it has been translated into thirty languages. It has been recorded with the author narrating to the accompaniment of the Philadelphia Philharmonic under Eugene Ormandy's baton. There is also an LP with Carol Channing reading and the Cincinnati Pops Orchestra playing the music. Recently *Tubby the Tuba* became an animated video disc.

When Tripp went on the air with *Mr. I. Magination* in the spring of 1949 the CBS television studio in New York City was literally still under construction. Within a month what began as a local show was taken on by stations in three other cities. Before long it was a network program.

Tripp was the host and often wrote the playlets that were presented. At his suggestion children wrote in telling about things they would like to see happen and famous people they would like to be. Paul, aided by his wife, their son and daughter, and the show's regulars would then dramatize their viewers' wishes.

Wearing candy-striped overalls he would "engineer" the train that took the audience to "Inventorsville," "I Wish I Were a Town," or "Ambitionville." Child actors played figures from history and fiction.

An award from *Look* magazine in 1950 was

one of the many the series received. CBS telecast eighty of the thirty-minute programs on a sustaining basis before Nestlé's took over partial sponsorship. *Mr. I. Magination* had garnered so much prestige that after it was canceled in June 1951 it was brought back by popular demand. Gary H. Grossman, in his book *Saturday Morning TV,* stated: "Its return was probably the first instance of public outrage reversing network cancellations."

After *Mr. I. Magination* finally left the air in April 1952 Paul emceed *It's Magic,* a network show on which well-known magicians performed their tricks, and *Carousel.* The latter won an Emmy as the Best Local Children's and Teenage Program of 1956. During the sixties he hosted *Birthday House,* another series for children that was seen on New York City's NBC station. He was featured in the movie *The Christmas That Almost Wasn't.*

Tripp toured in the national company of *1776* as "Benjamin Franklin" and took over when James Whitmore left the one-man show, *Will Rogers, U.S.A.*

He has written other stories for children, including *Rabbi Santa Claus.* A recent effort is *Diary of a Leaf,* the account of three days in the life of a leaf during the Battle of Gettysburg.

Tripp is very pleased to be recognized as he and his wife stroll near their apartment in Greenwich Village. He thinks that the generation that he helped to shape, on the whole, turned out *extremely* well.

He is concerned that the current generation of youngsters is not having their imaginations nurtured. He believes, "Children who do not read books are being deprived of one of the most precious aspects of thinking. I'm not just worried about the boy or girl who might go into the arts. The imagination is the source of all

original thought. Without it there would *be* no sciences."

Of children he has said, "They are *people.* Smaller in size and with limited language and life experience. To communicate with them you must respect them. Someone is always saying to me, 'You must just *love* kids!' Why should that be unusual? I love my own two, but we also *like* them, which, it seems, is a rare thing in families."

Paul Tripp and his wife, Ruth Enders, live in an apartment just off Washington Square in New York City.

"The great other woman of the screen" is how the book Who's Who on the Screen *describes Helen Vinson.*

Helen Vinson

The soignée actress of stage and screen was born Helen Rulfs in Beaumont, Texas, on September 17, 1907. Her father, an oil company executive, moved his family to Mobile and to Birmingham, settling finally in Houston.

Helen longed to go on the stage. Even though she was not accepted into the drama club of the University of Texas she persisted.

Her debut came in a little theater production in Houston. By then she had married the scion of a wealthy Philadelphia family who was almost fifteen years her senior.

Her Broadway debut was a walk-on in *Los Angeles* (1927), but she returned to Philadelphia after its short run. Her husband's business was seriously affected by the stock market crash of 1929. Within a year they were divorced.

Helen Vinson played opposite Sydney Greenstreet in *Berlin* (1931) and Charles Laughton in *The Fatal Alibi* (1932) on Broadway and then went to Hollywood with a Warner Brothers contract.

"That studio seemed to me like an absolute sea of short men," recalls Helen, who is 5 feet 7½ inches tall. "When I played with Jimmy Cagney, who is a lovely man but a little man, he had to stand on a box. Paul Muni was small and didn't like it a bit that I wasn't smaller. You should have seen what I had to go through when George Raft and I danced in *Midnight Club!* Even the production chief, Zanuck, was little. He didn't know how to cast me. I got my release after a year and freelanced very happily from then on."

Properly used, Helen Vinson smacked of finishing school and the *Social Register*. She was often bitchy and couldn't really be trusted even when she played the heroine's best friend. Her very sophisticated speech was softened by a slight Southern drawl. Probably she is best remembered for her role in *In Name Only* (1939).

Helen is usually thought of as a character actress in films, but she also played leads. She and Charles Bickford were top-billed in *A Notorious Gentleman* (1935). In England, where she made *Transatlantic Tunnel* (1935), she was co-starred with Clive Brook[8] in *Love in Exile* (1935) and Conrad Veidt in *King of the Damned* (1935). She and Richard Cromwell headed the cast of *Enemy Agent* (1940). In *Are These Our Parents?* (1944) she was co-starred with Lyle Talbot (married and living in Studio City, California).

Some of her other pictures were: *I Am a Fugitive from a Chain Gang* (1932); *The Little Giant* (1933) with Edward G. Robinson; *The Captain Hates the Sea* (1934) with John Gilbert; Frank Capra's *Broadway Bill* (1934); *Private Worlds* (1935); *The Wedding Night* (1935) as Gary Cooper's wife; *Two Against the World* (1936) with Humphrey Bogart; *Torrid Zone* (1940), and *Nothing But the Truth* (1941). *The Thin Man Goes Home* (1945) was her last.

Her second marriage was to British tennis champion Fred Perry in 1935. Like her first, it lasted five years.

In 1931 Helen was the leading lady on Broadway to Philip Merivale in *Death Takes a Holiday.* In it she played a young woman who is forced to choose literally between life and death, the latter being the play's main character. In the mid-forties, when she fell in love with Donald Hardenbrook, she was asked by the socialite stockbroker to give up her career after they married.

"It was extremely difficult for me in the first years," she admitted in 1984. "Acting meant a lot to me and I missed it. But I'm very, very glad I married my husband because we had the most wonderful life together. I lost Don eight years ago and that left a much greater void than the theater had been."

Early in the marriage she found herself at a loss as to how to fill her days and enrolled at the New York School of Interior Design. She says her husband was very proud of the degree she got after two years, but regarded interior decorating almost as unsuitable an occupation for his wife as acting. Helen contented herself

Jon Virzi

Helen Vinson is a widow living in Chapel Hill, North Carolina, and on Nantucket Island, Massachusetts.

with doing over their Manhattan apartment and summer home on Cape Cod.

Ms. Vinson, who has no children or family, lives by herself in a cooperative apartment in a retirement community in Chapel Hill, North Carolina, during the cold months. In summer she and her black Persian cat move to her home on Nantucket, which was built in 1790.

As "Voluptua" Gloria Pall lolled about on a white bearskin rug while wearing a nightie or pajama top. Life magazine called her "too much for TV" and Playboy *devoted five pages to her.*

"Voluptua" Gloria Pall

The brief sensation of late-night television was born Gloria Paletz in Brooklyn, New York. Her birthday is July 15.

Gloria decided while still in her teens to become a model. Her eventual goal was Hollywood stardom.

In the vernacular of the locker room, Gloria was "built!"

Magazines like *Pix, Gala,* and *Man to Man* featured her, often on their covers, projecting what was then called the "come-hither" look.

Her first publicity came when she was named "Miss Flatbush of 1947."

"I could tell I was getting somewhere," she recalls. "So I invested in my future. I had a nose job and then I went to Hollywood."

Shortly afterward *Stars and Stripes,* the veterans' magazine, chose her as "Miss Cleavage."

She insists that the character of "Voluptua" was her creation and that she owns the name. Hunt Stromberg, Jr., the executive producer of the program that skyrocketed her to notoriety, remembers it thusly: "I was the program director of Channel 7 in Los Angeles then. Very few good films were available to us in the early fifties and what we had were mostly real dogs. I chose from them every one that could by any stretch of the imagination be considered romantic. We called the series *Love Movies,* but I wanted a hostess to introduce them. I advertised in the trades for a well-proportioned gal to set the right mood. I felt this big blonde with a Brooklyn accent and a pair that wouldn't quit had the right attitude. Actually, she was a great camp in the way she came on to the men watching, but she seemed quite serious about her act."

"Voluptua" and the *Love Movies* began in December 1954. The complaints from viewers began almost immediately.

"Welcome to my boudoir" was her opening line as the camera revealed an oversized round satin couch, a gold telephone, and the voluptuous "Voluptua." The beauty mark on her cheek was heart-shaped.

Gloria would urge those watching to "take off your coats and ties—anything you want to take off. Just be comfortable." She returned at breaks to introduce the commercials and make insinuating remarks. At the conclusion the camera would close in on "Voluptua" who bid goodnight to her viewers by kissing the lens.

Gloria turned down offers to strip on stage in Las Vegas, but when she appeared poolside at the Dunes Hotel she engaged in something of a contest with Jayne Mansfield. The scene, which was witnessed by author Shelly Davis, was described by him twenty-nine years later: "Who could show the most seemed to be the game. Now, to be too much for Vegas, even in the fifties, sounds impossible and yet they were because they were both asked to leave. Neither did, by the way."

Maila Nurmi, who created "Vampira"[8] on the same TV station, remembers her contemporary: "A lot of married women were outraged that Gloria could come on to their husbands right in their own homes—often in their bedrooms. They felt these men were being seduced by her and since they couldn't keep them from watching the wives would call the station or write."

"I didn't do anything wrong," says Gloria Pall today. "I'd just flirt with the guys and maybe slink a little."

Her "pan mail," as she calls it, contained phrases such as "unspeakably vulgar" and "brazen hussy." Church groups organized call-in campaigns to the station, objecting to the way she was dressed and the remarks she made. Their name for her was "Corruptua." One petition demanding her removal from the air bore more than six hundred signatures.

When the FCC advised the president of ABC that Channel 7's license was in jeopardy, Stromberg was told to take Gloria off the air.

"I was really on my way," said Gloria in 1984. "And then the goddamn bluenoses had me fired!"

Shortly after her show was canceled Gloria Pall disappeared from a beach in Santa Monica. Some of her belongings were discovered at the ocean's edge.

"She milked it beautifully—for all it was worth," remembers her former producer. "She

Stanton Z. La Vey

Gloria Pall, the former "Voluptua," shares a townhouse in West Los Angeles with her son, Jefferson. She is separated from Alan Kane, a local Ford dealer.

got a million dollars' worth of publicity but, I guess, wasn't able to do much with it."

Gloria appeared in *The French Line* (1954) and *Son of Sinbad* (1955) with Lili St. Cyr (single and living in the Larchmont area of Los Angeles), and then faded from the news.

The name Gloria Pall appears on signs that advertise her real estate firm throughout West Los Angeles and Beverly Hills, but she would rather be working on television.

"If someone would give me a chance I could make it today," she insists. "I have different shtick now. I think of myself as a Mae West type and I still wear a 42C bra. You might say I resemble *two* Marilyn Monroes."

Johnny Whitaker with Mary Anissa Jones, who played his twin on the popular TV series Family Affair. *She died of a drug overdose in August 1976, shortly after her eighteenth birthday.*

Johnny Whitaker

The child star was born in Van Nuys, California, on December 13, 1959. His father is a high school teacher.

When he was three years old he was singing a solo of "I Am a Child of God" in a church choir which his mother was directing. Someone in the congregation suggested to Mrs. Whitaker

that she look into the prospects of work for her son in television commercials. On his first audition he was hired for a national ad for OK Used Cars.

"It went very quickly and easily," he recalls. "Then I played the little kid in the custody case on a couple of courtroom dramas. Everyone was so nice to me that I was eight years old before I realized that I was also being paid for my services." He originated the part of "Scotty Baldwin," a character that still appears from time to time on *General Hospital.*

During the filming of *The Russians Are Coming, the Russians Are Coming* (1966) Johnny had a hotel room next to Brian Keith. The star enjoyed the boy's company both on and off the set. When he signed to play the role of an uncle to three orphaned relatives on the TV series *Family Affair* Keith asked the producers to consider Johnny for the part of his nephew "Jody." The role had been written for a ten-year-old boy, but Whitaker, who was not quite seven, bore a striking resemblance to Anissa Jones who was already cast as "Buffy," one of Keith's two nieces. It was decided to make them twins. Johnny says that he now sees the shows as "much too sugar-and-spice. We never lied or cheated. No children are as angelic as we were supposed to be." The programs ran from 1966 to 1971 on CBS-TV and are still popular in syndication. By the second season Whitaker's face was a familiar one to most Americans.

His image was thought to be perfect for the family audience. In 1972 he made *Snowball Express* and *Napoleon and Samantha* for Walt Disney and starred on the Hallmark Hall of Fame TV special, *The Littlest Angel.* He was cast in the title role of the musical *Tom Sawyer* (1973) and began making national tours for the "Tom Sawyer" line of boys' clothing. Eventually, the same firm put out a "Johnny Whitaker" line as well. He considers this period the only regrettable result of a childhood spent in show business. His parents have eight children of their own and two foster sons. "Mom was with me whenever I traveled, which was a lot," he says. "The other kids resented that very much."

After Johnny was signed to head the cast of *Sigmund and the Sea Monster* he suggested Scott Kolden as the second lead. The two boys had worked together in Disney's two-part TV movie, *The Mystery in Dracula's Castle.* Their children's series lasted for three seasons on NBC-TV where it was telecast on Saturday mornings beginning in 1973.

About this time he insisted that his first name be spelled "Johnny." Until then he had been billed as "Johnnie Whitaker."

When he wasn't acting he played fairs along with two of his sisters and one brother in a variety act called *The Johnny Whitaker Show.* Frequently they performed also at "firesides," church-sponsored get-togethers for young Mormons. In August 1976, at the conclusion of one of these evenings, someone asked Johnny about the report of Anissa Jones's death. "I dismissed the story as an ugly rumor," recalls Whitaker. "But something within me sensed that it was true." The next morning he heard Rona Barrett on *Good Morning, America* give the details of the eighteen-year-old actresses's death by drug overdose.

Recently Whitaker talked about Anissa Jones: "Although we played twins we were poles apart as human beings. It didn't keep us from getting along well, but we were being raised in very different homes. I felt terrible about her death, but I wasn't all that much surprised."

Johnny presented himself to the missionary branch of the Mormon Church and was sent to Portugal, where he spent "the two greatest years of my life" attempting to win converts.

He is now a theater and cinematic arts major at Brigham Young University in Utah. He speaks seven languages and is interested in international politics.

He says he turned down two feature films because the scripts were "immoral." He would like to play Biblical characters such as "David." *Hamlet* is another of his goals.

He is still recognized frequently for his role on *Family Affair.* Usually, fans don't remember his name and call him "Buffy."

"I realize that my views on drugs, alcohol, and premarital sex seem strange to many people, especially to young people," he admitted during a recent interview. "But I have the security of knowing that what I am doing is right and that at the end of my life I will have something to look forward to."

Johnny Whitaker describes himself as a "serious Mormon."

John Whitaker, as he is now called, married a theatrical agent in June 1984.

Thelma White as "Mae Coleman" in Reefer Madness, *which has been released also under such titles as* Tell Your Children *and* The Burning Question. *The film purports to expose the dangerous effects of marijuana. It was directed by Louis Gasnier, who had directed some of the famous Pearl White serials. Also in its cast was the silent star Mary MacLaren and Dave O'Brien, who later became well known for his appearances in* Pete Smith Specialties.

Thelma White

The actress slated for stardom as "Blonde Poison" was born Thelma Wolpa in Lincoln, Nebraska, on December 4, 1910. Her parents were with the A. C. Wortham Carnivals and shortly after their daughter was born she became "Baby Dimples," one of the attractions.

By the mid-twenties Thelma had become a name on Broadway. After being featured by Earl Carroll in his *Vanities* of 1926 the impresario brought her back for the 1930 edition. In 1932 she was in *Tell Her the Truth* with Wil-

liam Frawley and Margaret Dumont and two years later she and Milton Berle did *Saluta* together.

Thelma White made her first motion picture in 1929, *A Night in a Dormitory.* It was a two-reeler and in it with her was Ginger Rogers.

When Thelma signed with RKO in the early thirties she was promised the title role in a melodrama to be called *Blonde Poison.* And there was going to be a big publicity buildup for her as the fair-haired wicked woman. But after much script trouble and change of studio administration she was, instead, used as support for Wheeler and Woolsey in *Hips, Hips Hooray* (1934) and on loan-out.

After two years she left the studio and freelanced thereafter in such B pictures as *Wanted by the Police* (1938), *Spy Train* (1943) with Richard Travis, and *Bowery Champs* (1944).

She returned to Broadway in *Right This Way* (1938) but the musical that introduced the song "I'll Be Seeing You" was not a hit.

Illnesses contracted on extensive tours with the USO in World War II lingered and were complicated by polio. When she completed *Mary Lou* (1948) with Frankie Carle (married and living in Mesa, Arizona), Thelma was hospitalized. She spent the next eight years in bed and has been a semi-invalid ever since.

By the time she was saluted on *This Is Your Life* in May 1957, she had become an agent. One of those who came on the show to thank Thelma for all she had done for his career was Robert Blake. She is in touch with another former client, Dolores Hart, who is now Mother Dolores, the head of a convent of cloistered nuns in Bethlehem, Connecticut.

Thelma appeared in some shorts with Edgar Kennedy and a few with Leon Erroll. She made *The Moon's Our Home* (1936) with Margaret Sullavan and Henry Fonda and *Song of the Open Road* (1944), but the picture that buffs know her for is *Reefer Madness* (1935).

She played "Mae Coleman," a hard-bitten blonde whose apartment is the scene of the marijuana parties that result in her arrest and the downfall of all who smoked the "devil's weed." The script of the exploitation feature allowed her character one glimmer of good. "Mae" is obviously uncomfortable about including teenagers in the evenings of reefer smoking at her place. Her retribution is suicide by jumping out of a window.

Howard W. Hays

Thelma White Productions produces fillers for cable TV channels. She is also a personal manager of actors.

In 1984 Thelma and Tony Millard, who was part of the Olsen and Johnson company for many years, celebrated their twenty-seventh wedding anniversary. They live in Encino with their Chihuahua.

It is only in recent years that Thelma White has become aware that *Reefer Madness* has found a new audience on college campuses and at midnight screenings in movie houses. She was both surprised and pleased not long ago when she made a personal appearance with the picture and received an ovation from a large crowd made up mostly of people who were born long after the film was made in 1935.

She was completely naïve about marijuana when she played "Mae Coleman" and was as serious about it as any other role. Today she calls it "a real camp!"

Before becoming one of **The Brady Bunch** *Barry Williams played Christopher Jones as a boy in* **Wild in the Streets** *(1968).*

Barry Williams

The teen favorite of the early seventies was born Barry Blenkhorn on September 30, in Santa Monica, California. His father owned a chain of loan offices.

When he was three years old Barry's playmate and neighbor was the daughter of Peter Graves, who was then appearing in *Fury.* He made up his mind then that he wanted to be an actor and told his parents so, but received no encouragement.

Four years later he tried again to get them to assist him in getting started in show business, but was told to "wait awhile." At age eleven he delivered what amounted to an ultimatum. They relented and took him to an agent.

Almost immediately he began to do television commercials. Shortly after his twelfth birthday Barry got a part, his first, on the TV show *Run for Your Life.* Then he appeared on *Dragnet, That Girl,* and *Mission Impossible.* Often he played New York City street kids, but on *Marcus Welby, M.D.* he gave a very effective performance as a boy stricken with leukemia. On *It Takes a Thief* he played a boy genius and on *Gomer Pyle* he was an autograph hound. It was that job that led to his audition for *The Brady Bunch.*

John Rich, who had directed him on *Gomer Pyle,* had been signed to do the pilot for *The Brady Bunch* and suggested Barry to the producers. At that point his goal in life was to have a running part on a TV series. On his fourteenth birthday the first script was hand-delivered to his home.

The situation comedy about the everyday happenings in a middle-class home ran from 1969 to 1974 on ABC-TV and is still popular in syndication.

On it Barry played "Greg," the oldest of the three "Brady" boys, and quickly became the cast member who drew the most fan mail. Although there were five other kids on the program as well as Williams, the fan magazines that catered to teens gave him the most attention.

In 1977 Barry and most of the original cast members were reassembled for *The Brady Bunch Hour,* a comedy-variety that showcased their musical talents. It only lasted a few months.

Barry Williams has said that he chose the acting profession because he felt it was the one that would most quickly get him what he wanted in life: "Money, fame, fast cars, and beautiful girls."

Although he met many pretty girls while making *The Brady Bunch* and had thousands more screaming for him at personal appearances, he soon realized that he was "basically monogamous." Barry took out a few fans, but found that they only wanted to date him to impress their girl friends. Maureen McCormick, another "Brady," and he were seen together for a while and enjoyed each other's company but they were never seriously involved.

Williams has worked almost continually, although much of his activity has been on the stage. He took his solo concert act to the Steel Pier in Atlantic City and Knott's Berry Farm and has starred in productions of *Oklahoma!, West Side Story,* and *Grease.* He did *Pippin* for seven months on the road and then played it on Broadway.

In early 1984 he played a very unlikable character on *General Hospital,* but on the whole he has found that "casting people for TV and films would much prefer it if I could be the same age and size as 'Greg' still."

The one part he wanted above all others was in *The Reivers* and not getting it was very difficult for him.

At present money is being raised to star him in a feature in which he will play the mass murderer—rapist Ted Bundy.

Casey Kasem and Lyle Waggoner are his close friends. His ambition is to be known as an "actor who sings" and to work in movie musicals.

Barry's house in Malibu is on the Pacific Ocean. He owns a boat and does lots of swimming and surfing.

He attributes the changes of late in his attitudes toward his career to the human potential movement. Williams spends several weekends every year at the Esalen Institute.

"I still enjoy acting and singing as much as I ever did," he said recently. "But I'm not quite sure how I feel about the business. I considered law for a while and medicine is still a possibility. I don't feel any less committed to acting, but I'm much less compulsive about it."

Richard Lamparski

Barry Williams with "Bubba," one of the pair of male Himalayan cats that share his house in Malibu.

Bill Williams made dozens of movies before starring in three TV series.

Bill Williams

The star of feature films and TV was born in Brooklyn, New York, on May 15, 1921. His father died when he was four years old. His German-born mother worked as a waitress to support them. "They were very hard times," Bill recalls. "She'd sleep on a narrow cot and I, being small, would spend the night in the bathtub." Eventually she boarded her son out with a series of Jewish families who raised him. At seventeen he was an orphan.

Bill was an all-round athlete from an early

age and held several national junior titles for 220- and 400-yard events. He was planning to enter the competition for the Olympics when he was noticed one day in the pool by a man who produced vaudeville acts. Still in his teens, Bill became part of an adagio team that went to London's Palladium for a year's engagement.

Williams toured in vaudeville and sang baritone with the St. Louis Opera before he went to Hollywood for a fifteen-month stay at Earl Carroll's theater. It was during this period that he became interested in an acting career. After bit parts in *Murder in the Blue Room* (1944) and *Thirty Seconds Over Tokyo* (1944), he got a break with a good part in *Those Endearing Young Charms* (1945). It was about this time that his marriage ended in divorce. "We never got along," he said recently. "She had no interest in anything I did."

Bill Williams went under contract to RKO at a beginning salary of $100 a week. He was staying with the Weir Brothers, a top dancing act of the day, and studying navigation in hopes of becoming a pilot. "I wasn't sure how serious the studio was about me," he says. "And I always wanted to fly." He was drafted but after eighty-nine days he was released because of a bad sacroiliac.

When the actor returned to his home lot he was publicized as RKO's answer to Van Johnson, a title that still amuses him. "Van was a great help to me," he recalls. "He explained how wholesome and young-guy-next-door we were supposed to be. I never saw it as funny until he pointed it out."

Bill was not, however, always cast as the male love interest or hero. He alternated between the good guy and the villain, playing the latter in more than thirty features.

Among his screen credits are: *The Stratton Story* (1949); *Fighting Man of the Plains* (1949) with Randolph Scott;[8] *A Dangerous Profession* (1949) with the late George Raft;[8]

Blue Grass of Kentucky (1950), *The Cariboo Trail* (1950); *California Passage* (1950) with Adele Mara (married to producer Roy Huggins and living in the Mandeville Canyon area of Los Angeles); *The Great Missouri Raid* (1951); *Son of Paleface* (1952); *Apache Ambush* (1955) with the late Tex Ritter; *Legion of the Doomed* (1959); *Hell to Eternity* (1960); and *Tickle Me* (1965) with Elvis Presley.

For almost four of the years he spent at RKO he was completely idle. Even though he drew a salary during that time that went as high as $1,200 a week he was anxious to work and took any role offered to him. One that he would have liked to play was the lead in *Till the End of Time* (1946). Guy Madison got the part and Williams was cast as his handicapped friend.

Bill Williams and Barbara Hale were both on the RKO lot for over nine months before they began dating. In 1946 they made the thriller *Deadline at Dawn* together and were married on June 22.

He frequently hosted several musical variety shows on television beginning as early as 1949. He co-starred with Betty White in *A Date with the Angels,* a domestic comedy that lasted from May 1957 to late January 1958. At the time he and Barbara were living on their houseboat whenever possible. The producers of *Sea Hunt* offered Bill the series but he turned it down, thinking that underwater adventure would not draw an audience on national TV. After Lloyd Bridges had a hit with the show Williams agreed to do *Assignment Underwater.* The thirty-nine half-hour programs featured him and Diane Mountford as a father-daughter sea-diving team in 1960.

When he is recognized, which is frequently, it is usually for his portrayal of the title role in *The Adventures of Kit Carson.* The series of 104 episodes about the frontier scout were filmed in 1951 and are still in syndication.

Iku Downey

Bill Williams photographed at Horace Heidt's apartment complex in Van Nuys, California, where he and his wife, Barbara Hale, live part of the time.

Bill Williams and his wife keep an apartment in Horace Heidt's residential complex in Van Nuys and own a mobile home in Palm Desert Greens. Bill spends most of his time maintaining their extensive rental holdings. He says the couple agreed when they were married to invest one-third of all their earnings in real estate. At one point they owned forty-two commercial and seven housing units. "I love to build and repair things," he says. "It's good to keep busy."

Their oldest daughter is a speech therapist. Another is married and the mother of two children. Bill says he is retired from acting, explaining that "the fun of the picture business ended for me a long time ago." He has, however, a keen interest and great pride in the career of his only son, who has starred in several movies and had his own TV series. What especially pleases his father is that Bill, Jr., made it on his own with no help from either parent and while using his father's real name, William Katt.

Cara Williams was the co-star of Pete and Gladys, *a sitcom that played on CBS-TV from 1960 to 1962. Harry Morgan had earlier played* "Pete" *on* December Bride, *but his wife* "Gladys," *to whom he constantly referred, never appeared.*

Cara Williams

The actress-comedienne was born Bernice Kamiat on June 29, in Brooklyn. Her parents were divorced when she was quite young. Her mother ran a beauty parlor next to a theater where Cara as a little girl spent hours watching movies.

Mrs. Kamiat, whom Cara has described as "the definitive stage mother," took her green-eyed, red-haired daughter to Hollywood. Her first job was doing her vocal impressions of movie stars which were dubbed in a "Porky Pig" cartoon. Shortly after that a Twentieth Century-Fox executive saw her in a little theater and signed her to a stock contract. At the time the studio's publicity department gave her year of birth as 1925. She says she was born in 1933.

As a starlet she did small parts in such films as *Happy Land* (1943) with Ann Rutherford,[8] *Something for the Boys* (1944), *The Spider* (1946), and *Boomerang* (1947).

She left Fox after five years and has since made: *The Saxon Charm* (1948); *Knock on Any Door* (1949); *The Girl Next Door* (1953); *Meet Me in Las Vegas* (1956); *The Helen Morgan Story* (1957); *Never Steal Anything Small* (1958), and *The Man from the Diners Club* (1963).

Her comedic skills were used to good advantage in *The Great Diamond Robbery* (1953) with Red Skelton, but by then she was Mrs. John Drew Barrymore. In 1952, when she married him, he appeared to be on the verge of stardom.

"I put John and his career before everything else," she has said. "I wanted *him* to be the star, but his insane jealousy destroyed our relationship. He wasn't even drinking heavily during the six years we were together. Cold sober he managed to create the most awful scenes over and over."

In 1958, after what one newspaper described as a "street brawl" with her husband, Barrymore was arrested. Cara held her own in the fracas, just as she had in 1948 when she and a starlet exchanged blows at Ciro's until they were separated by her friend Lila Leeds (single and living in Los Angeles).

Cara played in the national company of *Born Yesterday* and was tested for the role in the screen version that went to Judy Holliday.

Just when her marriage to Barrymore was breaking up Stanley Kramer cast her in *The Defiant Ones* (1958), which brought her an Academy Award nomination as Best Supporting Actress. Asked how she felt at the time she replied, "Just being considered for an Oscar was a great thrill, but I didn't even get a call from John to congratulate me. I don't know what I'd have said if I'd won because my mind was on my marriage, which I knew was over, and our little boy whom I would have to raise by myself."

Cara returned to Hollywood and was immediately cast in the lead of the TV series *Pete and Gladys*. She had not wanted to do television, believing it to be a step down professionally. However, her first salary check saved her home from foreclosure. Two years after it left the air she starred on *The Cara Williams Show* during the 1964–65 season.

Cara played "Mae" on *Rhoda* during the 1974–75 season and has been in the films *The White Buffalo* (1977) and *One Man Jury* (1978). Her almost total absence from the screen since then is because she feels she is thirty pounds overweight at 150.

She has a daughter by her present husband, Beverly Hills realtor Asher Dann. Cara has bought and sold antiques, designed clothing, and jewelry. Her skill as an interior designer has been featured in two dozen magazine and newspaper articles. Her real passion, however, is gambling, especially high stakes poker. In 1984 she was among the finalists in a national tournament.

"I never developed an ambition," she said recently. "My mother had enough for both of us. I've turned down dramatic roles because I want to do things that make people laugh, not cry. There's enough to cry about."

She was compared to Lucille Ball when she played "Gladys" and on the *Cara Williams Show*. Even Lucy complimented her comic

Cara Williams and her husband, Beverly Hills realtor Asher Dann.

timing. But on the set of both series she was considered the "heavy."

Cara's explanation: "I complained constantly about scripts that made no sense and a leading man who had no feeling for comedy. Was I wrong? *Pete and Gladys* began with a large following who left us as the writing worsened. And I haven't seen or heard of Frank Aletter since the *Cara Williams Show* went off the air. Any woman who dares to make waves in this business is disliked. Ask Barbra Streisand."

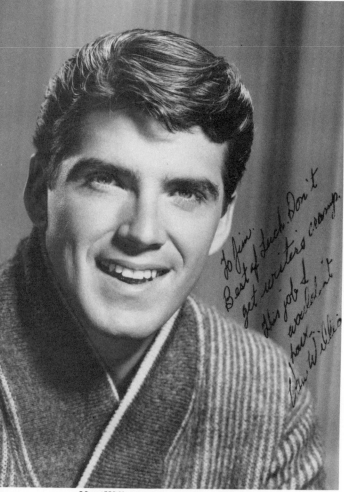

Van Williams was under contract for five years in the sixties to Warner Brothers.

Van Williams

Television's "Green Hornet" was born on a ranch on the outskirts of Fort Worth, Texas, on February 27, 1934. His full name is Van Zandt Jarvis Williams.

Williams won a football scholarship to Texas Christian University, marrying a co-ed in his freshman year. Two years later his wife had twin girls. Shortly afterward Van got a divorce and dropped out of school.

By the mid-fifties he had established a salvage business and skin-diving school in Hawaii. Mike Todd and his press agent Bill Doll became acquainted with him and felt he had strong potential as a leading man in movies. Before taking their advice and offer for help he went back to school for a degree in business administration. Then he headed for Hollywood.

Williams had absolutely no acting experience when he arrived in the film capital in 1958. "I'd never even been in a high school play," he admits. Yet within a few weeks he met an agent at a party who took him the next day to the producers of *General Electric Theater.* He made his debut opposite Ronald Reagan and was subsequently pacted. Four months later his contract was sold to Warner Brothers.

At the Burbank studio Van was cast as "Ken Madison," one of the members of a New Orleans private detective agency on *Bourbon Street Beat.* Although he played the junior partner in the firm, it was Williams who received most of the attention from the press as a "new face." When the series was canceled after a year on the ABC network he went right into *Surfside Six.* Again he played "Ken Madison," who now did his sleuthing in Miami Beach. Like *Bourbon Street Beat,* the sixty-minute shows were slotted on Mondays at 8:30 P.M. *Surfside Six* ran for two seasons and was popular for many years in syndication.

Next Williams was cast as "Pat Burns," the loyal young assistant and private pilot to Walter Brennan, who played the title role in *The Ty-*

coon. The half-hour shows played on ABC from September 1964 to the fall of 1965.

Van Williams is probably best remembered for his portrayal of "Britt Reid," the crusading editor and publisher who fights crime under the guise of "The Green Hornet." The series lasted only for the 1966–67 season but was edited and released as a feature in 1975 after the death of Bruce Lee, who played "Reid's" faithful manservant "Kato."

Van's feature film appearances were in *Tall Story* (1960) and the Joan Crawford starrer *The Caretakers* (1963). He would have been cast in a prominent role in a major feature had the film's star, Glenn Ford, not objected.

Williams began to lose what little interest he had in acting after *The Green Hornet.* The last part he played was a police lieutenant on one of James Garner's TV shows in late 1979. "About the only thing I enjoyed about the business was going on location," Van admitted recently. "I don't like crowds and being made a fuss over just embarrasses me. I never got used to the lack of privacy and the more successful you become the less you have. I'm a very private person."

Even when he was under contract he kept a close watch on the investments he was making. In 1966 he told an interviewer, "I've got the first dollar I ever made." Since then he has acquired a ranch in Texas and several businesses. The one he personally runs in Santa Monica sells and rents communications units and firearms to law enforcement agencies. He is a deputized captain with the Los Angeles County Sheriff's office.

Williams has three daughters by his second wife, whom he married in 1959. They live in Pacific Palisades. He is a grandfather by one of his twins.

Van Williams feels he is far removed from show business and has not kept in touch with anyone except his co-star on *Surfside Six,* Troy Donahue. Although he does not rule out a comeback, he turned down the offer of a running part on *Falcon Crest.* "It was a good role," said Van recently, "but when I realized that I couldn't do it and run my business, too, I opted to stay where I am. It didn't require any soul-searching. I happen to like where I am."

Ron Alexander

Van Williams owns and operates a firm that supplies communications equipment and firearms to law enforcement agencies.

Judith Wood originated the role in **Dinner at Eight** *(1932) on Broadway that was played in the motion picture by Jean Harlow. Her lover at the time was Franchot Tone.*

Judith Wood

The actress whose chance at movie stardom was ruined by a car crash was born Helen Johnson on August 1, 1906, in New York City. Her father was Merle Johnson, a noted commercial artist of the day. Helen frequently accompanied him when he covered the theatrical events he was assigned to illustrate for newspapers, and her ambition then was to become a "great artist."

Helen spent two years in Paris, where she studied under André L'Hote, then a major figure in the art world. But when she returned to the United States and presented her work to a well-known dealer she was told that it had "cleverness and personality" but nothing more.

Her first affair brought about what all her early exposure to the theater failed to do. She decided to act shortly after she and Franchot Tone became lovers. He eventually proposed, but by then she had made an auspicious Broadway debut in *Dinner at Eight* (1932). Fifty years later she commented, "I was what we'd now call a liberated woman. Of course, they called it something else, much less polite, in those days."

She bore a resemblance to Ann Harding, who was then quarreling with her studio. Helen was sent for and went to Hollywood by air, a rare occurrence at that time. Her pilot was Jimmy Doolittle.

Under contract first to M-G-M and then to Paramount, Helen Johnson was seen in such early talkies as *Soldiers and Women* (1930), *Sin Takes a Holiday* (1930), and *The Vice Squad* (1931).

David O. Selznick took a personal interest in her career and, after changing her hair and her eyebrows, Paramount began to give her a publicity buildup. At her own request her name was changed. As Judith Wood she made *Girls About Town* (1931) and *The Road to Reno* (1931).

Shortly after she played a woman whose face is disfigured in an automobile wreck in *The Divorcée* (1930), she was picked as a Wampus Baby Star of 1931, a big boost in her professional standing. But then she was thrown from her car during a collision and suffered a severely broken nose. After the many months it took her to recuperate the impetus of her career had been lost.

Franchot Tone, who had come to Hollywood, wanted to resume their relationship, but she declined, only to have second thoughts when he almost immediately became involved with Joan Crawford.

Darryl F. Zanuck signed her for his newly formed Twentieth Century Productions, put her in *Looking for Trouble* (1934), loaned her out for *Crime Doctor* (1934), and then failed to pick up her option.

"For Franchot it was too late," she once said. "And for Zanuck it was too early. By the time he had merged with Fox and could have used me I was in England making a film opposite the orchestra leader Harry Roy."

In London she lived with a diplomat who was the son of R. C. Wren, author of *Beau Geste*. They married just before he was transferred to the British Embassy in Tokyo.

"I went with him thinking that my acting career was over and glad of it," Judith recalls. "But I found that my whole life was now acting because he was there to do espionage and I was to help him."

In 1940 they left Japan just as they were about to be arrested by the secret police.

Her marriage and World War II ended about the same time. Judith did some acting on radio in New York City. She had been seriously interested in directing ever since she had made *Working Girls* (1931) under Dorothy Arzner's guidance. But, she found, "There was no breaking through the barrier against women."

In 1950 she returned to Hollywood, where she still lives and works as a costume designer for "everything from operas to porno films."

Now that most of the famous men who were her lovers are deceased she is considering writing her memoirs.

Referring recently to Robert Montgomery and William Powell, she said, "Small specks on an ocean of men. You might call them my real career—certainly wasn't a sideline. I never played this part on the screen, but I was a strong, intelligent woman searching for a man to look up to. My entire life has been a near-miss!"

Mathew Tombers

Judith Wood shares her house in Hollywood with a Siamese cat.

Donald Woods was a leading man in many B pictures, but also played supporting roles in important films, such as A Tale of Two Cities *(1935),* Anthony Adverse *(1936), and* Watch on the Rhine *(1943).*

Donald Woods

The durable actor was born Ralph Zink in Brandon, Manitoba, Canada. His birth date was December 2, 1904. His family moved to California when he was three years old.

He first aspired to write but, after playing a part he had written in a play presented at Burbank High School, he turned to acting. At the University of California at Berkeley Donald played football and majored in drama, but left before graduating to marry the daughter of a titled German family.

He went from younger leading man of a Long Beach stock company to the highly regarded Elitch Theater Company in Denver. By the time he arrived in Hollywood in 1934 he had made his Broadway debut and played more than two hundred different parts on the stage.

Warner Brothers believed his experience, good looks, and no-nonsense approach to acting could be turned into screen stardom. After he was pacted, the studio introduced him to moviegoers in a special trailer heralding their new star and his first film, *As the Earth Turns* (1934) with Jean Muir.

Since then Donald Woods has made more than sixty motion pictures. He was especially effective as the suave sleuth in such low-budget crime films as *The Florentine Dagger* (1935) and *The Black Doll* (1938). Don Miller felt that in *The Case of the Stuttering Bishop* (1937) he made "the most plausible Perry Mason until Raymond Burr made the character his own."

He played opposite Nan Grey (married to Frankie Laine and living in San Diego) on *Those We Love,* a popular radio drama and for three seasons hosted a weekly musical program sponsored by the Woolworth chain.

Some of his other screen roles were in: *Frisco Kid* (1935); *The Story of Louis Pasteur* (1936); *I Was a Prisoner on Devil's Island* (1941); *The Gay Sisters* (1942); *The Bridge of San Luis Rey* (1944); *Night and Day* (1946); *Roughly Speaking* (1945); *Kissin' Cousins* (1964), and *Dimension 5* (1965). He was also in two of the "Mexican Spitfire" films and starred in the serial, *Sky Raiders* (1941).

Woods headed the cast of many of the better early television dramatizations, such as *Robert Montgomery Presents, Philco Playhouse,* and *Armstrong Theater.* Probably the highlight of his TV career was his appearance opposite Julie Harris in *Wind from the South* on the *U.S. Steel Hour*. He hosted the *Damon Runyon Theater* on CBS-TV in the mid-fifties and starred in his own series, *Craig Kennedy, Criminologist*. Later he was a regular on *Tammy*.

Donald was on Broadway in *Quiet, Please!* (1940) and in Dore Schary's *One by One* (1964). In 1962 he did Ibsen's *Rosmersholm* off-Broadway. He has co-starred on and off-Broadway and around the country with Sylvia Sidney, Shirley Booth (living in Chatham, Massachusetts), Martha Scott, and Myrna Loy. The production of *Two for the Seesaw* that starred Woods and Madlyn Rhue ran for six months in Los Angeles in 1960.

Donald Woods never fulfilled the predictions made at the time of his screen debut, but his career has lasted much longer than those of most stars. He has also had the satisfaction of acting in all media, something almost impossible for someone who had achieved stardom. His face is known to any TV viewers who have been exposed to movies of the thirties and forties. He is still considered a marquee name to audiences of the plays he appears in several times a year. He plays parts on television occasionally, the latest being an irascible old man on *Mississippi* in 1984.

Approximately half of his annual income comes from acting. The rest comes from commissions on the real estate he sells in Palm Springs. The office he works from was founded by the late Eadie Adams who had been Kay Kyser's[8] band vocalist.

Donald's wife died in 1972. Four years later during a visit to London he married her best friend. Many paintings by his son Conrad hang on the walls of their Palm Springs home. He also has a daughter and five grandchildren. He gardens and plays what he calls "old man's tennis" every day.

The only role he really wanted that eluded him was in *Knute Rockne—All American* and was played by Ronald Reagan. Asked in 1984 what he thought might have happened had he got the part Donald Woods replied, "I don't know, but it's pretty certain I wouldn't be President today."

James Cury

The character actor—realtor in the den of his Palm Springs home.

Alan Young won the Best Actor Emmy in 1950 for performances on his own CBS-TV show. The same year the Alan Young Show *was chosen by the Academy of Television Arts as the Best Variety Show.*

Alan Young

The TV and movie star was born Angus Young in England on the Tyne River near the border of Scotland. His birth date was November 19, 1919. He was still a child when his parents emigrated to Vancouver, British Columbia.

Alan made his debut as a monologist at a function of the Caledonian Society when he was twelve years old. The next year he started appearing around Vancouver in vaudeville houses and private clubs where the teenager did impersonations of some of the favorite stars of the day.

He began working on local radio programs and within a few years was writing his own act as well as material for other personalities. At seventeen he was made a featured performer on *Stage Party* which within three months became the *Alan Young Show.* The Canadian Broadcasting Company brought him to Toronto to do his shows on network radio.

An American agent who heard him on the air sold Alan to Bristol Myers for his own program which was a summer replacement for Eddie Cantor. From that he was signed to do his comedy on the *Texaco Star Theater* on radio.

Twentieth Century-Fox brought him to Hollywood and cast him in *Margie* (1946), *Chicken Every Sunday* (1949), and *Mr. Belvedere Goes to College* (1949). While he obviously had comedic skills and a distinct personality, he was not the standard hero type and just missed being really good-looking.

It was in television that he clicked. The *Alan Young Show* on CBS was done live and had a pace that well suited the brief skits he did each week. *TV Guide* did a cover story on him in which he was hailed as the "Charlie Chaplin of Television." The program ran for three seasons and the network would have carried it for a fourth, but Alan declined.

His hayseed quality made him appear right for the title role of *Aaron Slick from Pumkin Crick* (1952), but the picture was a financial disaster and is now considered something of a cult film since its inclusion on several lists of the worst movies ever made. He tried again with *Androcles and the Lion* (1953). Although it is one of his two favorites among his screen credits, it, too, was a box-office flop.

"You only got two chances in those days," he said recently. "If they thought you had something they'd try twice, but two strikes and you're out!"

The Time Machine (1960) is his other favorite film role. He also appeared in *Gentlemen Marry Brunettes* (1955), *Tom Thumb* (1958), and his voice was used in *Mickey's Christmas Carol* (1983).

He went to England, where he made twenty-six variety shows for Granada Television. The day he returned from London he was approached to appear on *Mr. Ed.* The idea of playing straight man to a talking horse did not immediately appeal to him, but when he could find no better property and was given a part-ownership in the series he changed his mind. The half-hour shows ran from 1961 to 1965 and are still playing in syndication around the world. Alan played "Wilbur Post," an architect who lived in the country and had a horse named "Mr. Ed" that could speak, but refused to do so to anyone but its owner. When he is recognized today it is usually for that show.

After *Mr. Ed* ceased production Young made his Broadway bow in *The Girl in the Freudian Slip* (1967). When it closed after two performances he announced that he was leaving show business and would devote the rest of his life to Christian Science.

"I had come to the church when I was fifteen years old and was healed of asthma and anemia," he explains. "I had been blessed with professional fulfillment and a wonderful family. I wanted to help others to find Truth."

The Youngs moved to Boston, where he set up a broadcasting division for the Mother Church. He lectured throughout North America and spent three years as a practitioner, but eventually he became disillusioned with what he calls "administrology" and, after he failed to get the hierarchy to respond to criticism, returned to performing.

Alan dubs many cartoons. His voice is heard regularly on *Fat Cat, Mr. T.,* and *The Smurfs.*

He says that he wants to continue in comedy and has written for six TV sitcoms. He has also made Bible stories into playlets that are performed for children at Sunday schools.

The Youngs have four grandchildren, a large black cat, and a small white poodle.

He has played in several productions of *The Best Little Whorehouse in Texas,* a druggist on the 1976 series *Gibbsville,* and drinks coffee, but maintains that he is still a Christian Scientist, "but in my own way." Two of his four children are in the acting profession, but none belongs to the church.

Alan is an officer of AWAG, a dissident group of Screen Actors Guild members. He works closely in the organization with Charlton Heston.

When he was under contract to Fox, Alan Young was up for the part of the sadist in *Kiss of Death.* It went to Richard Widmark and launched his screen career.

Asked about the role recently Alan said, "I don't believe in regrets or mistakes or tragedies. It was not part of the Divine Plan and I accept that completely."

Howard W. Hays

Alan Young and his wife divide their time between a condominium in Encino and a beach house in Costa Mesa, California.

Victor Sen Yung had one of his best parts in the Bette Davis starrer, The Letter *(1940), as the scheming solicitor's clerk.*

Victor Sen Yung

The character actor best known for his appearances on *Bonanza* and in the "Charlie Chan" features was born in San Francisco on October 18, 1915. His parents had emigrated from China late in the nineteenth century. Shortly after his mother died in the flu epidemic of 1919 his father placed Victor and his sister in a shelter for children and returned to his homeland.

In the mid-twenties Victor's father returned from China and his children went back to live with him and his new wife. It was then that Victor first learned to speak Chinese.

He went to work as a houseboy when he was eleven years old and eventually saved enough money to enter the University of California at Berkeley. Working his way through, he graduated in the mid-thirties with a degree in economics.

Victor first acted in Hollywood as an extra. He played one of the peasants who kill the locusts in *The Good Earth* (1937), but worked also as a salesman for a chemical firm. When he got his real start in pictures he was trying to interest technicians at Fox studios in a flame-proofing compound. Someone suggested that he try out for the role of one of the sons of "Charlie Chan."

The series was undergoing a major change in cast upon the death of Warner Oland, who had played the Chinese detective almost from the beginning. When Sidney Toler took over the part he approved of Victor being hired and coached him as "Lee Chan" for *Charlie Chan in Honolulu* (1938). Although his character was to change to "Jimmy" and, eventually, to "Tommy Chan" he acted as one of the sons in seventeen subsequent features.

Yung worked steadily from then on except for the years he spent as a captain in the U.S. Air Force Intelligence during World War II. Until the early forties he was billed merely as "Sen Yung." Among his credits are: *Across the*

Pacific (1942); *China* (1943) with Loretta Young;[8] *The Crimson Key* (1947); *Breaking Point* (1950); *Peking Express* (1951) with Corinne Calvert (a member of the Arica Foundation, living in Santa Monica); *Forbidden* (1954) with Joanne Dru (married and living in Beverly Hills); *Blood Alley* (1955); *The Left Hand of God* (1955), and *Flower Drum Song* (1961) with Nancy Kwan (living in Beverly Hills, producing feature films). His last movie role was in *The Man with Bogart's Face* (1980).

He had two running parts on TV series. On *Bachelor Father* Victor played "Cousin Charlie Fong," the racetrack tout, who dropped by frequently to visit with John Forsythe's houseman "Peter Tong" and try to get him to bet on a horse. Sammee Tong, who played the role, committed suicide in 1965. Yung was probably even better known as "Hop Sing," cook to the Cartwright family on *Bonanza*.

Long after both series had gone into reruns he was earning his livelihood mainly from his culinary skills. He was an excellent cook and wrote a book on Chinese food, *The Great Wok,* which was published in 1974.

In 1972 Yung was returning to Los Angeles from Sacramento when his plane was hijacked by political dissidents. Although Yung's gunshot wound was superficial, the passenger in the seat in front of him was killed during a shootout with the FBI. Victor sued the airline for $500,000, but settled out of court for what his sister describes as "considerably less."

In 1977 at a dinner in his honor given by the Chinese Historical Society he explained why, after so many years as an actor, he was earning his living by giving cooking demonstrations on TV and in department stores: "The truth is that I appeared in about twenty percent of the *Bonanza* shows over fourteen seasons and that was not enough to sustain myself. You do all kinds of things. When someone needs a cook, I can cook."

Jon Virzi

Victor Sen Yung shortly before he died in 1980.

He was working on his second cookbook when he was found dead in November 1980. He had been heating his small San Fernando Valley bungalow with the kitchen stove and was asphyxiated by gas fumes. The coroner confirmed his family's assertion that it was accidental. "He was in particularly good spirits," said a friend. "It was rainy and exceptionally cold weather. That house was very hard to heat and I guess he was just careless."

The actor had a child from his one marriage, which had ended in divorce. The son and Victor's two grandchildren were living in Ohio at the time of his death.

Victor Sen Yung always wanted to visit China. The closest he ever came was a trip to Hong Kong.